JUÁREZ GIRLS RISING

Juárez Girls Rising

Transformative Education in Times of Dystopia

Claudia G. Cervantes-Soon

University of Minnesota Press
Minneapolis
London

Portions of chapter 4 were published in "Testimonios of Life and Learning in the Border-lands. Juárez Girls Speak," *Equity and Excellence in Education* 45, no. 3 (2012): 373–91. Reprinted by permission of the University of Massachusetts, Amherst, College of Education, www.umass.edu/education/, and by permission of the copyright owner, Taylor & Francis, http://www.tandfonline.com.

Published by the University of Minnesota Press
111 Third Avenue South, Suite 290
Minneapolis, MN 55401-2520
http://www.upress.umn.edu

The University of Minnesota is an equal-opportunity educator and employer.

Library of Congress Cataloging-in-Publication Data

Names: Cervantes-Soon, Claudia G., author.
Title: Juárez girls rising : transformative education in times of dystopia / Claudia G. Cervantes-Soon.
Description: Minneapolis : University of Minnesota Press, [2017] | Includes bibliographical references and index.
Identifiers: LCCN 2016036908 (print) | ISBN 978-0-8166-9647-5 (hc) | ISBN 978-0-8166-9654-3 (pb)
Subjects: LCSH: High school girls—Mexico—Ciudad Juárez—Social conditions—Case studies. | Transformative learning—Mexico—Ciudad Juárez—Case studies. | Young women—Education—Mexico—Ciudad Juárez—Case studies. | Young women—Mexico—Ciudad Juárez—Social conditions—Case studies.
Classification: LCC LC205.5.M6 C47 2017 (print) | DDC 370.11/5—dc23
LC record available at https://lccn.loc.gov/2016036908

Contents

Preface

WRITING A BOOK is a challenging journey of intense intellectual investment and unexpected detours of questions and ideas. This book is not an exception. But what led me to embark and remain on this journey has been more personal than I could foresee at the outset. At first, it did not seem like a timely project. Destiny sure seemed to have had a sly scheme on me when the drug wars erupted right around the time I planned to begin my fieldwork. As U.S. researchers were being urged to leave México, I was trying to get in. It was not that I was admirably brave or naïve or careless, but simply that the intimate connection I had with the city of Juárez could not be eroded by media alarms or institutional warnings. This intimacy with the city is what fueled my passion and my determination to complete the project. It was also what gave me the necessary insight and intuition to help me navigate the city in such complex and dangerous times. Today I can see more clearly that the personal is the breath of life that has maintained this intellectual project. It is also through the personal that I have been able to excavate relationships and mind-altering lessons about life, youth, and hope from the coldness of academic research.

The journey leading to this book began long before I started my fieldwork. In the summer of 2006, I left the El Paso/Juárez border area to begin a new journey away from "home." Having grown up in Juárez, and having lived in El Paso for most of my adult life working in the public schools as a bilingual educator, I had been a border crosser all my life. But that summer, I was turning the page from a painful divorce and was eager to leave the dry and dusty borderlands and the history of my life that it represented. I enrolled at the University of Texas at Austin to pursue my PhD. More than a career strategy, this was an intellectual and spiritual exercise, motivated by a desire to find a place that would cultivate critical thought and bring new meaning to my life as an educator. Austin, Texas, offered the perfect place to begin this process. It was sunny and cheery and a context away from anyone who knew me. I hoped that the happy-go-lucky attitude of this so-called weird city would be contagious. It was time to detach, to find the real me and to explore new and different directions away from my past — or so I thought.

On a Wednesday afternoon, during my first year as a graduate student in a critical pedagogy course, and after rushing through traffic in 95 degree weather, I walked late into class and into an unexpected encounter with the *home* that I was trying so hard to leave. The professor, fond of spontaneously using films to provoke thought and discussion, had chosen to show *Señorita Extraviada*. This film by Lourdes Portillo is a haunting investigation into the horrifying feminicides that had made Juárez world famous since the 1990s. There I sat, surrounded by a handful of peers who barely knew me at all, unsuccessfully trying to prevent the tears from coming as a plethora of images of brutality and violence against Juárez women, corruption, and impunity appeared on the screen. How could I engage in intellectual and detached conversations about the unspeakable killings of women who had come of age at the same time and in the same place as I did? Without a doubt, my peers were shocked and deeply saddened by the heart-wrenching stories, but that night and many more to come I was not able to sleep, thinking that these women could have been my sisters, my friends, or me. Moreover, I had to once again face the exposure of my hometown as nothing more than a killing field. As necessary as this exposure was in order to raise consciousness, it contributed to the many depictions of Juárez as a human landfill, a stairwell to hell, where its hopeless residents could only clumsily cry for a help that would never come. I wondered what people really did with this so-called critical consciousness beyond nodding their heads in pity and helplessness. I especially questioned this—though not in this class—when hearing colleagues theorize and privilege the U.S. borderlands as a site of valuable knowledge and cultural production, while simultaneously continuing to frame Mexican border towns as nothing more than amusing open bars for repressed Americans.

Three years later, in 2009, when I returned to Juárez to conduct my study, the city was in its worst condition ever, devastated by violence, numbed by sorrow, covered by a dense and heavy cloud of death and fear. The media reports and discourses about Juárez that focused almost exclusively on the drug wars could hardly be avoided, but these often obscured the realities of most people who were holding on for dear life and who continued to work, raise families, and strive for their dreams despite the devastation of their communities. During these years of skyrocketing violence, heart attacks, miscarriages, accidents, and other illnesses began to make an appearance in the lives of even my own family members, sickened and burdened by the angst of living in a civil war against a deadly enemy of many blurry faces. And the violence against women did not dwindle, though it received much less attention from the media.

Yet in the midst of massive militarization, decapitated bodies, and terror, a dim light of hope in the possibility of collective action also emerged. *"Amor por Juarez"* bumper stickers were everywhere, and messages of peace, resistance to U.S. gun sales, and calls for solidarity among the youth began to substitute for a few of the political party slogans painted on fences and walls. Many people refused to give up on their city, clinging to it as a home worth fighting for. "Esos criminales no me van a sacar de aquí, y si me muero pues moriré aquí" (those criminals will not drive me out of here, and if I die I will die here), my father would say. Was it possible to tell a story that captured this resiliency and struggle for justice, survival, and dignity, especially among young working-class women of Juárez?

While I did not want to write a romanticized story, I cannot deny that my own subjectivity as a *mujer fronteriza* with loved ones and personal ties to the area affected this project. Thus, in writing this book, I also wish to be open about how my positionality as a self-identified Chicana and my own story growing up in Juárez have contributed to my analysis (Simon and Dippo 1986; Delgado Bernal 1998; Foley 2002). In navigating the borderlands and the school, I relied heavily on my *cultural intuition*, which Dolores Delgado Bernal (1998) defines as a complex, intuitive, and dynamic process that involves the unique perspectives that many Chicana researchers bring to the research process, including insights from the literature and community memory, as well as personal and collective experience. I was a partial insider whose experiences growing up and going to school in Juárez during the emergence of the *maquiladora* industry as its main source of economic subsistence and through the appearance of the first feminicide graveyards in the early 1990s helped me understand to some extent what this context meant for young women.

I also drew on family memory to understand this border city as a land of hope for the many migrants who had populated it in the past several decades. In the 1930s my maternal grandparents emigrated from a remote town in Canton China to settle permanently in Juárez, motivated by the poverty and lack of opportunities in China and by my grandfather's previous experience working in the building of the Mexican railroad during the Mexican Revolution. Several years into their new country, they still struggled to raise a family of now eleven children. Despite their extremely hard work, discipline, and resourcefulness, they lost three children to illnesses that could perhaps have been prevented or overcome if they had only had the necessary financial resources. My mother and all her siblings worked hard at the small convenience store in downtown Juárez, which my grandfather managed. Hunger tended to be a regular family member and hard work part of everyone's daily life. The children learned to cooperate in everything and to develop creative ways to help the family stay afloat. Their story is not unique. It resembles the stories of many other migrants in México as well as immigrant families in the United States and around the world. All their work, they figured, would eventually pay off if they invested in education. However, for my Chinese family, education was reserved for the men. At the time, my family's cultural tradition viewed women as destined to get married and serve another family's interests. Therefore, in order for my mother to fulfill her unlikely dream of going to middle school, high school, and college, she began working at age thirteen, not only to pay for her own education but also to contribute to the family and help pay for her brothers' education—an obligation that she had to honor before she could think about her own educational pursuits. Eventually, my mother became a mathematics teacher, who worked hard—if not excessively—to get an education and move, if barely, into the middle class. She did it all by herself, including raising my siblings and me as a single mother, always working, learning, teaching, worrying, and striving to survive and give her children an education as a single parent.

It could be said that all of this was worth it, except brain cancer took her life at thirty-nine, when I was only nine years old. She left me behind in a scary world, with a house, a car, and a small savings account for college but also with the loneliness and the heartbreaking image of my little brother and sister, who did not know what to do with the idea of losing their mother.

In part, the stories of the young women in this study sound all too familiar. True, I was quite privileged in many ways growing up in the lower-middle-class sector in which my mother worked so hard to become a member. But I also grew up alone and scared, wounded by memories of epileptic seizures, having to come to terms with losing the most precious and important person in my life, facing an uncertain present and future, and having many child-rearing responsibilities at an early age. As a teenage girl, not only did I have to deal with the daily challenges that a city poses on any young person, but I also returned daily to an empty home as a latchkey kid raising myself and my siblings alone. Street harassment was a common experience when I walked home from school, and I often worried about the safety of my younger brother and sister in the rise of drug addictions, gang activity, and violence against women. Maintaining my sanity through my precarious childhood and adolescence was nothing less than a miracle. If someone were to tell me about my future at the time, I would have never believed it.

This book is not about me, but having come of age in difficult circumstances on the border, as well as having witnessed the roles that women must undertake for their survival and that of their families, has helped me understand, to some extent, life on the border as an educator, as a child of migrants, and as a child and young woman with responsibilities beyond what is imagined in hegemonic, Eurocentric constructions of girlhood. My mother's experience also gives me some insight into the dreams and hopes that many young women put in the hands of education.

It has been several years now since I left the U.S.–México border, and I have realized that the distance has allowed me to appreciate it from a different perspective, to analyze its problems with an insider's insight. I have also become more sensitive and have grown keenly aware of discourses that demonize Juárez and render its residents as facing disaster without taking into consideration the complex contradictions of the city. This journey has helped me recognize why, to many Mexicans, Juárez did not necessarily represent a killing field for women or a doomed drug war zone, but rather a land where they could get a chance for survival in the global capitalism that had swallowed the country. Sure, many joined the large exodus of people fleeing the city during the most violent years, but many more stayed. How did those who did not have the means or desire to leave grapple with their current circumstances? What tools for survival, hope, and social transformation were available to them, especially among marginalized women and youth? How did institutions of education respond to the increasingly difficult social realities?

This book is not an answer to all these questions. Instead, it is an attempt to uncover the ways in which young working-class women in a unique school community resist victimization and hopelessness and about the ways in which education can offer a space for critical consciousness, agency, and healing. Living in Juárez today is not the same as it was thirty years ago. There have been too many wounds that have not been healed, but people refuse to give up. I hope the reader will find that the women in this book are not incoherently or naïvely begging for pity, protection, or help, nor do they invoke a postfeminist "girl power" based on individualist pursuits (Harris 2004; McRobbie 2004; Ringrose 2007). Instead, I aim to provide an empirical account of the complex relationship between schooling, identity, agency, and collective struggles. The story I present here cannot be generalized to be applied to any other border city, school, or community, but I hope it can offer hopeful insight about the possibility of meaningful and liberating education for marginalized youth and women in Juárez and elsewhere.

Countering Despair and Stigma
through *Autogestión*

It was 10:00 p.m. and Karla was already in her pajamas. It had been a long day. If not for the incident earlier that afternoon, she would have had less trouble falling asleep. As she walked home from school, a stranger in an oversize, shiny white truck had chased and harassed her. She had run to hide at a supermarket for several minutes and had missed her bus. When she got home later than usual, she was still very frightened. No matter how often something like this happened to her, the thought of ending up in the hands of some stranger always terrified her. "Thank God for his protection; tomorrow should be a better day," Karla told herself.

Everything was quiet now. Her small old house and aging furniture revealed her family's humble lifestyle. But there was also evidence of the love and the many sacrifices her parents had made for her. The photograph on the dresser of her *quinceañera* brought back happy memories; she never felt as beautiful as when she wore her satin white gown and tiara. Her father was lucky to still have a job at the factory when so many were being laid off, but his earnings made it almost impossible to afford the luxury of a party to complete the traditional rite of passage into womanhood at the age of fifteen. Still, her parents did all they could to celebrate her fifteenth birthday. Her mother sold used clothes at a flea market, and her father worked extra hours. Although they were in their late forties, lately they both looked older and weary. Karla knew it was all for her, so that she could finish high school and be the first one in the family to attend college. "I can't disappoint them," she often told herself.

But there was also a photograph she kept in her room even though it brought her deep sadness. It was a photograph of her favorite uncle, who had recently been murdered. He had been brave enough to refuse to give in to an extortioner's demands, and now he was gone forever. Making any profit from his used-car business was hard enough, but having to give it all to some cowards making anonymous calls was just enraging. "¡Yo no voy a andar manteniendo cabrones!" (I refuse to support assholes!), he had told Karla. Only six months after his murder, she still missed him dearly. Like every night, she closed her eyes and said a prayer for the two small children and wife her uncle left behind.

Karla was getting ready to finally get some rest when suddenly a loud knock on the door interrupted her plans.

"Someone is at the door!" Karla's mother exclaimed. "Who could it be at this time? It's almost eleven! Don't people have manners anymore?" Karla's father peeked through the window and saw a military jeep with four soldiers and two more at the door. Karla's father looked alarmed. Their big riffles were threatening enough, but given all the stories of abuse that circulated the city, a military crew was to be avoided as much as the criminals.

"Papá, I'll open the door. Don't you worry, Mamá; we have nothing to hide." Wanting to protect her parents, and with her usual decisive and bold attitude, Karla opened the door.

"Please step outside," a soldier demanded. "Where is your husband?"

"I don't have a husband; I am a minor."

The soldier stared at Karla's curvy body. She was only seventeen, but he saw her as a woman, not a kid. "Where is your husband?" he demanded.

"Didn't you hear me? I don't have a husband. I am a minor and my parents are inside. What do you want?"

"There was an accusation about drugs being hidden in this house, so we have to come in to investigate." As usual, since the city was militarized, the soldiers carried no search warrant or any proof of their accusations.

"We don't have any drugs."

"That's what you say, but we have to come inside and check."

"OK, come in. We have nothing to hide."

"Alright, you will come with me and show me around."

"Fine."

Three soldiers entered the house. They all looked young, ranging from their early twenties to their midthirties, but their heavy weapons demanded absolute obedience.

"Ma'am, you will stay here in the kitchen with me," one ordered, and Karla's father was sent to wait outside with another soldier.

The other two soldiers ordered Karla to take them to her bedroom. "Open that drawer, and that one too," one demanded. The soldiers looked through every drawer, every corner of the room. One of the soldiers was carrying a digital camera and took pictures of the open drawers and other objects in the room. Karla wondered why they were so interested in her bedroom and did not care to search the kitchen or her parents' bedroom. She also wondered which feeling was stronger, fear or fury. She was still wearing her nightgown, and both soldiers kept staring her up and down at every chance they had.

"What else do you have?" asked the soldier with the camera as he took a snapshot of Karla. Then he took another, and another.

"Why are you taking photos of me?" she protested.

Ignoring her question, the soldier pointed at the photograph of her uncle on the dresser. "Who is he?"

"He's my uncle."

"What's his name?"

"Arturo." He was known by his middle name, Isaac, so she gave them his first name instead. Just in case.

"And where is he?"

"He passed away."

"Oh, OK. Guys, let's go!"

"Hey, but before you go, tell me why you were taking pictures of me!"

"Uh . . . because I have to submit a report."

"But you took a picture of me. Why did you? You don't need that for a report. Let me see! Show me!"

"I can't."

"I know that's a digital camera." Karla wanted to take the camera and delete her pictures. "You can show me. Show it to me!"

"No, I can't show it to you."

"But why did you take it!"

"Hey guys, let's go! Come on, let's go!"

I arrived at Preparatoria Altavista on the morning of October 2, 2009, to a crowd of students and teachers organizing and working outside under the bright sun. They were preparing for a march to commemorate the Tlatelolco massacre and at the same time voice resistance against the violence and militarization in the city. Karla was sitting on the ground painting a large banner with an artistic image of a swastika symbol melting and turning into the image of a dove. "I created it myself. It represents the possibility of turning violence and hate into peace," she explained.

It was my first week of fieldwork when Karla shared with me the story of military invasion into her home, which I have presented here almost exactly in the same way she told it to me. I had managed to listen attentively and remained poised, but once I was alone in my car, her story drove me to tears. I had seen countless headlines of Juárez crime and violence, I had heard the rumors of military abuse, I had read numerous articles and books on the violence invading the city, but all of that did not prepare me to hear about Karla's experiences from her own lips. I thought of how much I did not want this study to be about tragedy, loss, and despair. Realizing that Karla's story was neither unusual nor the most dramatic, it seemed that writing about hope would be an impossible task. Yet as I continued to immerse myself in the world of young Juárez women, I was intrigued by the many other facets that encompassed their lives. The precarious and oppressive context in which Karla and the other protagonists of this book were coming of age, needless to say, influenced their outlook on life. But I would soon learn that Karla's life, as the other women's, was not limited by fear or paralyzed by tragedy. She was a high academic achiever who resisted the likelihood of becoming a maquiladora worker. She was a mentor to many younger peers, a theater actress and talented artist, a caring daughter, and, as the second vignette illustrates, an involved participant and organizer of social justice activities at her school—the very images that are seldom offered in depictions of young Juárez women.

This book is about the lives of young women coming of age in an extremely complex and challenging context shaped by many factors, including neoliberalism, patriarchy, militarization, gendered violence, and economic inequality, to name just a few.[1] But this book is also about a high school that offered a safe and sacred space to cultivate a critical hope and nurture their agency. Rather than limiting my analysis to the difficulties of their lives, this book aims to offer an alternative narrative that illuminates other aspects of young Juárez women's lives that tend to be obscured in the popular discourses and depictions of these women. In particular, this book attempts to uncover the decisive role that schooling, and especially critical education, played in the young women's identity formation and in the direction that they gave to their agency. While Juárez girls are often described as students, and while education is often referred to as the road to liberation for subaltern women, little is known about the type of education to which young Juárez women have access or whether that education offers any possibilities for liberation. This book centers their high school, Preparatoria Altavista, as a crucial context of emancipatory potential for these women.

Bringing together the life stories and voices of ten adolescent working-class females attempting to trace a path for their lives in the complex context of Juárez during an unparalleled violent era, as well as the story of their high school as the space that served as an incubator for their development of politicized identities and agency, the book aims to illuminate the notion of *autogestión.* Autogestión emerged as a holistic and dialectical approach to humanization and a unique form of agency and self-authorship in which young Juárez women engaged individually and collectively, and it was the central goal of Altavista, leading its pedagogical and structural practices. Autogestión also became the moving force in the young women's identity formation and agency as the school capitalized on the women's subaltern knowledge and experiences in ways that are rarely cultivated by Juárez education systems.

Thus, in order to understand how the young women became *autogestivas,* this book takes a careful look at their school and gives serious consideration to their experiences and voices. It does so in two major ways. First, because autogestión involved a reciprocal process, the book aims to offer insight about the ways the young women contributed and shaped the cultural production of the school and their collective identities as they developed their autogestión. Second, this book reveals four pathways to autogestión as part of the intimate lives of these women. This analysis offers a window into their individual process of self-authorship as they orchestrate the multiple discourses of the various realms they inhabit, as well as the lessons learned from their lived experiences, with particular attention to the role their school played in this process.

Identity, agency, and transformative education among subaltern Juárez girls are then the main themes that allow us to conceptualize autogestión. In the following sections, I discuss the theory that grounds the analysis in this book, as well as the methodological approaches to the study. The purpose is to present the reader with the theoretical framework to better understand the epistemological stance, structure, contributions, and direction of the book. I conclude with a brief description of the chapters.

Considerations in the Study of Young Juárez Women

Understanding Constructions of Subaltern Juárez Girls

Adolescence is generally considered a pivotal time in a person's life course in which concerns about self become more salient. But for women, adolescence takes an additional dimension. As made clear by Mary Pipher's (1994) suffering Ophelias, who produced international concern about the so-called girls in crisis, the image of girls from almost any background as victims of their circumstances and desperately waiting to be rescued is widespread. In this conception of adolescence, hegemonic notions of femininity tend to result in a great loss for young women (Stern 1991; Brown and Gilligan 1992). But girls of color, from marginalized communities and in the so-called Global South have further acquired an almost permanent image of the uneducated, apolitical, and victimized girl without agency of her own.

It often appears that popular narratives about subaltern girls converge into a story of perpetual crisis and vulnerability in which girls' assumed underdeveloped and childish condition added to a backwardness inherent in their cultural and social contexts make them incapable of framing their circumstances, much less overcoming them or crafting intelligent solutions for their lives. Even in analyses of youth activism, whether in the United States or even in Latin America, the voices and determining roles played by teenage girls and young women tend to be ignored (Taft 2011). Much of this assumed backwardness is framed by dominant U.S. and middle-class orientations toward the construction of girlhood (Saldaña-Portillo 2003). These conceptions are also reminiscent of colonial and patronizing orientalist ideas of womanhood that render women as in need of protection and incapable of social awareness and critique, of transformative action, or of politicized identities—hence not fully human (Mohanty 2003).

As the typical sad story goes, the traumas of violence, war, and dispossession that subaltern girls experience near and far curtail their innocence and force them into abrupt womanhood. But reaching adult womanhood does not necessarily mean that they achieve full humanization. As Chandra Mohanty (2003) points out:

> Third World women as a group or category are automatically and necessarily defined as religious (read: not progressive), family-oriented (read: traditional), legally unsophisticated (read: they are still not conscious of their rights), illiterate (read: ignorant), domestic (read: backward), and sometimes revolutionary (read: their country is in a state of war, they must fight!). This is how the "Third World Difference" is produced. (40)

On the other hand, while Western-based human rights campaigns and corporate philanthropy have increasingly focused their attention on saving the racialized, vulnerable girls in crisis in some remote part of the world (Gilmore and Marshall 2010), the perception of urban girls—who are typically poor girls of color—is felt as a much more nearby problem in the popular imagination, loaded with stigma and a mix of pity and contempt. Urban girls are depicted as both potential victims and enablers of domestic violence and as pathological threats to society by their propensity to teen pregnancy, addictions, and school dropout (Leadbeater and Way 1996, 2007). Prevalent discourses of risk in urban centers, as well as victory narratives of exceptional girls who "make it," mask the real experiences, resiliency, and navigational strategies of most girls in marginalized communities.

Young Juárez women fit both the Third World and the urban girl mythologies. They also have had to deal with the contradictory expectations of colonialism and Mexican patriarchy, as well as a highly predatory context in which feminicide and drug wars have become iconic.[2] As such, the image of Juárez women has become representative of gendered violence, a depiction that subjects them to not only perpetual victimization but also the commodification of their bodies as a fetishized illustration of women's violent death (e.g., Bowden 1998, 1999), to be consumed by international popular culture and products—from movies to makeup.[3]

In attempting to interrupt these discourses and images, this book avoids popular developmental frameworks because it is precisely the discourse of development that tends to perceive girlhood as a troubling stage prone to the formation of fragile identities that, rooted in racist and sexist conceptions of the ultimate attainment of human perfectibility, may lead to framing Latin America and the feminine as primitivistic (Saldaña-Portillo 2003). Although I use the terms "women" and "girls" interchangeably throughout the book, I would like to stress that these uses are merely for practical reasons, as I deliberately intend to divert from the infantilization of young women that is often connoted by referring to them as "girls." The problematic nature of this term in part involves conceptions of adolescence as a stage in a linear life trajectory that ultimately reflect homogenizing Western paradigms, impose definitions of empowerment and civility, and further erase any possibility for young women's agency in their own terms. These ideas of empowerment tend to point to the need for rescue, typically in the form of education and initiatives shaped by global capitalism (Gilmore and Marshall 2010). Certainly, the young women in this book would not want to be conceived as underdeveloped, incapable, immature, or naïve, in perpetual need for protection, especially considering that the circumstances in their lives do not grant them the privileges necessary to adopt such a position (Butcher 2015).

Therefore, although I do not necessarily advocate an antidevelopmental stance, my analysis draws on alternative frameworks that have proven more useful in offering a more nuanced and fair representation of young Juárez women's lives and their complexities and of their capacity for self-authorship and agency. Rather than viewing identity as limited to the labels that individuals acquire from the social categories already defined for them or as a particular stage in a linear conception of one's life trajectory, this book draws on the *sociocultural practice theory of identity* (Holland et al. 1998) and the *mujerista pedagogies* theory (Hernández 1997; Elenes et al. 2001). Respectively, these frameworks offer the possibility to situate identity as a culturally and socially mediated, fluctuating, and nonlinear understanding of one's self, as well as the ability to include and seriously consider subaltern women's voices without trivializing their experiences and subjectivities.

The sociocultural practice theory of identity, which draws from various schools of thought and from the work of Lev Vygotsky and Mikhail Bakhtin, proposes that cultural production and experience-based learning are fundamental in the understanding of identity because they allow us to recognize the improvisations and innovations as forms of agency that permit individuals to interrupt cultural and situational determinism (Urrieta 2007). In this way, identities form in a process of activity, involving perceptions and narratives of self that link the past to the present as well as continuous and nonlinear transformation. Identity is also socially constructed in that it "figuratively combines the intimate or personal world with the collective space of cultural forms and social relations" (Holland et al. 1998, 5).

In recognizing the importance of heuristic processes in conceptions of identity, Chicana/Latina/Mexicana feminist thought also offers important theoretical grounding for the analysis of Juárez women's identity. This school of thought has long pointed to the significance of lived experience in gendered, classed, and racialized contexts and of everyday women's discourse as sources of knowledge and agency. A theory generated in this school of thought, mujerista pedagogy, allows us to recognize the unique pedagogical tools and processes that the young Juárez women in this book utilized to engage in a collective and autonomous process of identity formation and negotiation. This involves moving from *self*-consciousness to *collective* consciousness through a "'womanist' sensibility or approach to power, knowledge, and relationships rooted in convictions for community uplift" (Villenas et al. 2006, 7). In this way, mujerista theories allow us to emphasize community goals by beginning with women's and children's concerns.

I will return in later sections to the significance of testimonio and mujerista pedagogies in the women's enactment of autogestión and the meaning they give to education. What warrants attention in this discussion is that by framing identity from sociocultural and mujerista perspectives we are better able to appreciate the self-authorship of subaltern young women that is produced not by a developmental state of personal crisis but from a multiplicity of experiences and participation in a variety of social realms, as well as to recognize the ways in which girls enact their agency—even in seemingly trivial ways—and generate ruptures in the predictable destiny to which Juárez women have been alluded.

Agency, Resistance, and Empowerment

A salient theme in the growing field of girls' studies is empowerment. An important body of work has uncovered the fallacy of the postfeminist and media-driven notion of "girl power," itself rooted in Western white, capitalist paradigms, including competition, individualism, consumerism, and a deceptive meritocracy (Harris 2003; McRobbie 2004; Taft 2004; Ringrose 2007). Relying on the uncritical pursuit and consumption of hegemonic and commercially produced representations of feminine beauty, sexuality, and power, this postfeminism is founded on the idea that feminism is no longer necessary, as women can be as successful as men, as long as they are determined and disciplined (Harris 2003). The image of girls and women in peripheral nations and in marginalized communities as perpetual victims rather than as agents of their own destiny stains the illusive progress and liberation assumed in postfeminist ideas of girl empowerment. This is not surprising, considering that generally, these popular postfeminist notions of the empowered girl are attractive and easy to adopt only by those with consumer power, but, more important, subaltern women around the world may find them absurd and the pursuit of the uncritical

"girl power" as irrelevant to their circumstances and at odds with their own
moral and ethical goals.

On the other hand, a growing body of work has highlighted the agency
that emerges among subaltern young women, not so much in attempts to
fit in the world as it is but rather in the form of resistance. Research on
adolescent girls in the United States has offered insight into the many ways
in which young women resist discourses of pathology and victimization,
underscoring women's acute ability to find spaces to enact their opposition despite the context of power inequalities in which their lives un-
fold. This body of work offers theories of resistance that articulate young
women's responses to gender stereotypes, naturalized gender roles, race,
class, culture and language, and media messages and images that consider
both conscious and unconscious rejections of social and cultural norms
(Lykes 1985; Goodenow and Espin 1993; Valdés 1998; Duke 2002; Abrams
2003; Taft 2011). More recently, research has also pointed at the innovative
cultural production that results from girls' enactment of agency in negotiating, redefining, and appropriating in creative ways, rather than completely
eliminating oppressive conditions and discourses (e.g., Bettie 2003, Taft
2004; Kearney 2006; Bae 2011; Adely 2012).

In addition, in contrast to the isolation and interruption of relatedness
to themselves and others that young white women are alleged to experience
during adolescence (Gilligan 2014), research on young women of color
has revealed that maintaining their relationships and a sense of connectedness has been an important source of strength in their resistance against
oppression (hooks 1991; Robinson and Ward 1991; Goodenow & Espin
1993). In fact, recent research on girls in various parts of the world has challenged the discourse of passivity and underdevelopment by emphasizing
girls' agency in reclaiming the right to their own self-definition (Adely
2012), in the formation of politicized identities, and in their ability to organize and join activist struggles for social justice (Taft 2011).

Considering these advancements in the study of girls, a fair analysis of
young Juárez women's identity and agency, moving away from masculinistic
frameworks that emphasize autonomous and independent forms of resistance, is important (Durham 1999). However, it is just as important that
independent activities not be trivialized as devoid of political consideration by patriarchal constructions of activism that privilege formally organized political activities. Therefore, this analysis aims to recognize the ways
in which subaltern Juárez girls move their agency past improvised resistance

through an individual process of reflection, interrogation, and critique of social practices and power, stemming from the merging of lived experience and collective struggles for social justice. These individual and intimate journeys are important, as they have an impact on the young women's possibilities for collective action. Moreover, it is important to identify the ways in which educational institutions can support these processes.

To this end, one of the goals of this book is to underscore models of agency that stem from ordinary life, which, while unique at the individual level, affirm the collective and relational aspect of girl culture. The mujerista pedagogies theory again offers useful lenses that center the young women's "articulations of teaching and learning, along with ways of knowing—rooted in the diverse and everyday living of Chicanas/Latinas as members of families, communities, and a global society" (Villenas et al. 2006, 3). Hence, the ways in which subaltern Juárez girls actively engage their minds, souls, and bodies in everyday life to survive oppression, abandon defeat, find healing, and live joyous lives constitute important forms of agency that, while evident at the individual level, can be directed toward building solidarity for communal uplift.

Subaltern Women and Education

In considering young women's oppositional strategies, Jennifer Pastor, Jennifer McCormick, and Michelle Fine (1996) argue that because of the lack of opportunities to develop collective forms of resistance, marginalized girls often manifest their critical consciousness by developing isolated, rather than collective, strategies to negotiate the contradictory demands and needs of family, friends, and school, while resisting oppression. On the other hand, Tracy Robinson and Janie Ward (1991) have noted that in some cases young women's resistance results in liberation and change, but other times their oppositional behavior against subjugation and injustice comes in the form of quick fixes that may lead to self-damage or may create situations that further disadvantage them. These concerns point to the capacity of social institutions, or lack thereof, to allow girls to cultivate their agency and direct it in truly empowering ways. Schools then are important sites of analysis where many girls spend much of their time hoping to improve their living conditions.

It is true that formal education has long been considered to be crucial in the struggle for equality in the global era (Coatsworth 2004) and for women's social mobility in economically developing countries (Chant 2003). In fact, globalization debates often point to education as a panacea for women's empowerment. Nevertheless, economic globalization has resulted in finance-driven reforms such as decentralization, privatization, and reduced governmental spending on education (Carnoy 2000), as well as in schooling practices that increasingly follow a business model of efficiency and productivity. These trends in current school systems have increasingly and significantly undermined issues of equality, critical consciousness, and democracy, all of which are particularly relevant to subaltern young women today (Stromquist and Monkman 2000).

Nelly Stromquist (1995) argues that schools still have the potential to empower women by fostering the development of four dimensions: (1) the cognitive, or critical understanding of one's reality; (2) the psychological, such as feelings of self-esteem; (3) the political, such as the awareness of power inequalities and the ability to organize and mobilize; and (4) the economic, which is the capacity to produce independent income. But in Juárez schools, most of these goals—except the last one—tend to be disregarded. On the one hand, in Juárez the purpose of education has been perceived almost exclusively as a means for obtaining a "better" job (Silva 2006). On the other hand, mass schooling in México has developed conjointly with the political hegemony of the nation-state, resulting in the infusion of colonialist and capitalist models, dominated by Western and homogenizing infrastructure, curricula, and teaching styles, benefiting the interests of the dominant classes (Juárez and Comboni Salinas 2003) and where hegemonic ideas of nationalism continue to be reproduced from the early grades through daily rituals and discourses (Rippberger and Staudt 2003). Considering these contradictions, even the promise of economic advancement still offers but a dubious road to gender equality—highly educated Juárez women continue to receive 30 percent lower salaries compared to men in all job markets (Brugués Rodríguez 2005).

Despite the limitations that constrain educational systems' abilities to offer the oppressed real possibilities for emancipation, the arguments of this book are founded on the idea that schools are still significant sites of cultural production, both through the official curriculum that aims to instill a set of ideas in students as well as through the norms, values, and beliefs conveyed and circulated in the social environment. In this conception, schools offer a fertile ground to investigate the ways in which all actors involved play an active role in reproducing, appropriating, and resisting oppression, as well as in negotiating their own sense of self and shaping new collective identities.

Defining *Autogestión*

Originated in Gerard Mendel's ideas of democratic education, the Spanish term "autogestión" in Mexican educational practice refers to the autonomous and free process of creation and negotiation of pedagogical methods and curriculum by and within the educational community—including both teachers and students—and according to their own interests (Mendel and Vogt 1975). During my time in the field, teachers and students often used the term, but it became evident that it had a unique meaning to them that was not limited to a pedagogical practice in the classroom.

Autogestión, as related to the young women in this book, refers to the process of self-authorship of one's politicized identity and thoughtful self-government, which involves the shaping of one's personal life as part of a collective. This involves a degree of both planned and reflexive action as well as flexible improvisations founded on the awareness of one's material and social realities, the discernment of power dimensions, and a sense of responsibility toward self and communal humanization and liberation. In this way, autogestión is a form of agency rooted in the collective and resulting from a critically conscious sense of self. This involves a process that, far from linear, is continuously contested by the cultural hegemony of society and is constantly evolving. In other words, the women of this book take an active role in constructing their own meaning of autogestión by determining what they consider liberating and empowering for their own lives.

In order to better understand the unique characteristics of autogestión as manifested by some of the young women at Preparatoria Altavista, critical pedagogy, decolonial theory, and Chicana/Mexicana/Latina feminist thought offer useful lenses. Below, I attempt to explain how these bodies of work weave together to offer the theoretical grounding that has guided this analysis and definition of autogestión.

Conscientization

Critical consciousness or conscientization is foundational to autogestión, as in order for individuals to engage in liberating action and self-authorship, they must be able to recognize the elements of power shaping the material conditions of their lives and be able to engage in self-reflection about their role in this dynamic. From the beginning of my fieldwork, it was clear that Preparatoria Altavista's philosophy and practice were guided by theories of critical pedagogy and democratic education, which offered its students a language in which to name their social realities and the agency to do some thing about them.

More than a theory of teaching and learning, critical pedagogy conveys a philosophy of praxis-oriented education for social transformation. In this sense, critical pedagogy embodies a social movement. First proposed by Paulo Freire (1970) through his work with peasants in Brazil and in his seminal book *Pedagogy of the Oppressed,* ideas of critical pedagogy are founded on the premise that human beings are thinking subjects with the capacity to reflect on and rise above their material realities to re-create their world and that education and literacy are about people becoming aware of their collective power to overcome oppression.

While Freire's theory of critical pedagogy is ultimately utopian, his anti-authoritarian philosophy relies on people's consciousness to determine and reinvent their own vision for a new society and personal existence. Consciousness is then a fundamental concept in Freire's theory, which is shaped by the interchange of socioeconomic and political structures and the cultural context of one's upbringing, education, religion, and other social influences. Because oppression tends to obscure the structures and myths created by powerful social forces that serve the interests of those in power and systematically subjugate people by virtue of their manipulative qualities, according to Freire, it is through critical consciousness— or *conscientizao*—that the oppressed can become aware of their potential for collective agency and engage in liberating action. At Altavista, critical consciousness gave students the language with which to name, interrogate, and critique the social structures and power dimensions that framed their everyday lives at local, national, transbordal, and global levels.

However, critical pedagogy in and of itself, while foundational, was not sufficient for the young women to develop the type of reflexive consciousness characteristic of their autogestión. I should pause here to note that from the shortcomings of dialogue as a liberating pedagogy (Burbules 2000) and the teacher's position and power in the role of emancipator to the predetermined discourse that assumes that a critique of power constitutes empowerment (Rickert 2001), critical pedagogy—particularly as envisioned by Freire—has not gone without critiques (Giroux 1988; Weiler

1991). Thomas Ricket (2001), in particular, argues that there could be a risk, especially in postmodern societies, of generating sociopolitical cynicism stemming from the violence and surveillance that sabotages any actions toward liberation. This is indeed a relevant concern in the highly repressive context of Juárez. Furthermore, the resulting cynicism could also generate identities defined only by oppression and dispossession, with the potential to perpetuate the prevalent narrative of victimization about Juárez women.

Another compelling critique, particularly relevant to subaltern Juárez women, has been raised by poststructuralist feminists, who have questioned whether progressive educational theory constitutes another regime of truth imposed over diverse students and teachers under a universalized rhetoric of social and educational transformation (Ellsworth 1989; Orner 1992; Maher 2001). In her influential essay, Elizabeth Ellsworth exposed the fallacy of arriving at universal truths by enforcing the rules of reason, the only vehicle available to the critical pedagogue and her students. As she notes:

> Literary criticism, cultural studies, post-structuralism, feminist
> studies, comparative studies, and media studies have by now
> amassed overwhelming evidence of the extent to which the myths
> of the ideal rational person and the "universality" of propositions
> have been oppressive to those who are not European, White,
> male, middle class, Christian, able-bodied, thin, and heterosexual.
> (1989, 304)

In other words, rationalism as a discursive practice, with its roots in Cartesian dualism and patriarchy, negates the validity of physical, spiritual, and emotional experiences as sources of knowledge and truth and consequently silences the voices and epistemological tools of those—namely women and people of color—who have been constructed by scientism as irrational others. Therefore, while young, subaltern Juárez women could use their social and material realities to read the word and the world, the wisdom and knowledge generated by their everyday bodily experiences, feelings, and spirituality could be easily neglected as possible sources of truth and empowerment.

Furthermore, Ruth Trinidad Galván (2001) emphasizes the importance of place, a factor often unrecognized by critical pedagogues, particularly in relation to teaching and learning among women. She argues that the sites of *convivencia* situated in a complex web of interpersonal relationships of the everyday encompass unique pedagogical sites where women can construct knowledge and produce new identities. Thus, I draw on decolonial and Chicana/Latina/Mexicana feminist epistemologies in order to recognize the elements beyond critical pedagogy involved in the autogestión that the young Juárez women enacted.

Theory in the Flesh and Testimonio

That the autogestión promoted by Altavista and exhibited by some of the young women was not limited to a language of critique or to the conventional rationalism of modernity could be explained in part by the school's embracement and legitimization of their students' and teachers' subaltern knowledges, or what Walter Mignolo (2000) refers to as *border thinking*. Border thinking draws on macronarratives to "bring to the foreground the force and creativity of knowledges subalternized during a long process of colonization" (13). According to Mignolo, border thinking counters the hegemonic knowledges and modern reason of Western thought articulated and propagated by Occidentalism—namely the set of myths used to conceptualize the colonial difference and the ranking of the rest of the world in relation to imperialist and capitalist powers. Thus, these subaltern knowledges have the potential to decolonize dominant intellectual thought and Eurocentric knowledges by challenging the content, perspectives, and discourses of new projects toward global conviviality. In many spaces, Altavista legitimized at least to some extent this border thinking by including the students' experiences of life in the barrio and narratives from their own perspectives as central to the curriculum that teachers used and to help them frame the theories, histories, and perspectives promoted by the standardized official curriculum. And as will be clear in the chapters, the school furthered this border thinking inside and outside the classroom and through a variety of pedagogical strategies.

What is more, among the women, the border thinking that was generated reflected an additional layer of awareness of their gendered experiences as frameworks that they used—albeit to various degrees—to organize their actions and oppositional strategies. Rather than following Cartesian conceptions of knowledge and truth that validate the rational but dismiss the emotional, physical, and spiritual subject or internalizing the stigma with which others in the city viewed them—as ignorant, deviant, and dangerous—the young women featured in this book embraced a barrio identity reflecting their class consciousness. But in addition, they recognized their own social, physical, emotional, and spiritual experiences and living conditions as Juárez women as valuable sources of knowledge, which they used to inform their analyses of and responses to their social realities.

This gendered and decolonizing subaltern knowledge characteristic of the girls' enactment of autogestión resembles what Chicana feminists have referred to as *theory in the flesh* and *mujerista pedagogies*. Cherríe Moraga (in Moraga and Anzaldúa 1983) posited that theory in the flesh is an epistemological, Third World feminist project, situated in subaltern women's bodily experiences, that has helped them negotiate and generate knowledge and praxis from the various systematic forms of oppression in their lives.

> A theory in the flesh means one where the physical realities of our lives—our skin color, the land or concrete we grew up on, our sexual longings—all fuse to create a politic born out of necessity.... We do this bridging by naming our selves and by telling our stories in our own words. (23)

Cindy Cruz highlights the revolutionary idea in theories of the flesh that, contrary to Cartesian understandings of knowledge, conceptualizes women's brown bodies as the very channels and agents of intellectual theory and praxis (Cruz 2001), rooted in emotional investment and inescapably grounded in politics of resistance and liberation (Moya 2002).

That theories in the flesh are generated and enacted by women's brown bodies points to the critical role that testimonial discourse plays in using subaltern knowledges to produce healing, reflection, wisdom, transformation, and action in individual and collective ways. Just as for many years marginalized women and other oppressed groups in the Americas have used testimonio as a decolonizing method to demand attention to their oppression (Menchú 1984; Smith 1999), historicize their own subjugated experience in their own terms (Menchú 1984; Elenes 2000), validate their experiences as sources of legitimate knowledge (Latina Feminist Group 2001), and express their solidarity with others (Saldívar-Hull 2000) as "refugees of a world on fire" (Moraga 1983), the girls at Altavista themselves were the vehicles for transmission and circulation of their theory in the flesh through the sharing of their testimonios.

Congruent with more recent theorizations of testimonio as a pedagogy (Delgado Bernal, Burciaga, and Flores Carmona 2012), I posit that their common practice of testimonial discourse as a form of autonomous mujerista pedagogy, fostered by their school and normalized among the young women, supported the young women's cultivation of politicized identities (Cervantes-Soon 2012). This, I suggest, allowed the young women to acknowledge their everyday gendered experiences as sources of wisdom and their shared stories as counternarratives that more clearly helped the women link their intimate worlds to the sociopolitical structures and forces that shaped their material conditions.

Through their testimonios, girls like Karla debunked and critiqued the various forces of oppression in their lives, such as normative and gendered notions of beauty, the media, gender roles, domestic violence, homophobia, gang membership, narcotraffic and drug use, classism and racism in schools and universities, capitalism, the authorities' corruption, and the repression of activists, among other things. In this way, their narratives became the means to transmit the longings and sense of urgency that stemmed from their own brown bodies. By sharing their testimonios with others around them, the young women broke taboos, negotiated contradictions, and re-created new identities beyond the injuries of global capitalism, violence, colonization, and patriarchy (Moraga 1993). Through their sharing of testimonios, they also strengthened and helped each other heal, socializing each other into a counterhegemonic discourse. Testimonio, then, constituted a normalized practice of their autogestión—a vehicle of praxis for their theory in the flesh—manifested inside and outside the classroom, in formal and informal conversations. Through their testimonial and politicized stories shared spontaneously or through the poetry and raps that they wrote, the young women offered alternative possibilities to predetermined ideas of Juárez women's fate.

Preparatoria Altavista played a crucial role in this process. Although not necessarily referred to in these terms, narratives in the form of testimonios, due to their politicized and heuristic nature, took center stage both in the regular curriculum and in informal spaces, giving precedence to the knowledge that came from lived experience. As the following chapters will illustrate, some of the teachers also used testimonial discourse as a form of pedagogy both in their classes and in their advising sessions, hoping that students would learn from their experiences, mistakes, and forms of agency. While not eliminating all the contradictions in critical pedagogy, students' and teachers' articulations of subaltern knowledge that transgressed traditional foundations of rationality were legitimized and centered in many spaces at the school. What transpired from these transgressions was the emergence of the school as a *sacred space* (Soto et al. 2009), where girls could actively embrace their theory in the flesh and pursue autogestión, all while critically interrogating assumptions and encouraging each other's self-reflexivity. Moreover, as students and teachers developed bonds that helped them cope with, understand, and overcome their personal difficulties and systemic oppression, as well as build coalitions with other subaltern community members, they worked together toward their own healing and liberation.

The prominence of testimonial discourse as well as of the school as a sacred space will become evident throughout the book. The way that both students and teachers protected their school, its philosophical foundations, and each one of their community members from external impositions of power, and the various ways in which they collectively built it into what they wanted it to be, revealed its sacredness. Specifically, the influence of the collective knowledge generated at their school will be revealed through the four intimate pathways of self-authorship and autogestión enacted by the young women as *Refugees* and as *Redirectors, Reinventors,* and *Redefiners,* which are presented respectively in chapters 4 and 5 of this book.

The Ethnographic Study

Since the 1960s, school ethnographies have offered in-depth analyses of life in schools. Many of them have shed light on how the legitimization and exclusion of specific kinds of knowledge and cultures and the implementation of particular pedagogical practices and forms of student tracking serve to maintain the marginalization of students on the basis of race, class, gender, and language and generate particular cultural processes, identities, and forms of resistance (see, e.g., Willis 1977; Apple [1979] 2004; Oakes 1985; McLaren 1986; Foley [1990] 2010; Levinson 1996; Soto 1997; Valenzuela 1999; Luykx 1999; Bettie 2003; Luttrell 2003). Nonetheless, most of this research has tended to be situated in U.S. schools—even when focusing on schooling contexts along the U.S.–México border. Moreover, much of this body of work has focused on schools where the perpetuation of inequalities is readily visible or in contexts where various groups of actors within the school work in opposition to one another (e.g., students vs. teachers). In contrast, this book aims to contribute to alternative accounts— those in which schooling is organized to deliberately foster youth's emancipation. In addition, this analysis takes into account that resistance processes are also shaped by a specific geopolitical position and historical background in México's struggle for education, which is deeply rooted in socialist movements and, needless to say, differs significantly from that in the United States. This ethnography seeks to contribute to the more limited available scholarship that focuses on not only revolutionary schooling practices but also forms of student agency in Latin America (Luykx 1999).

Standing out as a deliberately counterhegemonic school with a strong political orientation, Preparatoria Altavista offers a unique and enlightening setting. While the formal and informal curricula merit attention in and of themselves, what is important in this analysis is the way that the school's critical philosophy of education gave way to a space where young women were able to nurture their mujerista pedagogies and engage in liberating forms of agency. In this context, the women's agency and self-authorship were also evident in that rather than adopting and reproducing the school's ideas unproblematically, they creatively used them and shaped them to fit and enact their own ideas of liberation and to reflect their own heuristic knowledge. Therefore, the school's open-ended goal of autogestión offers insight into what is still possible through education, even with the most limited financial resources and for some of the most marginalized youth.

A critical ethnographic approach allowed me to experience life at Preparatoria Altavista and get a better understanding of the students' perspectives without the fallacy of assumed objectivity. As a critical ethnographer, I used critical theory to focus on the implicit values, ideologies, and symbolic devices revealed during my fieldwork to understand the behavior of teachers and students within the specific historic, sociocultural, and geopolitical context of Juárez (Madison 2011). I also carried out my research from a feminist perspective, following Shulamit Reinharz's (1992) goals: to focus on women as full members of their social, economic, and political realms; to study women's experiences from their own perspectives and reject androcentric interpretations that trivialize them; and to understand the role of the social context in the shaping of women's behavior.

Recognizing that my project was inherently political, aiming to disrupt discourses of passive victimization and de-intellectualization of young

Juarez women and support goals of transformative education (Simon and Dippo 1986; Foley and Valenzuela 2005), I eschewed any ideas of objectivity and detachment. Instead, I strived to be reflexive throughout my fieldwork, keeping a personal written and audio recorded journal in which I collected the manifestations of my own subjectivity. While the written journal helped me unravel my own ideas, the audio recorded journal helped me keep my sanity, becoming the silent ear that documented the feelings of guilt, rage, despair, fear, love, anticipation, and hope each day as I crossed the border driving to and from the school.

Since 2007, I began to visit the city with the goal of gaining a better understanding of the context from a researcher's perspective. Although this was the town of my youth, it had been at least ten years since I had moved permanently into the United States. Moreover, while Juárez was still a familiar place, my own understanding of it was framed by my immediate social circle and my middle-class life experiences. Therefore, I spent several months reading current research about Juárez, interviewing researchers and educators in the area, and in general trying to piece together the social complexities of the city as they related to the education of young working-class women and girls. What I soon learned was that the poorest girls in the city rarely attended high school, and some of the people I contacted did not seem too optimistic about the feasibility of my study. Luckily, I had other personal contacts that could provide further insight. My father, who was a high school principal himself and a well-known educational leader in the city, suggested that I consider Preparatoria Altavista. With his help I was able to meet with Altavista's principal. Altavista turned out to be a unique site not only because it served some of the most disenfranchised colonias in the city but also because it had a distinctive philosophy of education.

With Altavista's doors open to my research, I conducted fieldwork throughout the 2009–10 school year. This involved observing numerous classes and spending many of my days outside the classroom informally conversing with students, teachers, and administrators to get to understand the general culture of the school. The principal and assistant principal were my most helpful guides. They suggested classes to observe, and their approval seemed to immediately help me gain trust with teachers and even students. This was not surprising given how much both students and colleagues respected, admired, and loved them.

I observed classes taught by both veteran and beginning teachers and in almost every subject area. I also interviewed and had lengthy conversations with several teachers—though not all—including the principal, assistant principal, and curriculum specialist, which helped me gain a deeper understanding of the school's history, vision, and pedagogical orientation. These interviews happened in a natural way, often after classroom observations, in which teachers themselves volunteered to be interviewed. Not surprisingly, these educators tended to be the ones with the most leadership in the school and the ones who more strongly embraced its critical philosophy of education. Therefore, it should be noted that the voices of these teachers do not necessarily represent the entire faculty. I also did not request interviews from very novice teachers or from those who rushed out after teaching their classes or worked at the school on a part-time basis. However, much of what I learned from teachers came from spontaneous conversations in the courtyards when they approached me as they saw me writing field notes or when I simply joined them in socializing and conversing with students.

In order to get a better understanding of what it meant to be an adolescent Juárez female at Altavista, I followed ten girls more closely. Besides conducting in-depth life-history interviews, I simply "hung out" with these girls and their friends throughout the school day, inside and outside their classes. This allowed me to observe the girls in their own context and learn from their friends and develop relationships with other girls as well.

I also conducted a photovoice activity with them to learn about their perceptions of self. Auto-photography uses photos taken by informants to speak for themselves and display their own notions of self without the constraints of preselected categories generated by the researcher in interview protocols or other research instruments. The auto-photography technique has been utilized in various anthropological and psychological studies of identity, giving participants the freedom to select the people and elements of their surroundings that are most important in their constructions of self (see Combs and Ziller 1977; Ziller and Lewis 1981; Ziller, Vern, and Camacho de Santoya 1988; Ziller 1990; Campos Montero and Dollinger 1998; Noland 2006). Photovoice, another technique that has been increasingly used in participatory and community-engaged research, promotes community representations coming from those living in the community by using photographs taken by participants—along with their narratives—to develop collective forms of action that are relevant and significant to the ways in which participants, particularly those from marginalized groups, experience their social realities (Wallerstein and Bernstein 1988; Strack,

Magill, and McDonagh 2004; Wang 2006). Chapter 2 describes in more detail my selection choices in relation to the young women participating in the study, further details about the data collection process, and the procedures to complete the photography activity.

Working the Hyphen

By now, knowing my personal connection with the site, one might be wondering about my positionality and the nature of my relationships with the young women and the school community, as well as about my justification of these relationships during and after the fieldwork. This was not a traditional ethnographic study in which I remained a distant fly on the wall. On the contrary, this project exemplifies the feminist tradition that rejects the fallacy of "objectivity" in traditional ethnography (Harding 1993). Nonetheless, I also recognize the potential for colonizing practices within ethnographic work that arguably aims to *give voice to the voiceless* (Visweswaran 1994). Given my relationship with the young women and the school, it is important that I be open about my approach as a Chicana researcher throughout and after the fieldwork.

In looking for less exploitative research approaches, Judith Stacey (1988) urges feminist researchers to acknowledge the unavoidable power imbalances in research relationships and warns us against masking harming practices and representations with better-intentioned ethnography. To reduce these dangers, Stacey encourages the researcher to recognize the limitations of her work, reduce her claims, and view the research participants as collaborators, all while relinquishing control over the research process. In doing so, the researcher must be willing to embrace a "less comfortable social science . . . characterized by the loss of certainties and absolute frames of reference" (Lather 2001, 210), as well as to engage in a rigorous reflexivity (Harding 1993; Foley 2002) that can help her recognize and disrupt her colonizing and othering gaze (Pratt 1986; Stacey 1988; Rosaldo 1989; Fine 1994).

When members of historically marginalized groups engage in research projects with their own people, they must confront these tensions as well as the additional challenges of negotiating issues of identity, privilege, and colonization on the field (Villenas 1996; Brayboy 2000; Téllez 2005; Subedi and Rhee 2008; Sánchez 2012; Cervantes-Soon 2014). As a border-crossing Chicana conducting research in my former community, I experienced the paradoxical position of being both a "native" to the scholarly community and a *"gringa"*—which is what some of the students called me and which also pointed to my outsider and privileged status. While I looked and sounded in many ways just like my participants, I inevitably represented a U.S. university and brought with me a heavy baggage of U.S. history with México characterized by imperialism, colonization, and white supremacy. In addition, as a middle-class, border-crosser graduate student, I embodied immense privilege despite my insistence in identifying with my participants and their experiences and despite my marginalized social position as a Chicana in the United States. All these factors inevitably contributed to how both my participants and I constructed my research and my presence among them (Cervantes-Soon 2014). These ambivalences were among the most difficult aspects of the research, as my greatest fear was to harm, exploit, or misrepresent my informants.

Michelle Fine (1994) recognizes the complexities of the relationship between researchers and participants and views this liminal and tangled relationship as a hyphen that must not be ignored or resisted but rather worked.

> This relationship . . . is typically obscured in social science texts, protecting privilege, securing distance, and laminating the contradictions. . . . When we opt, instead, to engage in social struggles with those who have been exploited and subjugated, we work the hyphen, revealing far more about ourselves, and far more about the structures of othering. (135)

In order to work this hyphen, I must acknowledge that as a border-crossing Chicana not only did I embody a collision of the multiple layers of power and privilege and simultaneous subalternity in the United States (Anzaldúa 1987), but my bonds with the site and the participants were intellectual and political as well as personal. While my border-crossing Chicana positionality was complex and I was not exempt from the pitfalls of colonizing research, it also compelled me to maintain higher ethical standards and a commitment to my participants that went beyond academic pursuits. In Michelle Téllez's (2005) words:

> I have had to acknowledge that in some ways my own interests are being served, and that I could very well walk away from the community and not be held responsible for my subsequent

actions. Because I see myself reflected in the community and because of my consciousness as a Chicana feminist, I cannot remove myself from the commitment that I have to continue my relationship with [the community]. (52)

Moreover, as a Chicana feminist ethnographer, I interpreted the narratives the women shared as more than stories. These were rather testimonios—full of urgency and intention—which immediately turned me, more than a listener and researcher, into a witness. As such, I am compelled to action, commitment, solidarity, compassion, and inevitably love. While this is not a good example of objective science, it is the way I have worked the hyphen. This process has allowed me and my participants to move into a type of *transborder convivencia* that promotes research and actions committed to the collection and production of knowledge for transformative purposes across physical and symbolic borders (Trinidad Galván 2011). The consequences have been new possibilities for healing and for meaningful pathways to build solidarity with my research participants (Mohanty 2003). Through these organic processes I have been able to engage in the type of feminism on the border (Saldívar Hull 2000) that calls Chicanas to build solidarities with Third World feminists to reveal the oppression induced by global capitalism as well as women's agency and to build a global solidarity that recenters local epistemologies from the South (within and outside the North), extending transborderly to move toward collective feminist politics (Trinidad Galván 2014). Nonetheless, I acknowledge that even this work is far from innocent and that there is a long way to go to decolonize knowledge production processes and recognize, include, and center in substantial ways the subaltern knowledges of the South *outside* the North as Trinidad Galván urges us to do.

Writing Choices

Except for the principal, who noted that "Altavista has no secrets" and insisted that I use her real name as well as the school's, I utilize pseudonyms for all my informants to provide some degree of anonymity. In addition, I use first names when referring to Altavista's educators. While this is an uncommon practice, it reflects more closely the way students referred to many of their teachers as well as the intimacy and democratic values characteristic of the school.

I should again note that I did not pretend to be a neutral ethnographer or an objective writer, and my own reflections and emotions will be evident along the way. I believe that this emotion is important to my research, as it humanized the researcher-researched relationship and might reduce, even if to a small degree and at least on my part, the commodification and trivialization of the lives of those who so graciously shared their stories with me.

Furthermore, through my writing, I wish to communicate a glimpse of the feelings, thoughts, and reflections that the young women in this book expressed to me and to others as I got to know them through their narratives, their photographs, and the songs and poetry they wrote and shared with me. I have drawn significantly on testimonio as a method for writing. Therefore, as exemplified by the introductory vignette about Karla, writing this book has involved a careful assembling of all these pieces, which includes my own translations of my informants' statements, hoping to bring a nuanced picture of their lives without betraying their trust and authenticity. I quote my informants extensively to maintain the faithfulness to their voices as much as possible. If the stories sound dramatic, it is not to sensationalize but to reveal the urgency of the social realities that they experience every day and the meaning that these have in their lives and developing identities. Nonetheless, I should also clarify that none of the stories are of my own making or exaggeration, but all reveal, as much as possible, the women's own words.

Also, because of the length of their quotes, I usually include just the English translation. While all informants spoke to me in Spanish, needless to say, there are many variations. In order to capture the essence of their message, I have translated the girls' local linguistic practices when appropriate, but in some cases, I provide select phrases of their own words along with my translation to give room to other interpretations. Although I believe I had the capacity to adequately translate their narratives, not only because of my knowledge of the local culture and vernacular but also because of my knowledge of the speakers themselves, I realize that still much can be lost in translation, and I am responsible for any misrepresentations.

Structure of the Book

The fact that there are arguably no in-depth analyses of the impact education can have in the lives of subaltern young Juárez women, and considering the centrality of schooling in the formation of identities, a fundamental goal of this book has been to present the stories of the women in the context of Preparatoria Altavista. But in contrast to other school ethnographies that offer an extensive analysis of the site, given the extraordinary significance that Altavista had in these women's lives, this book seeks to more deliberately illuminate the ways in which this school promoted the young women's autogestión. Therefore, as previously mentioned, and at the risk of shortchanging both, this book merges the stories of the school and the young women to offer a more nuanced understanding of the potential that critical education can have in the promotion of autogestión. Without this nuanced illustration, notions of what counts as transformative education for subaltern women would continue to be obscured by the assumption that any given school could foster autogestión in the highly repressive context of Juárez, and "education" can again be trapped in the neoliberal discourse of development and economic empowerment. On the other hand, a nuanced analysis of the girls' self-authorship also seeks to demonstrate that the young women are not passive victims who can be simply rescued by a school with a missionary calling. Instead, the book aims to reveal the dialectical ways in which the young women were able to remake and redefine the terms of their liberation in the sacred space that Altavista offered them—a space that the girls themselves helped create.

With this in mind, chapter 1 provides a synopsis of the context that frames the lives of the protagonists of this book. The first part of the chapter provides a historical perspective of the city of Juárez that may help the reader understand the source of the demonizing discourses about the Mexican side of the border, with an emphasis on contemporary Juárez. The second part of the chapter focuses on the context of Preparatoria Altavista, including historical information about the school to understand its grassroots orientation and philosophical framework, and some of the challenges that the school has faced in order to maintain its critical and social justice orientation.

Chapter 2 introduces the protagonists of this book and offers an analysis of their lives drawing from their own perspectives. It also incorporates the insights gained into the protagonists' identities through an adaptation of a photovoice activity. The goal is to provide a more detailed portrait of the inner worlds and everyday lives of these young women.

Chapter 3 provides a more detailed illustration of the distinct elements that characterize Altavista's own articulation of critical pedagogy. It illustrates the ways in which the Altavista community, including teachers and students, resists hegemonic educational trends and policies to enact a pedagogy of freedom, revolutionary love, critical discourse, and activism with the ultimate goal of fostering autogestión.

Chapter 4 reveals some of the dialectical and cultural practices that make Altavista unique and liberating for young women. The chapter offers an analysis of the steps that teachers and students take to create a space as *Refugees* in the school that recognizes young women's subaltern knowledge and in which the young women can engage their own pedagogical practices, feel safe to envision their own forms of liberation, and engage in collective agency.

Chapter 5 provides a nuanced typology of three pathways conducive to autogestión cultivated by Altavista and focusing on its development at the individual level. The chapter illustrates the pathways through portraits of women whom I have identified as the *Redirectors,* the *Reinventors,* and the *Redefiners* to reveal the process of self-authorship at the intersections of the many realms in the women's lives and the ways in which Altavista played a role.

An epilogue concludes the book and offers an afterthought of personal reflections on this journey. It also provides a synopsis of life after high school graduation for each one of the women in the study with whom I was able to maintain a relationship.

The narratives and snapshots of autogestión presented in this book bear witness to the critical consciousness, agency, and intellectual capacity that subaltern Juárez girls can have in dismantling discourses of perpetual victimization, naïveté, and immaturity. By shedding light on the centrality of the school in the development of autogestión, this analysis also hopes to counter the hopelessness propagated by much of the discourse about urban high schools and illustrate the possibility of schools in proposing viable paths for liberation and for interrupting, to some extent, the culture of cynicism and sociopolitical disengagement among poor youth in urban centers and contexts of unrest. What we can hope to gain is a more humanizing portrait of subaltern Juárez girls and a better interpretation of what may count as empowering education for marginalized youth.

CHAPTER 1

Border Paradoxes, Dystopia, and Revolutionary Education

The U.S.-Mexican border es una herida abierta where the Third World grates against the first and bleeds. And before a scab forms it hemorrhages again, the lifeblood of two worlds merging to form a third country—a border culture.

—Gloria Anzaldúa, *Borderlands/La Frontera: The New Mestiza*

D IVIDED IN TWO PARTS, this chapter provides a sketch of the context that helps frame the lives of the women in this book. Knowledge of these contexts is crucial in order to better understand the stories of the young women presented in subsequent chapters as well as the factors that contribute to the young women's everyday life experiences and the socioeconomic and political histories that frame their aspirations, constraints, and struggles. Moreover, understanding their context allows us to better recognize the women's agency, their processes of self-authorship, and the knowledge they generate within these spaces.

The first part of this chapter aims to offer a portrait of Juárez by discussing some of the complexities and multiplicity of factors that have given way to the city's condition at the time of the study and that may further illuminate the implications for young women. With this background in mind, the second part introduces Preparatoria Altavista, the main setting where I observed and interacted with the young women in this study, emphasizing its grassroots origins and the way the school has evolved to offer a space of liberation for marginalized youth. While the perspectives of the young women about Altavista are crucial in this book, they will be provided in length in other chapters. My intention here is to provide a sociohistorical look at the school in order to better understand the context that was presented to the girls. Therefore, this part has been informed mainly by Armida, the principal of Altavista, and other veteran teachers, such as Jorge and Rigoberto, all of whom graciously and candidly shared their perspectives during interviews and informal conversations, as well as by documentary analyses of the local research and the events taking place in the city at the time.

Ciudad Juárez: City of Dreams, City of Nightmares

Ciudad Juárez, Chihuahua, has drawn international attention for almost two decades. Located on the U.S.–México border, across El Paso, Texas, and with over one million residents, Juárez is one of the largest industrialized border cities in the world (see Figure 1).[1] There is perhaps no better illustration of Gloria Anzaldúa's framing of the border as an open wound than this city, whose hemorrhage, more than a metaphor, is a literal reality. Since the 1990s, Juárez has been known as a violent city, first as a killing field for women with the hundreds of unspeakable feminicides that continue to be an issue today and since 2008 as the epicenter of the war on drugs that led to over six thousand cartel-related deaths. Not surprisingly, Juárez has been the topic of a plethora of media reports and public discourses that sensationalize and demonize the city and its residents, particularly the youth and the poor, and render women as doomed, fragile, and voiceless victims.

But in order to have a more nuanced understanding of the current complexities of Juárez, the city must be analyzed in the larger historical, economic, and political contexts of the Juárez/New Mexico/El Paso, Texas, region (Lugo 2008). Violent and forceful power struggles and bitter contestations over territory between different groups have characterized the area since the first settlements of Spaniard colonizers and U.S. expansionism that demarked the current geopolitical borders and more recently through economic globalization, drug trafficking, and militarization. This legacy of power struggles and conflict has inevitably contributed to the identity of the area.

Marking Borders, Creating Identities

Historian Oscar Martínez (2006) notes that the U.S.–México border has long been framed by both the United States and México as a deeply troubled periphery of cultural deviance from both national cores. On the one hand, many U.S. residents associate the border with uncontrolled illegal migration, racial battles, and various kinds of criminal behaviors—from

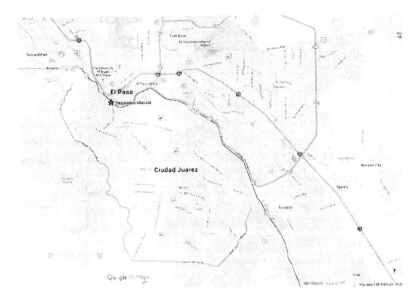

Figure 1. Juárez/El Paso Metropolitan Area and Preparatoria Altavista. Map data copyright 2016 by Google Maps.

underage drinking to corruption and prostitution. On the other hand, Mexicans feel apprehension and distrust toward the United States. This is not surprising, given the history of unequal power relations that have obligated México to give in to the United States' forceful and ambitious demands on many occasions (Martínez 2006). Hence México's northern region often receives considerable criticism from México's interior for its close relation to the United States. Border residents are often stereotyped as culturally *"agringados"* or Americanized and as morally permissive in their desire to attract U.S. tourism or adopt an American lifestyle. While stereotypes of people on both sides of the border exist, the geopolitical boundary of the U.S.–México border emphasizes the stark contrasts between the two countries, reifies an implicit rivalry, and ascribes national and cultural identities in the public imagination (Vila 2000, 2003).

Take for instance the unilateral border policies that have governed this political boundary (Coronado 2008). Prior to 1917, border residents were able to move relatively freely across the Juárez–El Paso area, but after 1917, U.S. immigration reform has imposed increasingly rigorous restrictions, documentation requirements, and inspections for those who want to enter the United States, and these have helped to frame Mexicans as undesirable, as a potential burden, or as latent criminals unless proven differently. Moreover, lifestyles on either sides of the border differ significantly. The U.S. minimum wages during the time of the study were eleven times the minimum wages of Juárez, and paradoxically, while Juárez is considered an economically advantaged city in contrast to the rest of México, El Paso is one of the poorest cities in the United States.[2] Another significant difference between these so-called sister cities is their reputations in the public imagination. Whereas El Paso has been rated as one of the safest American cities for many years, Juárez has been increasingly viewed as a center of perdition, and much more so during the recent years of the drug wars when international media considered it to be among the most violent cities in the world.

But much of Juárez's negative reputation originated after the passage in 1917 of the "Ley Seca," a Texas law that prohibited the production, sale, or consumption of alcohol (González de la Vara 2002). As El Pasoans turned to their Mexican neighbor as their exhaust valve to engage in these and other morally permissive activities, they fostered an industry that thrived due to consumer demand often from affluent tourists, the U.S. military, and other clandestine clientele wishing to enjoy alcohol, sex, and drugs not readily available in the United States. Americans were the main beneficiaries of the revenues of these activities—approximately 40 percent of the businesses were American owned (Martínez 2006). Americans were also the main consumers, which led to the uncontainable smuggling of alcohol and drugs into the United States. This highlights the fallacy of moral superiority that has been assigned to El Paso (González de la Vara 2002). By the early 1930s, the "sin city" industry declined and other types of business and activities developed to attract tourists, such as Mexican souvenir stores, hotels, restaurants, theaters, and even the Juárez Coliseum, where a variety of shows, bazaars, and athletic competitions took place. Juárez also became a cheaper source of healthcare for El Paso residents willing to cross. Despite these and other attractions that continued to bring in people from El Paso and other parts of the United States, the depiction of Juárez as in need of redemption remains today.

In sum, the stark differences between El Paso and Juárez as well as a history characterized by asymmetrical power relations have contributed to their collective identities, often positioning their residents in dichotomous ways, as winners and losers, criminals and puritans, legal and illegal (Lugo

2008). Despite these separations and disparities, hybridity and liminal spaces exist, and codependency patterns of supply and demand, as well as kinship and friendships that bind people on both sides of the border in complicit relationships, have pushed institutions, at least to some extent, toward binational cooperation (Staudt 2008).

The Social Consequences of Industrialization and Economic Globalization

While gender issues in Juárez did not receive worldwide attention until the early 1990s, they have been in the works since the founding of the area and greatly influenced by transborder dynamics. In part, everyday life in Juárez and the evolution of gender relations have been shaped by a series of economic phenomena that have taken place in the region. Since the 1890s (with the exception of the 1930s), the Juárez–El Paso area functioned as a "labor depot" attracting mainly males from central and southern México (Lugo 2008, 181) to European American–owned border markets, including the mining industry, ranching, agriculture, and railroad construction. Also, for over twenty years, the El Paso–Juárez area (like other border towns) played a key role as a site of recruitment and gathering in the implementation of the Bracero Program in the United States.[3] This program, which hired only males, brought more than 80,000 *braceros* from rural México every year to the area (Vogel 2004). Many were not able to join the program and ended up settling in Juárez, and when the program was terminated in 1964, it left 200,000 unemployed braceros along the border in addition to large numbers of agricultural workers from southern México who continued to migrate north (Fernández-Kelly 1983).

With these developments, unemployment rates along the Mexican border reached 50 percent and Mexican officials sought to address this problem with the implementation of the Border Industrialization Program (BIP), which introduced the export processing industrialization or maquiladora industry in 1965.[4] At the initial stages, the BIP temporarily solved the unemployment problem by hiring men in the construction of industrial parks and residential buildings, which were needed due to increased migration (Fernández-Kelly 1983). Yet, as Juárez became an Export Processing Zone (EPZ) with an increasing number of maquiladoras, the unemployment issue remained unsolved, and an unprecedented gender shift emerged.[5]

Transnational corporations in Juárez belonged to the textile and electronic industry and preferred to hire women for the assembly sector. Female workers were considered cheaper to employ, more docile, less likely to demand their rights, manually agile, more capable of withstanding repetitive monotonous assembly line work, and naturally disposable (by leaving work voluntarily) (Joekes and Weston 1994). Up to 90 percent of the maquiladora workforce before 1983 were women (Fernández-Kelly 1983; Lugo 2008). This stimulated a new wave of migration from central and southern México, but this time the migrants were women. Maquiladoras began to employ men in 1983, but it took twenty years to gradually increase the gender balance in the labor force.[6]

The implementation in 1994 of the North American Free Trade Agreement (NAFTA), which aimed to eliminate barriers to trade and investment between the United States, Canada, and México, fully opened up the city (and the country) to a neoliberal regime that has had profound effects on the city's social fabric. As Juárez's reputation grew as one of the best cities in Latin America for multinational corporations to do business, the maquiladora industry expanded to become a major source of employment in the city. As such, in the last several decades, Juárez became to many migrants the Mexican version of the American dream, where men and women could envision the possibility of better life and job prospects and increased opportunities to continue their education rather than remain in their declining rural towns.[7] Thus, with the continuous migration, the Juárez population saw a 900 percent increase in the second half of the twentieth century, reaching over 1.2 million people by 2000, the majority of whom were children and young adults (Rubio Salas 2005).

Nonetheless, while Juárez and México have benefited to some extent from this neoliberal regime, they have remained on the disadvantaged side of the bargain.[8] While the maquiladora industry considerably reduced the unemployment rate, it did not reduce poverty levels (Portes and Hoffman 2003; Rubio Salas 2005), which climbed above the national average at the end of the millennium due to the low wages and high cost of living in the city (Brugués Rodríguez 2005). The severity of economic inequality is such that more than half of the total Juárez income finds its way to only 11.3 percent of the population, and the poorest Juárez residents, who constitute almost 34 percent of the population, share 9.5 percent of the total income in the city (Pérez Molina 2008). Moreover, without the right to unionize, maquiladora workers' protection is nonexistent and labor conditions are harsh, forcing more than forty hours of labor a week, allowing child labor by failing to investigate fake IDs, and discriminating against women who may be pregnant. Not surprisingly, women workers tend to be at a greater disadvantage, as those who are mothers are forced to accept part-time employment or are subject to interrupted periods of work. This limits their ability to secure benefits like retirement savings, health and life insurance, and salary raises.

The unlikely conditions for making a living on maquiladora wages and the unfeasible social mobility that the industry offers to the working classes have stimulated the proliferation of an informal economic sector in Juárez that survives at the margins and in a variety of semiclandestine economic activities, such as street vendors, garage sales, and food stands, among many others.[9] The informal market is increasingly popular among women who are able to receive an income while working from their own porches, but they remain disenfranchised and unable to receive institutional benefits. Moreover, women also tend to be further disadvantaged when their domestic partners are the owners of the business, as women often do much of the work without receiving compensation (Chant 2003).

The rapid growth of the population in Juárez has also generated the abrupt expansion of emergent and incohesive spaces, inadequate urban infrastructure, and lack of public services (Cital Beltrán 2005). The slums of Juárez are characterized by poorly built homes, with extremely reduced spaces, where many family members live together often in a single room, and where children lack a bed to sleep (Moreno Acosta 2008). Pervasive problems of lack of clean water and electricity in these peripheral colonias, as well as lack of transportation and insufficient paved roads, increase costs on the most underresourced households and pose significant issues of public health, safety, and environmental pollution. Family healthcare, basic levels of emergency care, and medical specialty services are severely underfunded and understaffed. And the lack of economic and public resources and limited participation from the private sector make these challenges even more difficult to undertake.

Family and Gender Roles

In Juárez, women have played a significant role in the transformation of families. Most of the families that migrated from southern parts of México followed traditional gender roles in which the father is the breadwinner.

However, it is frequently the mother who finds employment. This rupture of traditional gender roles makes the undertaking of domestic chores and childcare a real challenge. Women are also more prone to live alone and to head multiple family or extended family households. The latter situation sheds light on the domestic arrangements promoted by the circumstances in the city, in which grandmothers take care of the grandchildren.

If the increase of women in the labor force has brought about new gender roles in the family, it has not been accompanied by males' undertaking of domestic work. Domestic labor continues to be considered inferior and is traditionally assigned to women. Thus, it has been viewed as automatically generated and readily available, and traditional perspectives on this patriarchal arrangement have only slowly and marginally begun to change. Mothers who opt to work the night shift in order to spend the day with their children or take care of domestic chores end up exhausted both physically and emotionally. And those who choose to work during the day often feel guilty when their children become involved in juvenile delinquency (Pérez Molina 2008).

Despite the magnitude of the issue, both the public and private sectors have been clearly insensitive and unresponsive to the needs of female workers. While for twenty years women were expected to take on the load of maquiladoras' assembly lines, insufficient services and incompatible work conditions forced them to put their children at risk for the sake of employment, not to mention the fact that households headed by women tend to be the poorest. Maquiladoras' irregular and long work schedules, the lengthy commutes to the workplace, and the high rates of single motherhood point to the adverse circumstances in which women were pushed to become breadwinners and at the same time provide for the affective and social needs of their children. Consequently, Juarenses between seventeen and forty years of age who were born to maquiladora homes most likely grew up in single-mother households, and many without the support of relatives or childcare services. Some fortunate ones were raised by their grandmothers or some other relative, but it is not farfetched to believe that a good number of them had no other company than their siblings and no choice but to assume parental roles. The youth in this type of situation spent much of their time in the barrio, where they formed relationships and shaped their identities. These are the type of circumstances in which many of the young women in this study, as well as their parents and siblings, grew up.

Feminicides and the Normalization of Violence against Women

As might be clear by now, the once male-oriented Juárez labor market that suddenly began to massively attract women did not necessarily translate into women's emancipation. While the maquiladora industry opened new opportunities for women's economic independence, working-class women's participation in the labor force has been and continues to be motivated more by necessity and oppressive conditions than by liberation from patriarchy and independence (Craigie 2005). In addition to increased responsibilities and poverty, disenfranchised women have had to cope with a pervasive lack of security, potential violence inside and outside the home, and uncertain access to justice (Limas and Ravelo 2002; Schmidt Camacho 2005). Some argue that the neoliberal governance in Juárez resulted in not only cheap women's labor (Fernández-Kelly 1983) but also the commodification and in many cases violent exploitation of their bodies (Schmidt Camacho 2005; Taylor 2010; Connell 2015).

The commodification of women's bodies was not a new phenomenon in Juárez. The city's history of catering to men's needs and wants from both sides of the border meant well-established centers of prostitution, and images of sexualized women's bodies as marketing strategies, had long begun to inundate the city (Wright 2001). But nothing manifested the devaluation of women like the hundreds of reported and unresolved feminicides committed in Juárez since 1993 (Fregoso 2000; Amnesty International 2003), with half of the victims being twenty years or younger (Moreno Acosta 2008; Palmer 2008). These crimes drew international attention as some of the murders fit a recurring pattern of distinct characteristics, such as daylight kidnappings, the victims' physical resemblance and working-class backgrounds, systematically mutilated bodies, and mass graves (Ballí 2009). While not all the feminicides were committed in these conditions (many of them occurred as part of domestic violence), they are all often considered collectively for their significance in reflecting the widespread aggression against women in the city.

Much of the risk for women or anyone else stems from structural factors such as poverty, a fragile democracy and weak institutions, corruption among the authorities, the lack of opportunities, and other global factors such as the illicit traffic of drugs and weapons and a degraded environment. But, especially in the barrios, women are safe neither in the streets nor at home. Very young wives and those in forced marriages are the most frequent victims of violence. Julia Monárrez Fregoso (2005) notes that young women are among the most vulnerable to domestic violence, especially when they have children, because they would rather remain in the family than face life with their children alone. The problem is of such magnitude that in the state of Chihuahua, one of every five women is a victim of domestic violence by her partner and two are victims of emotional abuse (Monárrez Fregoso 2005). Furthermore, Kathleen Staudt (2008) indicates that "one in four women with partners reports physical violence in the United States and Mexico, but despite these similarities, an average of six times more women and girls are murdered on one side of the border than the other" (5). These statistics demonstrate the high levels of impunity among Mexican perpetrators and corroborate Staudt's (2008) assertion that "domestic violence has become normalized and routine" (2). This pattern of violence and murder of women in Juárez threatens not only women's right to life but almost all their rights. It has profoundly affected women's freedom of movement, their right to work in safe conditions, their right to leisure activities, and even their right to physical and mental health.

According to the Instituto Municipal de Investigación y Planeación (IMIP) (2002) of Ciudad Juárez, the main causes of women's violent death were reported as "undetermined" or with no apparent cause, yet they were committed with excessive violence and brutality. In other words, they were viciously murdered for no other reason than for being women. The first explanation for the ghastly feminicides (those that followed a distinctive pattern and in which dead and tortured women's bodies were found buried in the desert) was that a pathological serial killer was loose in the city. This assumption freed Juarenses and any public or private institution from any responsibility. Staudt (2008), however, argues that violence against women is a more pervasive problem at the border and manifested in everyday life: two-thirds of the feminicides have involved "girls and women for whom death came at the hands of husbands, boyfriends, partners, or perhaps opportunistic friends or neighbors who transformed the interpersonal violence into murders" (2).

An analysis of the causes of this generalized and systematic violence against women is out of the scope of this book, but suffice it to say that the centuries of territorial conflicts in the region manifested in colonization, U.S. expansionism, narcotraffic, and neoliberalism have left a ripple effect that has been most devastatingly and profoundly felt in recent decades by women and the poor (including men, even if differently) who attempt to move through and make a living in the fractured public and intimate spaces of Juárez (Ballí 2009). Thus, Cecilia Ballí (2009) interprets the feminicides as a reflection of "the new kind of society that is under construction in Ciudad Juárez" (13), stemming from a variety of local and global factors and struggles for territory among wealthy landowners, politicians, drug cartels, and the citizenry, including young and poor women and men where "gender and power are continually renegotiated" (155). As disempowered and dispossessed men constantly seek to assert their threatened masculinity over public space, Ballí reasons, young women become the transgressors and, hence, normative and convenient recipients of their violence—men's ultimate expression of manhood. This is a learned hypermasculinity performed, reinforced, and reproduced by a militarized and highly repressive context.

Staudt (2008) also blames the widespread violence on flawed political and criminal justice institutions on the border. It is not new that patriarchal values are at the core of the Mexican government and its practices, and the poor responsiveness from the public and private sector to the needs of working women is a good example. Rather than seeing the crimes as a pervasive pattern of gendered violence with profound roots in a dominant patriarchal ideology, paradoxical depictions of the role of the Mexican woman as solely of motherhood, service to others, and the embodiment of moral virtue as well as the prevailing image of border women as sex laborers and promiscuous have been used by Mexican authorities to justify the violence, framing it as a natural consequence to women's own immorality, while simultaneously increasing labor demands and reducing citizenship (Wright 2001; Fregoso 2003; Craigie 2005; Schmidt Camacho 2005).

Although since the emergence of the feminicides to the present the families of the victims, women workers, and women's rights activists have continuously demanded justice, their mobilization is constantly being unmade by discourses that trivialize and normalize violence against women, and by neoliberal policies and sexist repressions from the state (Wright 2001, 2004; Castillo and Tabuenca Córdoba 2002; Fregoso 2003; Washington Valdez 2005; Lugo 2008; Staudt 2008). From dramatized performances and marches, black and pink crosses, altars, and poetry and songs to various ways of framing their protests and the victims, antifeminicide activists have utilized numbers as well as a variety of symbols, performances, and discourses to raise consciousness and draw more local and international support.

There has been considerable rhetoric and promises of justice on the part of the state, but the results have often been nothing but impunity and the torture and punishment of scapegoats utilized in the authorities' futile efforts to achieve credibility. Staudt (2008) considers that free press, the rule of law, and professional accountability are essential conditions in order for governments to respond adequately to violence against women. But according to Rocío Gallegos, the newspaper editing coordinator of *El Diario de Juárez* at the time of my fieldwork, Mexican journalists constantly fear repercussions from criminals, are faced with choosing between self-censorship and death, and are often victims of impunity (Conti 2011). In addition, most Juárez residents view the police with distrust and suspicion. And with the presence of the federal police and the military in Juárez due to the drug wars that erupted in 2008, women's sense of insecurity in the past decade has been worse than ever.

Youth and Life in the Barrio

Alejandro Portes and Kelly Hoffman (2003) assert that extreme levels of poverty—even for those who are employed—and excess of inequality in Latin American cities with neoliberal economies lead the masses to a dead-end road of indignation, especially in urban areas. This, they argue, has given rise to an intensification of violent crime and illegal transactions in the cities (including the dependence on a drug economy, extortions, and kidnappings) as a reaction to their hopeless and precarious living conditions. This analysis corroborates some of the possible reasons why Juárez working-class youth often consider the quick economic benefits of drug trafficking, especially when a low-level drug dealer will make more money in a single *"burrada"* or transaction than in various months of work at a maquiladora (Moreno Acosta 2008).

Bordering one of the countries with the highest illicit-drug consumption has been fundamental to the development of Juárez as a major drug trafficking area and to the consolidation of the Juárez Cartel as one of the most powerful in the world. Moreover, due to drug stagnation on the Mexican side of the border with post-9/11 increased border security, Juárez went from being a prominent pathway of drug traffic to becoming a site of major drug sales and consumption.[10] With this development, organized crime and violence in the form of retributions have also become a major issue.

Juárez youth are the most affected by the cycle of drugs and crime, both as victims and as perpetrators. This is particularly true for those living in the city's slums, who spend long hours at home alone and whose limited home space forces them to roam in the streets for much of their day. At as young as ten years of age, children are increasingly attracted to dealing and using illicit drugs (Moreno Acosta 2008). The use of cocaine and heroin is among the highest in the country, and thousands of "picaderos" or clandestine drug outlets abound.[11] A great number of young people live in zones where violence is normalized, where victims are seen as deserving of pain, and where life expectancy is significantly reduced by the deaths resulting from fights or retributions (Moreno Acosta 2008). In addition, approximately five hundred gangs exist in Juárez, comprised of many armed members, who were often recruited by cartels during the drug wars. Surely, youth who want to stay away from these risks must possess the necessary agency, intelligence, and skills to circumvent them as they navigate the barrio on a daily basis.

The west side of the city, where I conducted this study, is the most marginalized, and though it may well be faced with the most severe economic challenges, the youth in this zone are highly stigmatized and criminalized, even when they are students. They are feared and often discriminated against in jobs, schools, and other social institutions, further diminishing their opportunities. Misunderstood by a middle class whose lifestyle has little to do with them, these youth are often regarded as mediocre at best. They are also often and quickly blamed for the social problems in their communities, making them victims of arbitrary abuse and scapegoating from the police and the military.

Access to Education

What hope is there for Juárez marginalized youth? Some would argue that education is the only available path for social mobility. While in theory all Mexican youth have the right to public schooling at all levels, only basic education (grades kindergarten to 9) was compulsory and hence fully sponsored by the state at the time of this study.[12] And even then, parents are frequently asked to bring materials to school and pay for the required uniforms, supplies, and transportation. Teachers, whose salaries are meager, also tend to subsidize many of the classroom expenses. As one elementary teacher explained to me, "As a teacher, all you get your first day of work is a box of chalk and a blackboard eraser. After that, you're on your own."

Chihuahua is one of the states that has invested most heavily in education, yet it remains one of the states with the highest rates of illiteracy among people fifteen years of age and older, and Juárez is the city with the highest dropout rate in the state (Montero 2005). The reasons are not difficult to deduce. First, most public schools are overcrowded and under-resourced, and schools at the level of *preparatoria* or *bachillerato* (grades 10–12) only give access to about one-third of the adolescents who are of age to attend (Montero 2005). These schools are poorly distributed across the city, forcing poor students to travel very long distances, which is time consuming, expensive, and dangerous. For those who need to work to help support the family, this inconvenience represents an important obstacle to continued studying, effectively excluding the most vulnerable youth—those whose families subsist with incomes of less than two minimum salaries, such as members of the informal labor sector, the proletariat, and indigenous communities (Montero 2005). For youth living in the peripheral areas of the city, the lack of space at home also limits their ability to study or do homework, as they often have to wait until everyone has gone to sleep.

Women also tend to be underrepresented at a rate of 7 percent below that of men at the high school level (Montero 2005), as educating them may be perceived as an unnecessary burden when they are expected to get married and leave the household, or to stay home and help with childcare. Furthermore, it is well known that most of the murders and disappearances of women have occurred as they moved across public spaces, such as when commuting between home and work or school. Considering the lack of schools in the most marginalized areas, inadequate transportation, and unsafe streets of the shantytowns that women have to navigate on a daily basis, going to school can be perceived as an unnecessary risk and expense by many families.

Second, in Juárez, education has been perceived almost exclusively as a way to prepare youth for the job market, and both the state and the maquiladora industry have further promulgated these functional goals of schooling by providing support to technical high schools that will train students to become skilled workers. Nonetheless, given that many of the working-class youth have witnessed the oppressive work conditions of the maquiladora industry—the main job market available to them—the outcomes of education may not appear too attractive. Moreover, a curriculum that fails to recognize the experiences of urban youth and offer them the tools to analyze and transform their social realities may seem irrelevant and archaic and further discourage youth to invest their time, limited resources, efforts, and safety for the sake of formal education. As Susana Molina ("La Oveja Negra"), a working-class Juárez activist and MC of the hip-hop band Batallones Femeninos, stated to a listening crowd of college students during my fieldwork:

> The reality of this city does not allow us to dream of a wonderful world because we live in a disgusting world, where impunity, injustice, the already established, and normalcy leave us out of the game. At my twenty-five years of age I should have a college degree—because I'm brilliant! But I don't like the educational system; it doesn't satisfy me. It doesn't attract me because on the contrary, I feel that I'm wasting my time.

Juárez in Dystopia: The Years of the Drug Wars

Shortly after Felipe Calderón assumed México's presidency in 2006, he declared a war on drug trafficking, possibly as a way to gain control, authority, and credibility after a highly contested presidential election (Faux 2012). While initially his strategy appeared successful in his home state of Michoacán, his crackdown on the drug cartels soon evolved into an unprecedented era of violence and murder at the national level.

In Juárez, Calderon's war fueled an already bloody battle between the Sinaloa cartel (the largest in México) and the Juárez cartel (Campbell 2009). Thus, since 2008, over six thousand cartel-related deaths were reported in Juárez alone, making it Ground Zero of this bloody and uncontrolled war. Still under the shadow of the feminicides, and the impunity that reigns in the city, a multitude of additional crimes, ranging from armed robberies and assaults to extortions and kidnappings, proliferated exponentially. Though never a completely peaceful city, Juárez was hardly what it turned into as a consequence of the drug wars. Juárez became the deadliest city in the country from 2006 to 2010, and was fifth among those with the highest rates of homicides not attributed to organized crime (INEGI 2011). Clearly, murder was not only at the hands of the cartels but was becoming routine in Juárez, in part due to the pervasiveness of impunity that opened the doors to a growing market of kidnappings, extortions, and other crimes committed by ordinary people. It was not only low-level pushers who were being killed. Medical doctors, teachers, university professors, journalists, business owners, critics of the government, and even students and activists became the new targets of extortions, kidnappings, and violent murders. The massacres and drive by shootings were not limited to the rough areas of the city either; they occurred at bowling allies, all types of homes, rehabilitation centers, and even major avenues and intersections. As such, Juárez residents would wake up to decapitated bodies hanging from bridges at major intersections, schools and small business were threatened by extortionists, and parents were assaulted when picking up their children from school.

Between 2008 and 2011, and with U.S. support, President Calderón deployed eleven thousand troops of military and federal police to take control of the violence in Juárez to no avail (Goodman 2011). The violence actually seemed to be getting worse and the military and federal police seemed to consistently arrive late after almost every incident.

Almost everyone I knew in Juárez had been affected in one way or another by the rise in crime during these years. Although most of the casualties were men, the surviving women suffered enormous consequences as they carried the burden of sustaining the home on their own, while mourning the loss of sons, partners, fathers, and brothers, in the midst of fear and an increasingly hostile and militarized context. Those left behind, including children, also experienced an abysmal emotional and psychological trauma as well as health consequences. Many people changed their phone numbers to avoid extortions, and even the socialites' pages on the local newspapers ceased to include family names in their attempt to protect personal information.

Adding to the deep social agony in which the city was immersed, the U.S. economic recession also resulted in significant damage to the border area that was highly dependent on U.S. investments. By 2009 the maquiladora industry in Juárez lost more than 80,000 jobs and about 20 percent of maquiladora employees were given frozen contracts and reduced work hours and salaries.[13] The drug wars, extortions, and kidnappings also brought about the closure of about 10,000 businesses of all types, skyrocketing unemployment, and an exodus of about 100,000 people to El Paso and other parts of the country. Escaping, however, was clearly not a possibility for everyone, including the youth at Altavista. Approximately

7,000 orphans and widowers were among the ones who did not have a choice. Nonetheless, what may come as a surprise is that not all Juárez residents were looking to leave the city. A good number of Juárez's residents—those who remained hopeful or were too rooted in the city—continued their daily lives in the midst of chaos. Most of the people that I talked with during my year of fieldwork loved Juárez deeply and wanted their city back. Therefore, despite the terror, some Juárez residents across various social sectors also engaged in efforts to restore their community, and expressions of resistance against violence and impunity as well as acts of solidarity with victims began to emerge.

In particular, a massacre in the working-class neighborhood of Villas de Salvárcar on a cold December night in 2010 brought fury and a call to action to Juárez residents (Gómez Licón and Borunda 2010). A gunman had burst into a home where high school and college students were having a birthday party. Sixteen people were killed and twelve more were critically injured. Most of the victims were children and teenagers who parents described as good kids, studious, hardworking, and athletes—not the typical targets in a drug war.

The massacre, and especially the reaction from the authorities—which included lack of protection after investigations that led to further retributions and even the Mexican president's suggestion that the victims were most likely gang members[14]—fueled a wave of indignation and outcry. University and high school students across the city, including most of the women in this study, and numerous organizations and people of all ages, rose in solidarity and fury to demand justice. On February 13 over three hundred people marched fearlessly in one of the largest demonstrations against violence, impunity, and militarization since the eruption of the drug wars. But a march of three hundred people in a city of over one million suggests that a good number stayed home paralyzed by fear. This comes as little surprise in a city where activists and the families of victims are often forcefully repressed by both the authorities and other "mysterious enemies," and many have been silenced to death.[15] In learning about these cases, one cannot help but suspect that there is a complicit relationship between everyday criminals of all levels and the authorities.

This is the context that the young protagonists of this book navigated every day, and the consequences were felt by some in very personal ways. The drug wars added a new layer of fear and restraint to the lives of youth, particularly girls. Nothing seemed to stop the massacres, and matters only seemed to get worse as the numbers of casualties grew, women continued to disappear, and activists were murdered. Spending a year of fieldwork in that context was both heartbreaking and terrifying, but in searching for a light of hope, however dim, I found Preparatoria Altavista.

Preparatoria Altavista: A Legacy of Revolutionary Education

I visited Preparatoria Altavista for the first time on a sunny day in March 2008, just a few months before the drug wars put the entire city on edge. In a previous phone call, Armida Valverde, the school principal, had generously agreed to be interviewed. Although I had driven by the school many times before, it was not until this day that I noticed Altavista's peculiar location. It was located at the crossroads of many borders. The school stands only yards away from the Río Bravo (or Rio Grande River) and in very close proximity to El Paso's downtown area. In fact, U.S. buildings such as Wells Fargo and the El Paso City Hall can be easily seen from the school grounds. As I stood in the parking lot, I could see the nicely delineated freeways of El Paso and could not help but notice the stark difference from the unpaved and crooked roads of the dusty shantytown across the Juárez valley covering the hills of the colonias right behind me. Altavista's neighbor to the east is the local juvenile detention center, four miles to the west is the border with New Mexico, and only a few streets down is the largest distribution center of illicit drugs in the city.

The three buildings that made up the school had the typical flat and squared architecture of Mexican offices. They were almost colorless, blending seamlessly with the desert dirt and the city's cement. It appeared to have been a nice-looking school some decades ago, but now it was in urgent need of renovation. Yet the few big trees around it and its large green areas adjacent to the Río Bravo gave it some charm, and I felt a nice calming effect that was in extreme contrast to the chaotic and dangerous feeling of the city as soon as I walked onto the grounds.

Having attended high school in Juárez myself, I was quite familiar with the policies and general culture of Juárez high schools. Contrary to the notion of urban schools in the United States as dangerous and hostile, I expected to find a rather tranquil environment—even in the city that would soon gain the label of being the "murder capital of the world."[16] I knew I would not encounter metal detectors or be expected to sign in at the office and wear a visitor's badge like in many U.S. urban schools. However, I did expect some degree of bureaucracy and formality. I also anticipated that students would wear uniforms, as they do in most Mexican high schools, and a prefect would usher them to class and scrutinize the boys' hair and the length of the girls' skirts.

As soon as I parked my car I was surprised by what I saw. There were a few kids hanging out in the courtyard outside the office. It was ten thirty in the morning, so they surely should have been in class—or so I thought. In my high school days, the office areas would be the last place one would want to be seen when skipping class. Students were not wearing uniforms or military-looking hairstyles as I expected. In fact, some boys had big Afro hairdos and some girls wore punk-style clothes. Maybe these were not Altavista's students, classes were over, or perhaps this was a holiday, I figured.

I walked into the administrative building looking for the principal. There was no front desk or counter. Instead there were four small offices with open doors and big glass windows facing the small hallway. Students and adults came in and out of the offices talking and moving in what I sensed to be a busy but jovial atmosphere. A small group of teenagers sat on the hallway floor writing in their notebooks. I wondered if they were in some kind of detention, but they were talking to some of the people flowing in and out of the offices with no hint of shame or annoyance.

A slender woman seemingly in her midforties and dressed in jeans, sandals, and a buttoned-up brown shirt came out to meet me. It was Armida (as she later urged me to call her), the principal, who welcomed me with her energetic personality. "I'm sorry I couldn't see you earlier; I teach a class in the mornings," she said as she shook my hand. I wondered if she taught at a university like my high school teachers did or if, like my father, she took a double role as principal and teacher. I realized it was the latter when she explained that in addition to being the principal, she was the sociology teacher at Altavista. She walked me to a small room right behind her office. It was functionally furnished with a couch, a chair, a small desk, a mini refrigerator, and a kitchen counter. The room served as both a teachers' lounge and a meeting room. "We will have a little more privacy here than in my office," she explained as she offered me a cold Coca-Cola. Indeed, people came in and out of her office, and a young woman—who I later learned was a student—sat at her desk. I could not tell precisely because no one wore uniforms. Armida seemed quite comfortable at the idea of being interviewed, as interviews were not unusual at Altavista. I had already discussed the purpose of my visit over the phone, so after a brief chitchat, she began to passionately talk about her school.

According to Armida's description, Altavista's student body was composed of approximately three hundred students, of which 49 percent were females and 51 percent were males, ranging from fifteen to eighteen years of age. Most of the students, about 70 percent, came from the barrios of Anapra, one of the poorest areas in the city. "I have been working here since 1985, and in previous years the students came from the Altavista neighborhood and the downtown area, but that is not the case anymore," Armida explained. Not only were these two areas slightly less underprivileged than Anapra, but the population there was getting older as well.

Most students were working class whose parents had completed elementary school, and some came from conditions of extreme poverty and with illiterate parents. But there was some socioeconomic diversity in that a small minority enjoyed a higher degree of privilege; their parents had bachelor's or master's degrees or owned small businesses, such as a mechanic shop or small store. There was also a small sector of the student population whose parents worked in El Paso "legally" (as permanent residents) or "illegally" (using a border visa), as gardeners or maids. But most of the students' families worked in the maquiladora industry or in the informal market. Some of the girls also had part-time jobs at the shoe stores, the two supermarkets right across the street from the school, or the small mall kiosks selling cellular phones. Armida explained that some other students worked at the maquiladora industry: "We have a girl here that works the third shift. She gets out of work and comes directly to school. Her living conditions are very precarious, and that is the case for most of the girls."

In order to have a better understanding of Altavista, I will provide some information about how schooling in México is organized. High school education in Juárez includes grades 10 to 12. It is offered by private and public schools, as well as by *schools by cooperation*. Public schools are funded by the state, and hence are closely controlled by it, but they have limited and selective enrollment typically based on admissions exams. In most cases, even at public high schools, students are still responsible for at least an annual enrollment fee, textbooks, and uniforms. Many middle- and upper-class families send their children to private schools, which can be quite costly.

Altavista is an example of a school by cooperation, which functions almost like a public school but is funded by a combination of federal, state, and local entities in cooperation with social organizations and "those who have a special interest in the community's educational development" (Cámara de Diputados 2007). In other words, while the government provides the building, funding for consumable materials, and some of the teachers' salaries (of those who have "a plaza," namely who are tenured and unionized), schools by cooperation depend on students' monthly tuition fees to cover additional costs, including nonunionized teachers' salaries (which at Altavista are the majority). Given Altavista students' socioeconomic status, they were extremely underresourced. As Armida explained, most of Altavista's students were there because of their parents' efforts and courage; their parents have to be brave enough to take on the expense that education entails. Considering these families' economic situations, the fees that Altavista charged were marginal, and more often than not, students still fell behind on their payments, especially during the harsh economic recession. This, in turn, directly affected the teachers' paychecks and Altavista was often behind on teachers' salaries by at least one month. Therefore, most teachers worked multiple jobs in order to sustain their families, even when working full time at Altavista. That also led a good number of the students, mostly girls, to drop out by their second semester.

Funding from the government was not necessarily more stable. In recent years it had been delayed several months every semester. In addition, restrictions on how to spend the money prevented Altavista's administration from utilizing government funds to pay part-time teachers or purchase furniture, books, or technology. With these limitations, the school was not able to offer some of the basic things that would have supported its students, such as free or reduced enrollment fees, transportation, textbooks, computers, or after-school activities.

Altavista was one of the very few high schools by cooperation that remained in the city, as most had been taken over by the government. Although a school of this kind places a burden on the students and their families and faces severe funding challenges, it also enjoys some degree of freedom from absolute governmental control. Armida revealed that it was this freedom that, while limited, allowed Altavista to frame and enact its distinct philosophy.

> If this school were turned into a Colegio de Bachilleres or a
> CBETIS [public schools fully funded by the state], we would lose
> what in some ways keeps us far away from the center, because
> those are centralized schools. We do not have a supervisor

surveilling us and telling us exactly what to do all of the time. Because there was a time when the teachers used to say, "Let's demand plazas." But then we thought, what would happen if there were plazas? A series of forces would infiltrate into the school trying to control it: the teachers' union, the issue of commissioned teachers, uniforms, and what not. So it's better like this. At least by not receiving resources from the city council and the state, by not receiving plazas, we have a certain margin of autonomy.

But why was autonomy so important to Altavista that teachers were willing to work for such unstable and meager salaries? The answer to this question requires both a look at the past and an understanding of Altavista's philosophy of education, the driving forces of its idealistic teachers.

Altavista's Vision: Thinking Subjects versus Objects of Production

In spite of the growing support for technical and vocational schools aiming to produce skilled workers, *"preparatorias"* or preparatory schools like Altavista have managed to maintain to a certain extent their focus on preparing students for college. They usually offer a program of studies that must be completed in grades 10 to 12 and includes various areas of specialty that provide students with basic knowledge necessary for higher education. During the first three semesters, students take general courses in language arts, literature, philosophy, research methods, mathematics, and both social and natural sciences. By their third or fourth semester, students begin to choose one or two courses related to their field of interest, and by their fifth semester, they are able to choose the discipline cohort that they want to be part of and that will offer a very specific curriculum. These cohorts include: physics and mathematics, economics and administration, chemistry and biology, and social sciences and humanities.

However, at Altavista, preparing students for college is viewed more as a byproduct of the entire schooling experience. While it still maintains the curricular choices described above so that students can begin to prepare for a specific field of study, the main goal that was continuously articulated and emphasized from the first interview with Armida until the very last day of my fieldwork was that of offering a space where youth can affirm their own identities and where they can critically analyze their social realities, learn to question the world around them, and hopefully feel compelled to become agents of change. While some may perceive this as an idealistic and perhaps naïve vision, Armida took into account the contradictions inherent in human agency.

So this is what we insist: if the tendency today is to form technocrats, our emphasis is on the formation of thinking human beings who will take charge of their lives—of their existence—who will question the world in which they live, and do something to change it. Or if they like it, they can keep it the way it is. Because that we cannot define. Because we don't believe that we can completely form anyone. Some accuse us of shaping students as if we were cutting out paper dolls, all looking the same. But those who think in that way must not know anything about schools. We are neither able nor wanting to do that. There is no reason why we must define our students' lives, but it is not true either that we don't seek to form—not leaders nor competitive individuals, but thinking subjects? Yes. Competent beings? That too. Because the one who is competent knows how to do something, the one who can, the one who is able.

Armida's philosophy of education, shared among several of the teachers and founded in a critical view of the current state of education, deserves to be quoted at length.

I believe that there are many truths about education that we have considered as fundamental principles for many years, but how valid and how real are they today? I think that schooling has lost the significance that it represented to society, or the regard it used to receive in our country, where schools and teachers were highly respected. It is not the case anymore because schools are seen as the place to go get a degree, a credential, a certification to get a job, and that's it. Schools are not the place to develop culturally, where you could read this or that person, where you could learn about philosophy and science. No, schools are now oriented to the productive apparatus and that is how the curriculum works. . . . But now, that is the hegemony of the economic analysis of schools. They are meant to form human capital, they say. But wait, it turns out that these are no longer human beings, subjects of rights, they are now human capital, objects of production. They are not meant to think!

After a two-hour conversation on my first visit, Armida took me to a small, dark room that seemed more like a large storage closet at the end of the hallway. When she opened the door, a skinny teenage boy with a big Afro hairdo was sitting in front of a desk operating a set of mismatching technological tools. Armida explained that this room served as the cabin for a radio station that the students had created for the school. Then Armida closed the door. I did not know if this was for the sake of privacy, but then she pointed to the wall behind the door displaying a picture drawn and dedicated to Altavista by Subcomandante Insurgente Marcos (Figure 2), a lead figure of the Zapatista Army of National Liberation (EZLN).[17] The way this mural was protected behind the door of this dark room at the end of the hallway made me think that it represented not a celebrity's autograph but rather a symbol that would remind the coming generations of their political orientation, social justice goals, and solidarity with indigenous and peasant groups. This was important at Altavista, where teachers strived to maintain a connection between each new generation of students with the school's origins in grassroots movements.

Preparatoria Altavista in a Historical Perspective

Schools are neither blank slates nor neutral spaces. Every school embodies a heritage, a set of ideas that led to its invention. Founded by graduates of the Normal School of Salaices in 1968—a peasant teachers' college in a small rural town of Chihuahua that became a driving force in populist movements—Altavista maintains, at least to some extent, its original revolutionary vision. In order to better understand the vision and context that the school provides to its students, it is important to understand the past and current links to grassroots social movements and the way the school has evolved.

Toward the end of the 1960s, México saw important social transformations. On the surface, the country appeared to enjoy prosperity with an emerging and growing middle class. But while consumerism grew among the middle and upper classes in a seemingly peaceful period, the peasantry and urban proletariat were relegated to poverty, marginality, and limited life prospects. Motivated by college and high school students' liberal ideas

Figure 2. Mural drawn by Subcomandante Marcos on one of Preparatoria Altavista's walls.

whose values and styles clashed with the older generation and who began to express their discontent with the social condition of the time, and externally by the various ideological revolutions of the 1960s taking place around the world,[18] several peasant and student movements erupted across the country—with the ones in Chihuahua being the strongest up until 1960 (Office of Special Prosecutor Ignacio Carrillo Prieto 2006).

The teachers' college of Salaices was one of the leading schools in which both students and teachers embraced a leftist position. In all these rural normal schools, students confronted the state's educational authorities, demanding better economic conditions that would allow them to complete their studies. In addition to claiming their own interests, students fought in solidarity with other popular struggles developed at the state and national levels. Rural educators thus played an important role in organizing the peasant and indigenous masses, and many provided the political and military direction to the Mexican socialist guerrillas of 1964 (Office of Special Prosecutor Ignacio Carillo Prieto 2006).

Gustavo Díaz Ordaz, the Mexican president at the time, was extremely authoritarian and insisted on keeping México's image of stability and peace by maintaining absolute control and repressing any kind of protest, especially in anticipation of the upcoming Olympic Games of 1968 that were to take place in México.[19] Numerous people were arrested and put in prison, accused of provoking social turbulence. This included railway workers, politicians, leaders of the medical doctors' strikes, and peasant teachers and leaders of student movements from various states, including some from the Normal School of Salaices (Office of Special Prosecutor Ignacio Carrillo Prieto 2006). This fueled even stronger demands from student, teacher, and peasant movements. But state repression grew as well, climaxing in the Tlatelolco massacre of 1968 in México City, which resulted in the injury, killing, and disappearance of thousands of students, and in the subsequent closing of fourteen teachers' colleges around the country, including the normal teachers' college in Salaices in 1969.[20]

It was in this context of student movements across the nation, unprecedented social challenges, and the simultaneous emergence of Juárez as a modern and industrial city that Preparatoria Altavista was founded in 1968. Coming from the Normal School of Salaices, the founding teachers' Marxist ideology and grassroots backgrounds framed the philosophy of a new urban school. Armida, who was doing research on the history of the school at the time of my fieldwork, explained:

This school has a history of social dissidence since the beginning. And it was created for poor kids. So that is the foundation of the school; that is our foundational legend: that this is the school where the *"rojillos"* are, the rebels. That's how many people see us.

Altavista was indeed established against the current, for in that era, the focus on educational expansion favored technical efficiency over critical and social consciousness, and competition over solidarity, particularly in Juárez, where the maquiladora industry was beginning to flourish. This reputation as *rojillos* or "reds," which represents a tendency toward leftist ideals, had followed them until today.

Nonetheless, the neoliberal trends of the 1980s trickled down to the education sector, which began to increasingly adopt initiatives that aimed to prepare students for the labor force—and in Juárez this meant the maquiladora industry (Rincones, Hampton, and Silva 2008). Schools were considered effective only insofar as students were able to find employment, and curricular transformations began to embrace market goals of productivity and the development of human capital (Silva 2006). These ideas permeated Altavista, and during the 1980s its revolutionary ideology eroded with a new generation of leadership that followed the hegemonic educational trend of efficiency, competition, and technocratic goals. Moreover, Altavista became highly repressive, going along with the authoritarian model of most schools. In the 1980s, the principal, who was very well supported and protected by teachers' unions, was extremely strict and severe, frequently sanctioning students for any minor infraction. This, however, was only a temporary period, for the late 1980s and 1990s brought about key events that played an important role in reconnecting Altavista's current identity to its revolutionary roots.

Several new teachers joined the school in the mid-1980s. They came from various walks of life, but what many of them had in common was a counterculture orientation. They were not involved in political parties but rather in other forms of sociopolitical resistance expressed through music and social movements. These new teachers, who had been influenced by the social movements of the 1960s, included much of the leadership and other faculty at the time of my fieldwork, such as Armida, the principal; Jorge, the assistant principal; and Manuel, an English teacher—all of whom had come from strikes at their universities—as well as Juan, the curriculum specialist, who had been fired from several jobs due to his tendency toward social critique. A few other veteran teachers like Gilberto, the chemistry teacher; Rigoberto, a history teacher; and even Lolo, a younger philosophy teacher, had also had a background of activism in student and peasant movements. Thus their common ideas brought them together and helped them bond.

In 1987 the principal in turn decided to teach a course to the senior class. This did not go well for him, as students soon lost patience with his repressive approach and went on strike demanding that he leave the school. For twenty to thirty days they took over the school until the principal resigned. The state sent a new principal, who was very lenient—mostly because he was often absent juggling multiple jobs and uninvolved with the school. Those teachers with a critical orientation saw this as an opportunity to revive the original project of the school and to enact their own philosophy of education. Rigoberto, a veteran history teacher who had been at Altavista during those years, revealed how crucial this period was.

> This school has a leftist history since its founders. Except during the period of 1983 to 1993, when it was forced to maintain a repressive administration. It clashed with the founders' philosophy. . . .
> But the following administration stopped doing that, more than anything because the principal had three jobs and was not here most of the day. So we lived that experience, which he allowed to happen because he stopped tending to the school. So all the critical ideas, ideas of a Zapatista nature, Marxist, some more moderate, and even some right wing, but the majority tended to be on the left, started to rise. So we began to fight for a more democratic school. . . . I teach a university class, and I was telling them that one of the best periods of my life was that, when all of this erupted, the struggle to take back our school.

Armida also recalled how they began to reconstruct their ideal school during this era.

> We began to create workshops and had the possibility to de-institutionalize what had been established. We started out by creating contracts with students, but then we got rid of them because we realized that this was a very capitalistic approach. Little by little we evolved into a more counterhegemonic school. Not

that we got rid of everything; we still maintain many structures, otherwise it would be completely unstructured, but we began to reject authoritarian and bureaucratic approaches. The principal at the time would get annoyed because we never followed the same system to solve problems—it all depended on its unique circumstances.

According to two teachers' accounts, including Lolo, a philosophy teacher who had been an Altavista student during those years, students organized again in the late 1980s, insisting, among other things, on a new change in leadership. The students succeeded in their demands and it was then that the school regained its original goals and philosophy, and Armida Valverde, who was a full-time teacher at the time, was instituted as Altavista's new principal. However, she never left the classroom, which she saw as crucial in her leadership.

I have realized that remaining in the classroom is what keeps me grounded. When the teachers come to me complaining about how hot the classrooms are and asking me to fix the air conditioner, I'm able to understand them because I'm there too, so I try to hurry up to get what they need. Otherwise, it would be too easy to forget how it feels to be in the trenches. Teaching also helps me get to know most of the students, their needs and their interests.

The other two administrators, Jorge and Juan, took the same approach. During my year at Altavista, Jorge was the assistant principal, but he also taught twelfth-grade communication studies and eleventh-grade literature. Juan, the curriculum specialist, taught tenth-grade language arts. All of them also taught at the Autonomous University of Ciudad Juárez (UACJ).

During a conversation with Armida and Jorge, Armida explained that Altavista's history was not a linear one: "As you can see, it started with a revolutionary vision, then it was lost, and then it was recovered. We have tried several approaches, we have abandoned some, substituted others."

"And we have stagnated too," Jorge added, reminding me that this was not a story of a great vision that gets institutionalized and teachers and students live happily ever after. Altavista has been a contested space where victories, struggles, failures, and new experiments take place in a continuous quest for self-invention and utopia.

Moreover, Preparatoria Altavista has not been untouched by the series of events of the 1990s that took place in the city, including the signing of NAFTA, an increase of drug trafficking and organized crime, and the emergence of brutal violence against women. Rather, they might have also served as a catalyst to recover its revolutionary vision.

In the 1990s, many of the Juárez feminicide victims' bodies were found in the colonias where Altavista's students lived, and an unknown young victim was found on Altavista's school grounds, right at the edge of the Rio Grande River on June 13, 1993. Her body showed evidence of having been violently raped, knifed, stabbed with a tree branch, and killed by a blow to the head with a concrete block (Grupo Ocho de Marzo de Ciudad Juárez 1993–98). Surely, whether the young woman had any relationship with the school or not, the emotional toll on students, teachers, and the wider community in general caused by this and other feminicides impacted Altavista for many years to come. In fact, visual artist Gracia Chávez notes, "Definitely, la prepa Altavista was one of the schools most severely punished by the topic of kidnappings and feminicides," as it served almost as a perfect spot for predators to observe and learn the girls' routines (Hidalgo Glez 2013).

But perhaps equally crucial to Altavista were the activism and critical consciousness that emerged in the city and the world around the feminicides. Furthermore, the rise of the Zapatista movement in 1994 may have also helped revive Altavista's revolutionary spirit. Because Chihuahua had been one of the leading states in past guerrilla and peasant movements, and several of the teachers had a history of activism, there are reasons to believe that these events, as well as the new climate of crime and feminicide in Juárez, triggered Preparatoria Altavista's collective and historical memory.

Preparatoria Altavista in the New Millennium

In the early 2000s, during Vicente Fox's presidency, educational reform furthered the neoliberal path established since the 1980s and education was considered an expense rather than an investment when it did not result in employment. It was simply accepted that schooling in México must prepare students for the menial jobs of production, rather than for the design of systems or technology in the growing industrialization of the country (Silva 2006), much less for questioning asymmetrical power relations between core and peripheral nations in this global economy.

But Altavista had a new administration, and in the midst of compelling events in the history of Juárez and the pervasive educational ideology that pushed schools to produce the students that could fulfill the market's demands, the school initiated a return to its origins. This began with a process of eliminating hierarchies between teachers and students. According to Armida, "freedom" became a foundational element of what they wished their students to experience.

Before, everything was closed. So we began knocking down walls, and the students are now able to go into every space. We don't have any restricted spaces. There are no exclusive restrooms for teachers. No, nothing. But it's part of the experience. Some teachers also stopped taking attendance and substituted exams with other forms of assessment.

This explained the absence of uniforms and the gathering of students in most of the spaces of the administrative offices that I saw during my first visit. They would often use these spaces for their own study groups, to plan activities for the school, or simply to work on their assignments whenever they wished.

Part of the transformation also included a curricular reform based on action research. A group of teachers collected data from students to identify the topics of interest and dedicated many hours to collectively design a relevant curriculum based on the results. All of this took great effort on the part of the teachers, who for the most part had to take second jobs to support their families. Nevertheless, there were teachers who did not fully agree with the orientation of the school. Mateo, a teacher who favored a more traditional and authoritative style, harshly criticized the deviation from the government's mandated curriculum. He took matters into his own hands and complained to the federal government that the school was not following the official guidelines. A delegation of the Secretaría de Educación Pública (SEP) or Office of Public Education officials was sent to Altavista some years before my fieldwork, taking away the curriculum that the teachers had created with threats of closing the school if this ever happened again. The school was put on probation and the annual subsidy provided by SEP was taken away for a few years.

Since then, Altavista has tried, in various ways, to offer a relevant curriculum despite the many impositions from the state that tend to discourage youth to finish their studies. In Armida's view, the increasingly standardized state curriculum is outdated, lacks relevancy and depth, and discourages students from finishing their studies.

> It's a curriculum that has little to do with the interests of today's
> youth and does not include an analysis of the current problems,
> such as issues of gender, which are important and are not covered.
> Issues of human rights and violence should be included in the
> curriculum also, but they are not. And when they are covered,
> it is only as a brush stroke.

Indeed, issues of human rights, violence, and other topics of interest to students are not easy to cover, particularly during an era in which Mexican education mimicked the U.S. trend toward a standardization and accountability. ENLACE, the standardized test mandated by SEP, had just been administered for the first time in April 2009,[21] but according to Armida, it was received with resistance and indifference from both teachers and students.

> There were students that refused to take it. But since this is a
> public school, it is subject to national policy. So we said, OK, here
> it is, but it has no relevance to us. It isn't relevant because the
> information that it provides is the one sought by the official sector.
> It's about the type of individuals that the SEP seeks to form. But
> we are interested in forming a different type of individual.

In the spring of 2010, it was my turn to witness the students' reactions to this state-mandated assessment, which were for the most part negative. Much of their discontent stemmed from seeing the inconsistency between the seriousness that the state demanded of students and the arbitrary way in which state officials administered the test. Although the official academic calendar of SEP specified that the assessments were to be administered from April 19 to 23, state representatives showed up unexpectedly on March 23 and 24, ENLACE tests in hand. Students were in the middle of final projects and had spent a considerable amount of time after school working on them. Several of them were even scheduled for final presentations. However, everything had to be stopped to administer the reading and mathematics exams.

Neither the students nor the teachers or administrators had been notified of this change. Because in their last semester of high school students only take classes relevant to their field of study, those in the social sciences and humanities as well as in the biology and chemistry cohorts had not taken a math course in almost a year. Needless to say, this put them at a great disadvantage on the math test, for which they were given no time to study. Some of the girls that I talked with felt insulted by this inconsiderate attitude of the state and some refused to respond to this portion of the exam. Others saw it just like a census and took the test without giving it much importance. But these inconsistencies were not insignificant. The results of these tests are made public and result in the labeling of schools. Because Altavista's students are already viewed with disdain by many in the outside community, an additional label of failure only aggravates the stereotypes associated with these youth and obscures the lack of formality and seriousness from educational authorities that plays a role in the outcomes. In this way, the state played a major role in the construction of Altavista as a deviant school. This, however, was not the only obstacle that the state had imposed on teachers and students wanting to keep their school. Other important events had also marked the history of Altavista, revealing its vulnerability as well as its strength and collective agency.

Gone with the River: Rebuilding Altavista's Community at the Margins

In the summer of 2006, a severe storm that lasted several days poured over the city of Juárez. Many residents in marginal areas lost their homes to flooding, and broken vehicles piled up in ditches. With the heavy rains, the Rio Grande River overflowed into Altavista, flooding many of the classrooms. The water and mud reached up to four feet high and caused significant destruction. In 2008, when I visited the damaged classrooms that were still in serious need of repair, I saw dozens of broken old computers and technological equipment completely covered by dry mud, shattered furniture, holes in the walls, and broken windows. The river's current had been so strong that it had broken the windows, flipped the tables where the computers were, and cracked the walls. The teachers had even found fish in the classrooms buried in mud. Most of their documents and archives, equipment, books, and supplies were destroyed.

What appeared to have been an attractive building now looked like an abandoned warehouse. The school garden that students had cultivated had been covered by mud that, once hardened, impeded the water from filtering down into the soil, killing the trees, vegetable plants, and flowers. Armida described the emotional devastation that this incident caused to teachers.

> Vanessa, one of the teachers, when she arrived and saw what happened she began to cry. Because truthfully, you felt like . . . all the work, everything had gone to waste, all the effort we invested and all of a sudden you didn't have what you had achieved, you just had a lot of work.

When I began my fieldwork in Altavista in 2009, three years had passed since the flood, but the sight of some of the buildings and classrooms was still quite depressing and the moldy smell had not completely vanished. The ruins stood there, as a reminder of what had been lost, but also of what they had built together. The flood had given Altavista an opportunity to enact their vision. Gone with the river were also admissions exams, which high schools utilize to determine acceptance into the school based on the score and available space. From that point on, Altavista stopped administering them and no efforts were made to replace them. Armida explained that at Altavista these exams were more like a ritual, with no real significance.

> They had no relevance to us. We have always known that many prospective students are academically needy, but that won't stop us from admitting them. What we have thought of doing is develop-ing a diagnostic assessment, but we are still debating whether a test would provide adequate information anyway.

The broken bell was never replaced either, and that served them well as they attempted to create a school where students took responsibility for their own learning and reduced their dependency on extrinsic motivators and behavioral regulation.

SEP never came to Altavista's rescue, but that devastating summer brought renewed solidarity, trust, and passion among teachers to continue the project they had begun during the late 1980s and early 1990s. Thus, a group of about fifteen teachers and staff, as well as some of their family members, rolled up their sleeves and took it upon themselves to clean up the mess and try to recover as much as possible. Many of these teachers got sick with stomach infections and rashes due to the mold and bacteria, but they continued working. Armida explained:

> We seriously worked from like eight in the morning to three in the afternoon every day during the summer. We would think, "Are we ever going to finish? Yes, but when?" My whole body ached! It was really an odyssey. But let me tell you that it really united us. It was like a re-founding of the school. There was a new enthusiasm.

Armida described how as faculty and staff spent time together, working in dire circumstances and sharing their resources, they built community in authentic and organic ways.

> So we created the Group of 50. We called it the G-50. So when the State Director of High School Education asked us who cleaned up, we responded, "The Group of 50." And he said, "Oh, that's good, you have a big group." "Oh, no, no," I said, "it's not a big group." There were only about fifteen people, a little less than half of the people who work here. But the thing was that on Fridays when we were done for the day, we would ask, "So should we get some beers? OK then, put down your fifty pesos!" [*Laughs*] And those who had money with them, because not everyone had money, would donate their fifty pesos and would buy the beer.

The teachers and staff were able to clean up the school to leave it at least in livable conditions. But they were unable to put many of the classrooms back into working order, such as the two science labs and the counseling room. In fact, almost an entire building was in need of complete renovation. When the students got back in the fall, they had to work with even more limited resources, no books, and having to choose between eating lunch or spending their money in an Internet café to keep up with assignments. "It's expensive. You don't eat that day," confessed a student to a reporter during a media interview (Paterson 2006). The student also indicated that together with a classmate, he collected money in order to purchase a computer for the small student-operated radio station in order to cheer up the school atmosphere with music. "This is our expression of gratitude to our school. We want this to be the best school. It's our school and we have to support it," he told the reporter. Students and teachers thus worked together to sustain the school, even in the bleakest conditions.

While the constraints imposed upon Altavista did not vanish after this incident, many of the teachers had demonstrated to themselves and to each other their commitment to the school. The students' love for their school may have also helped them see how important Altavista was to them. This encouraged teachers to continue to work within the contradictions that exist in every school, even in a democratic one where, if the diversity of ideas is really promoted, it will inevitably lead to conflict. Not that all teachers agreed from that point on, but perhaps those who did not help during the flood did not feel as entitled to impose their views or to hinder the philosophical ideas that held the school together.

Moreover, new loyalty and a sense of community emerged, which was crucial in continuing to build the type of school they envisioned and was also important for the students as they too became active participants in the type of human interactions that were the foundation of the school. It was clear that what transpired from the flood helped most teachers realize that all they had was each other. Armida explained:

> We saw that SEP did not care about us. They came and didn't even send us a chair. Nothing, just like that! And many teachers used to tell me, "The problem is that you never ask for help from SEP," and that made many colleagues see how the people at SEP were, and to stop waiting for them. We used to tell them that we shouldn't be waiting, that they wouldn't give us anything, especially with the type of project that we had. Quite the opposite; what they want is for this school to die.

Even if there was not a conspiracy against Altavista, SEP was surely not interested in supporting this school. In 2009 SEP collected benefits from the insurance company for the damages caused by the flood, but Altavista did not receive one peso. Given that this is such a revolutionary school, one would expect its community to revolt and demand sufficient support for maintenance, teachers' salaries, compensation for their extra hours of work, materials, equipment, and the insurance benefits that belonged to them. But again, instead, many of Altavista's teachers saw SEP's lack of financial support as their way to stay away from absolute governmental control.

A Barrio School: From and for the Community

How, then, did Altavista stay alive? Much of it was due to their relationships with the community, with those who knew them and shared a common philosophy. People and organizations that sympathized with their project offered resources—from the Autonomous University of Ciudad Juárez to NGOs and former students. Sometimes the help came in the form of a used computer or an old copy machine, and other times in the form of workshops and cultural events provided to students. This support was vital, but it was also the result of Altavista's long history of collaboration with the community's struggles for social justice, particularly those of the marginalized sectors.

On March 8, 2003, for example, in commemoration of International Women's Day, Altavista's students participated in one of the largest student protests against the feminicides. Hundreds of students from various institutions marched across the downtown international bridge led by local feminicide activists denouncing the impunity and human tragedies (Villamil 2003).

Another example of this collaboration with the community took place in November 2006, only five months after the devastating flood, when the school hosted Subcomandante Marcos's two-day visit to Juárez, as part of the national movement "La Otra Campaña" (The other campaign). Marcos met at Preparatoria Altavista with representatives from U.S.- and México-based groups to listen to local concerns on issues such as migration to the United States and labor.[22]

Altavista has continued to be a host of La Otra Campaña in 2010 and in 2012. And in 2007, Altavista would have hosted the Forum for Resistance and Defense of the Land if it had not been arbitrarily suppressed by the state. The forum was intended to disseminate at national and international levels the human rights violations against the residents of Granjas Lomas del Poleo, who had been evicted by wealthy magnates (Jesús 2007).[23]

These are only a few instances in which Altavista has taken part in the community's efforts for social justice, but most of their critical and social justice efforts lie in their everyday work with their students inside and outside the classroom, as will be explained in more detail in later chapters.

A School for the Disinherited

Altavista's collective identity was that of dispossession and resistance. Students and teachers were well aware of their marginalization, but they were able to turn their outcast condition into their main source of motivation to keep on going. Armida, rather than seeing her students as deserving only pity and low expectations, viewed them as daring fighters of promise.

I think the fact that they enroll in high school tells us about their desire to improve their living conditions. This gives us some insight, doesn't it? To those who want to get out of where they are, education is their only path because they are the disinherited and they don't have any other choice.

In addition to being severely underresourced, Altavista students, like most youth in the west side of the city, carried a strong social stigma that further limited their opportunities. "Do students actually go to class?" "Aren't they too lazy?" "Do teachers teach anything there?" "Be careful, there must be lots of gang members there." These were the types of comments I often got from middle-class Juarenses when they found out I was doing research at a school in the west side of the city—never mind the sacrifices on the part of the families or the incredible efforts that students made to overcome the many social barriers imposed by their economic situation. For example, contrary to the common construction of Juárez working-class families and particularly of Altavista students as unintelligent, unmotivated, uninterested in education, and ignorant, one of the boys at Altavista explained to me that although his father had been unable to attend high school and his earnings as a street vendor were rather humble, he had always promoted reading at home and had managed to build a large collection of books, ranging from Karl Marx to Isabel Allende.

But Altavista students knew very well that they were considered deviant, mediocre, and as potential criminals. Several students had been persecuted numerous times by the police and had been victims of arbitrary abuse. "Last month the police picked up Pablo, one of our students, when he was going home after a party and accused him of being in possession of marijuana," Armida told me one afternoon, "so they stole his watch, his clothes, and whatever cash he had, and left him naked in the desert." It took Pablo a couple of days to find his way home, completely humiliated and sunburnt and with his bare feet covered in blisters.

This social stigma was even blatantly communicated to the Altavista community one windy morning in February, a few days after President Felipe Calderón visited the city. A couple of state representatives had shown up at the school wanting to speak to Armida. They came to propose an initiative that was intended to increase safety and reduce crime in the city. The proposal included a series of workshops for the students that would focus on three specific topics with the following respective titles: Dropping Your Weapons, Overcoming Addictions, and Improving Your Self-esteem. Armida, as well as most of the teachers, was enraged by the implications of this proposal. To the government, these students were not much more than criminals, drug addicts, and insecure failures.

Rather than targeting the well-known *picaderos* around the city or focusing on enforcing the law in an ethical and consistent way, they chose to target students from the west side barrios, the very kids who were trying to remain hopeful in education despite their precarious living conditions. "So through these workshops they want to teach them to have a high self-esteem," Armida protested, "but then the police treat them like they're nothing but garbage. How hypocritical that is!" Moreover, if the proposal were accepted, the students would be required to attend the workshops at the Tecnológico de Monterrey, which was not only very far away but also perhaps the most expensive private university in Juárez, located in an affluent area. Clearly, through these initiatives, the authorities continued to blame the victim and refused to take responsibility for their own corrupt actions.

Armida and the rest of the faculty held an emergency meeting to talk about the proposal. "They weren't here to help us when the river almost destroyed us, and some of our students don't even have access to clean water. Who do they think they are that they can come and tell our kids how to live their lives? They don't even know them," Jorge complained, "but maybe we should let them come, so the kids will tell them how they feel. All of our kids are very critical, so I'd love to see how that would play out." After hours of deliberation, the final consensus was to reject the offer.

When I learned about this proposal, I went to my father's school, which is also a high school by cooperation but is located in the southeast side of the city and serves mostly middle-class students. He indicated that this proposal was never offered to them, corroborating Altavista teachers' perceptions that only their students were being targeted and thus demonized.

Students also responded with suspicion and were critical of the alleged offers of help from the government. In April, Armida began to disseminate information about a new scholarship offered by the state government. It was a meager amount of five hundred pesos, roughly thirty-eight dollars at the time, which would be administered on a one-time basis to those who qualified. "The state is doing this because the elections for governor and mayor are coming up and they want to boast about their generosity and dedication to education and the poor," she told me. While Armida saw this only as interest convergence from the party in power, she still urged students to apply to help them pay for their high school certification fee that was required by the state after graduation. But when the students went through the application process, they felt insulted as they realized that this would not be offered to the ones with the most need. Anyone whose family members received any kind of support from the federal or state government would not qualify. This was the case even when just one person or a member in the extended family received any kind of governmental support.

Some of the twelfth-grade girls who had been encouraged to apply for the scholarship shared with me their feelings about this so-called help from the state. "I'm not convinced at all," said Gabriela. "The government wants to deceive us. Those five hundred *varos* [pesos] are the work of my *jefa* [mother], the taxes that she pays."

"And they also put a lot of obstacles," Marsella replied, "because my half sister was going to get it but they told her that since I already have a federal scholarship—though I have yet to see any money—that she wouldn't get it. So then she explained to them that she lives in a separate home, but since my grandmother gets a pension, they still denied it to her. So they make it almost impossible."

"And if at least you knew that you were gonna get those five hundred *varos* on a weekly or monthly basis, you could say, 'Oh, OK, that helps,' but no, it's just a one-time thing! That's a fucking joke, a slap in the face!" Gabriela complained. "And then they say that they're giving it to those who need it the most. Come on."

"And I can tell you that many of the scholarships were given to people who don't need them. Like Maria, I know it's going to sound ugly, but she doesn't really need it; both of her parents have jobs. So with her scholarship she doesn't pay her tuition; instead she goes somewhere else to spend the money," said Karla.

"Yeah, like Celia; that fool doesn't even go to class," Gabriela confirmed.

These girls then, who were not only among the highest achieving students but also among the ones with the most financial need, saw the hypocrisy of it all. If these scholarships were to benefit anyone, it would be those whose families' income was enough to not depend on any other social program. Clearly, this was nothing but a political game to get voters' support.

In conclusion, Altavista had been formed as a grassroots school that continued to live up to its legacy by working collectively. Although this was a highly disenfranchised school, remaining at the margins was also beneficial as teachers and students were able to maintain a relatively greater level of autonomy. While the students resented the negative light in which others in the outside community perceived them, at Altavista they had the opportunity to develop a barrio identity of which they felt proud. "I want people to see that there's talent in the barrio," Gabriela told me once. Several students repeatedly declared that they were not normal, but they enjoyed the fact that Altavista allowed them to display a collective identity of "weirdness," of being different in various ways. Mónica, one of the quietest and shyest girls, explained her appreciation. "I really like that people here don't criticize you. I think we are all weird. Some are hippies, emos, rockers, cholos. There are no normal people, but that's OK. Yes, that we are all different."

As noted throughout the book, this autonomy and ability to be different at Altavista was of crucial importance for the young women. Not only did this provide a space where they enjoyed greater freedom to self-author their identities, inventing and reinventing themselves as necessary and without judgment or without the push toward assimilation into a middle-class culture that did not reflect the realities of their lives. What is more, it provided a space where young women could think critically about their world and connect with others, past and present, in a struggle for social justice.

Conclusion

From day one, poor girls in Juárez carry a baggage of fear and a narrative of violence against women that is difficult to escape. They are shaping their lives in precarious conditions, while their aspirations, spaces, roles, and freedom are in continuous contestation. The stigma and criminalization assigned to these youth add one more layer of obstacles. "It's so hard in these times to find people who will support you, for it seems that there are more bad than good people," Nora, a twelfth grade student, confessed to me in an e-mail, "and when I see the things that are happening in society, sometimes you feel like you don't want to keep on going, and you wonder, for what, if this is only getting worse?" Altavista then is charged with the challenge of promoting a language of hope and a spirit of resistance in a city that continuously represses demands for social justice. Arguably, no other high school in Juárez has engaged in activism as persistently as Altavista, and these activities as well as its history inevitably help shape the culture of the school and the identities of its students. The struggle often begins inside and outside its own classrooms, where Altavista continues to pursue a counterhegemonic discourse that extends out to the world. As will be evident in the remaining chapters, Altavista girls participate in this discourse and also create their own, and in this way they become agents of change in their own terms—whether the change is internal or collective. Hopefully, the merging of stories of this school and of some of its students, which are presented in this book, will offer a window into the possibilities and complexities of coming of age and learning in meaningful ways in an increasingly dystopic Juárez, where youth hold onto their hope even as the options for the future appear to crumble before their eyes.

CHAPTER 2

Through Girls' Eyes

Coming of Age in Ciudad Juárez

I never paint dreams or nightmares. I paint my own reality.

—Frida Kahlo, quoted in Francisco Márquez,
"Art: Mexican Autobiography"

IT ONLY TAKES A FEW MINUTES walking in the streets of Juárez to regret having been born female. Stares, whistles, and sexual slurs are things a young woman has to endure as she walks home from school. Careful not to deviate her sight and walking sternly and quickly, she must pretend that she is immune to harassment, which has become normalized. That is the way I remember feeling as a teenager in Juárez in the 1980s. At the time the word "feminicide" had not entered my vocabulary or my imagination, but I knew that existing in a female body was a dangerous thing. Since the early 1990s, when the initial widespread news of hundreds of feminicides cast a permanent shadow over the city, working-class women in Juárez have experienced the same feelings I did, but they carry a heavier burden. Pushing away thoughts of their own raped and mutilated bodies drying out in the desert may become habitual for many young women.

The explosion of drug-related crimes in 2008 put the feminicides on the back burner, but violence against women has continued to occur at high rates, becoming normalized as part of life on the border (Staudt 2008). The young women in this study were born into the era of the feminicides. Many have witnessed violence in the home, have been directly affected by the rise in crime and impunity in the city, and have experienced a perpetual sense of insecurity and risk throughout their lives. Furthermore, these young women and their families represent the sources of cheap labor and dispossession in the arrangements of a predatory capitalist globalization and the obscene economic inequalities characterizing this border city. Nonetheless, these girls' subjectivities have also been influenced by the political consciousness emerging from women's activism and student grassroots movements that have denounced police impunity and violence against women as well as other activists in the city. In other words, there is more to these women's lives than fear. There is agency and a critical consciousness that has been nurtured by their own struggle for their right to a meaningful life and dignity in this context as well as by their school. Indeed, Preparatoria Altavista has, to a certain extent, provided a space for them to explore new alternatives.

This chapter introduces the protagonists of this book and offers a window into these young women's definitions of their lives beyond the feminicides, the violence, and fear, as they embarked on their last years of adolescence. In order to offer some general insight into the everyday lives of these young women, I draw on my analysis of observations, interviews, and informal conversations. To offer a richer portrait, I also present some of the girls' expressions of self-identity and perspectives of life in Juárez, through an analysis of photographs taken by seven of the girls. The purpose is to shed light on the coming of age in this city, through the girls' own eyes.

The Women of This Study

I had the privilege of getting to know ten unique young women at Preparatoria Altavista, mainly by "hanging out" with them and observing them in various school contexts. Several of them also shared their life histories and perspectives with me through interviews and an autophotography/photovoice activity. All but one of them had been at Altavista for at least one full academic year. The girls belonged to different social groups within the school that often overlapped, and with a few exceptions, most seemed to get along with each other. Some were very close friends, and three of them were related.

The girls ranged from sixteen to eighteen years of age and were all eleventh and twelfth graders. All the twelfth graders were part of the same social sciences and humanities cohort, who generally attended the same classes and had a similar schedule. The reason for this was both practical and accidental. Having most of my informants in the same cohort allowed me to observe several of them at the same time. Also, this was the cohort that spent the most time in courses taught by the leading teachers of the school—the ones who enacted the vision of the school most deliberately and who were also the ones most open to my study and consequently whom I observed the most. Therefore, not only did I get to know these students better, but it also took relatively less time to gain their trust. Furthermore, I was able to see them interact with more or less the same people over the course of the school year, which offered greater insight into the pedagogical sites that the students themselves co-created with their peers.

The selection process of my informants was both intentional and organic. I wanted a diverse group of students who had been in the school for at least one year, but in efforts to avoid imposing myself, I tried to let the field guide me. Indeed, the first girls to join the study did so moved by their own initial interest. Curious about who I was and what I was doing, they approached me first after class observations or when they saw me taking field notes in the courtyards. They often asked me to join them in their conversations, activities, and classes. This in turn allowed me to meet some of their friends, whom I also invited to participate in interviews. Others intrigued me from the first time I observed them, and I approached them myself.

There was also some variation in the data collection activities, mostly due to the nuances of working with adolescent girls and the unexpected turns of ethnographic research. I was able to spend a lot of time in naturalistic activities with some, while with others we had almost a strictly formal researcher-informant relationship. Nine out of the ten girls participated in interviews, and only seven participated in the photovoice activity. Two of the girls who did not participate in the photovoice activity were those with whom I spent the least time—mainly because of logistical constraints or because I did not sense much of a desire on their part to have me around. One of them, Lizette, was extremely busy, having to rush home immediately after school every day to take care of her family. She took the camera and intended to participate, but although she said that she had taken the photographs, she was never able to return the camera to me. The other, Cristina, gradually reduced her involvement in the study until she completely stopped a few months before the end of the school year. From the interviews, I knew that Cristina was going through difficult times, but I also sensed that she was the most guarded of all. Despite the many tears she shed during interviews, she would only share partial and often obscured information. During the last months Cristina also became truant and spent most of her time outside with friends. Whenever I approached her in this context I sensed her need for privacy, as she avoided eye contact and remained surrounded by peers as if trying to avoid personal conversations with me. Therefore, I did not push her to converse with me privately in the last few months of fieldwork and was unable to invite her into the photovoice activity. I never found out the reason for her distrust. She had had a fallout with another participant (Marsella), and perhaps because of that, she might have felt that she could not trust me. All I knew was that I would not push the girls to do anything that felt uncomfortable to them and I chose not to pursue her participation anymore.

Only one girl, Nora, did not participate in either the interviews or the photovoice activity. At first I did not intend to include her in the group because she appeared to be of middle-class background. Also, since I noticed that in contrast to most girls at Altavista, she spent most of her free time with her boyfriend, I—perhaps very mistakenly—assumed that she would not be interested in being involved in the study. Even after I realized that she, too, was from a working-class background, I never asked her to be formally interviewed or to participate in the photovoice activity. However, after looking at my data, I realized that most of my observations included her. She also approached me to ask me for help and advice about applying for admission to the University of Texas at El Paso (UTEP). Since then, we had numerous conversations that allowed me to get to know her quite well.

Although chapter 5 offers a detailed portrait of some of the girls and an in-depth analysis of their identities, in the next few sections I provide a brief introduction about each one of the ten young women I got to know. The purpose is to introduce the protagonists and help the reader get some sense of the type of experiences and backgrounds that filled the lives of these women to better understand their perspectives. The introductory information is also summarized in Figure 3, which provides a few basic and key characteristics, as well as a list of the data sources, to help the reader identify the girls and keep track of them through the rest of the book.

Alejandra and Gabriela

Because I rarely saw them together in school, I did not realize that Gabriela and Alejandra were sisters until I interviewed Alejandra. The two sisters lived together with their mother, who worked late and had long shifts as a supermarket supervisor. They had two more sisters and a brother, all married. One older sister had graduated from the major local university and was a lawyer (at the time unemployed) interested in human rights. The other older brother and sister lived in El Paso and Las Cruces, respectively.

Their parents divorced when the girls were very young, and the two sisters had witnessed their mother fall victim to domestic violence, at the hands of both their father and their stepfather. The latter had been a casualty of the drug wars in December 2008, when he was confused for another man and murdered while sitting inside a car. While none of the girls cared for their stepfather, they felt sorry for their mother, who had to continue working while still grieving her loss.

Despite sharing a common background, Alejandra and Gabriela could not be more different. Alejandra was a sixteen-year-old eleventh grader who was a member of Altavista's women's soccer team and a former track-and-field athlete. She was slender and slightly taller than most of her peers. Her big, beautiful brown eyes complemented her light brown skin, which, together with her easy smile, made her attractive to many of the boys. Nonetheless, she was hardly an easy target for romance. Alejandra was an assertive young woman and had no problems opening herself up to me during interviews. She enjoyed sewing and fixing her clothes, as well as spending time with her select group of friends. She also enjoyed working during the summer at a hardware store.

Gabriela's friendly, laid-back, and reflexive personality, as well as her outspoken and alternative style of dressing, made her one of the most popular girls in the school. She was seventeen years old at the time of the study. Both her style and her demeanor were influenced by Rasta philosophy and music. She wore her hair in dreadlocks, had dark brown skin, and tended to stand out as a leader of the group of friends that many referred to as "los hippies." She, however, did not seem to be looking for popularity.

Gabriela was very independent, and although she had a boyfriend, she seemed to maintain a strong sense of individuality and autonomy. Gabriela described herself as having grown up in the streets and thus was very street savvy. She enjoyed playing her guitar and writing poetry and raps—all of which had a strong political and critical orientation. Gabriela was also an articulate and vocal participant in all her classes and got along well with her teachers and peers. To get a few pesos, she sold her own handmade bracelets and crafts in the informal market.

Diana

Diana was a sixteen-year-old eleventh grader with a strong personality. She was intelligent, high achieving, and well liked by her teachers, though not so much by some of her peers, who at times saw her as conceited or domineering. Her intentions were probably misinterpreted by peers who were unaccustomed to such a confident, outspoken, and frank young woman, who set very clear boundaries with others to ensure that everyone respected her. She liked being a leader and was enthusiastic about initiating projects and learning and experiencing new things. She had even enrolled in a military middle school for a year just because she was curious. Diana lived with her mother and younger brother. Out of all the girls I met, Diana had the most solid financial situation. Though not necessarily of middle-class status, her mother, who was a single parent, was a psychologist. Therefore, compared to the other girls, Diana and her family had experienced better economic times. When Diana was seven years old, her mother's company transferred her to Portugal. After two years, the company closed and the job ended, so Diana's family returned to Juárez, but this experience had given Diana a chance to learn some Portuguese and live abroad for some time as well as to experience a middle-class life. Diana was very close to her mother, who had very progressive views and was a feminist activist.

Cristina

Cristina was an outgoing and sensitive eighteen-year-old. She was an average student at best, often truant, and seemed to enjoy spending time with her friends. She was thin and light-skinned, and had dark, shoulder-length straight hair that was layered in a modern style. She dressed in a feminine and revealing fashion and wore more makeup that the other girls. This, and her playful, flirtatious, and sweet personality, often drew much attention from her male peers. She had been very close to Marsella in the past, but recently, some kind of gossip had irreversibly injured their relationship. This might have been a reason why Cristina was a lot more cautious than the other girls in opening herself up to me. In addition, there were memories of past events in her life that still hurt her. During interviews, she could not prevent the tears from rolling down her cheeks when attempting to disclose even limited information. Therefore, she did not seem ready to talk in complete detail about those experiences, particularly to a stranger like me. She lived with her parents and two younger brothers—a fifteen-year-old and a toddler. Cristina's mother was a hairdresser, and her father worked in the informal market. Cristina had never worked outside the home, but with two working parents, she was responsible for a lot of the household chores, including childcare, cooking, and cleaning.

Karla

Karla was the first girl who approached me and who introduced me into the world of Altavista's students. She was seventeen years old and lived with her parents and brother. Her father was a kitchen supervisor at a maquiladora and her mother sometimes worked selling clothes in the informal market. Karla was a very outgoing girl, whose bubbly and warm personality was contagious. She had friends in every grade level and was particularly sought after by gay peers. Sometimes she worried about being overweight but was quite proud of her blonde hair and expressive green eyes. She loved acting, singing, dancing, and drawing. Her peers considered her to be one of the highest academically achieving students. She was often the leader of group projects due to her outgoing personality, creativity, sense of responsibility, and intelligence. She was hardly ever absent and turned in all her work on time and with great attention to detail and excellence. As a very confident young woman, who liked to mentor younger peers, she also enjoyed organizing extracurricular activities like singing and theater clubs. At home, she was a loving daughter whose most important goal was to make her parents proud and reciprocate the hard work and investment that they had devoted to her education.

Iliana

Among the oldest girls was Iliana, an eighteen-year-old with a quiet and serene demeanor. Her natural beauty and tender smile were hard to ignore. She had long, curly, and dark hair, dark skin, and big, brown expressive eyes. She dressed in jeans or long skirts and blouses and liked wearing indigenous jewelry and accessories. She was the second to youngest of five sisters and lived with her parents. Her mother was a homemaker and her father was a carpenter working in the informal market. All of her three older sisters had wanted to go to college, but due to financial limitations, only one was currently enrolled. Iliana also hoped that she would have the opportunity. Iliana was Alejandra and Gabriela's cousin and had a boyfriend outside of school. In school, she often hung out with *"los hippies,"* and in her free time, she read books, made bracelets, or listened to music. She also belonged to the school's women's soccer team and often participated in feminist groups and theater activities.

Lizette

Lizette was an eighteen-year-old who lived with her paternal grandmother. Her parents had divorced when she was ten, and her mother had taken her and her two other sisters to live in her native town of Torreón, Coahuila. But after eight years, when her mother began to struggle financially and could no longer help her pay for her education expenses, she decided to move back to Juárez. Her father, a carpenter in the informal market, was an alcoholic and had promised her that he would change and help her with her education expenses if she moved in with him. So she returned to Juárez, with the main goal of helping her father and finishing her high school education. The former had proved to be more challenging than she had hoped. Lizette was an outlier in the study because this was her first semester in the school. Nonetheless, she already had many friends, and while she was quiet in her classes, she enthusiastically participated in the school activities. She had a calm and sweet personality and dressed in skinny jeans, sneakers, and T-shirts, though her friends sometimes teased her, telling her that she dressed like a "chola" (female gang member).

Marsella

Marsella was an outspoken, expressive, articulate, and outgoing eighteen-year-old twelfth grader. Her big, beautiful brown eyes seemed to radiate enthusiasm for life. She was a very resourceful young woman who made her own jewelry and accessories. Her hair and clothes seemed to be deliberately fashioned in what seemed to be a combination of a pop-rock style. Therefore, first impressions easily masked the fact that Marsella was among some of the students who lived in the most precarious financial conditions. In fact, the only reason why she was able to attend Altavista was that one of the teachers, Rigoberto, had offered to sponsor her. Some weeks she hardly had money to purchase food. Also, her father died when she was very young, and for the last four years, since her mother remarried, Marsella had lived with her aging grandmother, who was sick and had difficulty walking. In spite of the dire circumstances in which she lived, in school, Marsella was a high-achieving student and had many friends from a variety of social groups.

Mónica

Mónica was a twelfth grader who, after turning eighteen, had just left the orphanage where she grew up. She did not have any parents but now lived with her sister, brother-in-law, and little niece. Her sister was unemployed and her brother-in-law was a city bus driver. Mónica was the quietest of all the girls and often struggled to put her thoughts and words together during interviews. She was more comfortable conversing informally with me, and she often shared her intricate drawings as well. She was slender and of a light complexion, dressed in jeans, T-shirts, and sneakers, and wore her long, dark blonde hair down. She described herself as very shy, but she seemed to have found comfort in her circle of friends, whose advice and encouragement she appreciated. She often hung out with Gabriela and others in the "hippie" group.

Nora

Nora was an intelligent, attentive, and participative twelfth grader of medium build and light complexion. She tended to be the first girl to ask questions or volunteer comments during class. This was Nora's second year at Altavista. She had transferred from Preparatoria El Parque, a highly reputable but more traditional high school where socioeconomic class differences were clearly demarked. Initially, her personal dressing style reflected this transition, as it still mirrored that of the middle-class students who attend Preparatoria El Parque. She wore her long, brown hair in wavy locks, and her feminine clothes and high wedge sandals later evolved into more simple jeans, T-shirt, and sneaker outfits. She lived with her parents, two younger brothers, and sister in a household where gender roles were quite traditional. Her father was a janitor for the city parks, and her mother was a homemaker. She also had a boyfriend in school who was the son of one of the teachers, and she spent most of her free time with him.

Learning, Loving, and Coming of Age in Ciudad Juárez

Despite the challenges that the social context of the city posed and the painful situations that many of the girls had experienced and were still experiencing, most of them described themselves as joyful and optimistic as well as unique, inquisitive, and open-minded. In some ways, these girls were no

Grade level	Name	Key Characteristics and Facts	Observations	Interviews	Photovoice	Naturalist activities / conversations
11th grade	Alejandra	Reserved and assertive. Athletic, soccer player, Gabriela's sister.	X	X	X	X
	Diana	Confident, critical, and outspoken. Academically high achiever. Mother was a feminist activist.	X	X	X	X
12th grade	Cristina	Sensitive and outgoing. Struggled academically. Responsible for most household chores.	X	X		
	Gabriela	Laid back, friendly, politically conscious, and street savvy. Popular in the "hippie" group. Alejandra's older sister.	X	X	X	X
	Karla	Upbeat, expressive, and outgoing. High achiever and artistic.	X	X	X	X
	Iliana	Serene, quiet, and friendly. Fond of indigenous inspired styles. Soccer player. Second year at Altavista. Gabriela and Alejandra's cousin.	X	X	X	X
	Lizette	Friendly and calm. First semester at Altavista. Wanted to help her father overcome his alcoholism.	X	X		X
	Marsella	Outgoing, friendly, and articulate. Sponsored by a teacher and academically high achiever. Lived with grandmother.	X	X	X	X
	Monica	Shy and quiet. Had just left the orphanage where she grew up.	X	X	X	X
	Nora	Participative and attentive in class. Second year at Altavista. Spent most of her time with her boyfriend.	X			X

Figure 3. Data sources and key characteristics of the young women participating in the study.

different from other young women around the world. Their youth and passion for life emanated from their eyes. They enjoyed listening to music, reading, and hanging out with friends, and most were artistically oriented and quite talented. They all had deliberate and individual styles of dress and music, which, for most, had evolved during their years at Altavista. Contrary to conventional thinking about what seems to be the norm for many adolescent females, most of the girls that I met appeared to have positive self-perceptions and feelings about their personalities, abilities, bodies, and choices. The few who did not, such as Cristina, Marsella, and to a lesser extent Karla, were generally not afraid to talk about it—even Cristina, the most reserved, as will be clear in chapter 4.

Home Life

All these young women were born in Ciudad Juárez and lived in the neighborhoods near the school. However, the school was not within walking distance, and they all took public transportation. The neighborhoods were a mix of shantytowns and zones with well-established, modest homes. Most of the girls lived in small and humble homes, often located in unpaved, hilly areas. The paved roads were usually dusty and uneven, and people would sometimes fill the many holes in the streets with sand to prevent flat tires or to keep cars from getting stuck—though little could be done to prevent the mess that rainy days would create. All my informants had access to basic services, such as running water (though not exactly clean) and electricity, and about half even enjoyed a few other amenities, like phone or Internet services, which their parents were able to afford.

Family was very important for all these girls, and many of them felt responsible for contributing to the well-being of their relatives, particularly their parents. The family configurations varied significantly. Four of the girls, including Cristina, Iliana, Karla, and Nora, lived in heterosexual two-parent households with at least one sibling at home; three—Alejandra, Diana, and Gabriela—lived in single-mother households; and three—Lizette, Marsella, and Mónica—lived with other relatives. In the latter cases, one or both parents had died or had abandoned the home, or the girl had chosen to move out.

Stories of struggle or emotional wounds abounded in the girls' narratives. Many of the challenges were related to their family life. While this is not unique to Juárez or to working-class and urban families, their experiences are in part related to the challenges posed by a city injured by stark social inequalities and violence. Three of the girls—Karla, Alejandra, and Gabriela—had lost family members as casualties of the drug wars or extortions. Stories of domestic violence were not uncommon, and they made a profound impact on the girls' lives. About half of them had seen their mothers, aunts, sisters, and grandmothers suffer domestic violence. Some of those who had been raised in single-parent households or by another relative, such as Gabriela, Alejandra, and Marsella, resented their parents' long hours at work or their mothers' choice of new partners and expressed feelings of loneliness and abandonment. Nonetheless, most repeatedly mentioned how much they cared for and were grateful for their family members, including mothers, fathers, siblings, and grandparents.

Financial struggles were among the most prevalent challenges. Most of the fathers of these girls had lost their employment or had precarious sources of income based on informal job arrangements. All, except one, of the girls' mothers in this study worked, mostly in the service sector or in the informal market. Only Diana's mother was a professional.

Despite their financial need, none of the girls worked at the time of the study, but some had experience with customer service jobs at local stores in the downtown area. They generally attributed their inability to work to the unavailability and incompatibility of part-time jobs with their school schedule, which they considered to be a priority. To most, the idea of working at a maquiladora was not at all appealing, and some girls rejected the idea completely. However, as graduation approached, a few thought they might not have a choice in the event that they were unable to afford or get funding for college.

Relationships

Most of the girls had been involved in romantic heterosexual relationships at some point at the time of the study. However, only three of the ten girls, Karla, Iliana, and Nora, were in a long-term relationship that they considered serious and with potential for marriage. Others who had boyfriends indicated that they were not thinking of marriage at the moment and wanted to wait until they finished college to consider it. Most girls had a more liberal view on long-term relationships and gender roles. A few considered open relationships to be more favorable than marriage. Some had seen, firsthand, the difficulties that came with marriage and were skeptical about their ability to stay committed to or in love with the same partner forever. However, most still thought of marriage as a desirable option for the future. Almost without exception, they discussed the idea of forming a family, centered on idealistic equitable relationships in which both partners would have the opportunity to grow professionally and in which household chores would be shared equitably.

When it came to friends, almost all the girls I spoke with showed an interesting pattern. Even after talking about their solidarity with women's goals and their belief that women were as strong and capable as men, many indicated that they preferred to socialize with male friends rather than with female friends or that they had more male than female friends. They viewed other young women with a certain degree of suspicion, believing that women were more likely to hurt them. Some also resented the discourses that were so prevalent among many teenage girls—or so they thought—which focused on boys, physical appearance, and fashion. In many cases, the girls spoke about "other girls" as being superficial and too engrossed in frivolous interests that prevented them from delving into meaningful and intelligent topics, such as politics, music, culture, and art. The only ones who did not make this type of comment were Lizette, Iliana, and Mónica, the quietest girls.

In contrast, my observation was that although all the girls did have male friends, all except Nora still spent most of their time with female friends. When I pointed this out, the girls, including Alejandra, Diana, Gabriela, and Marsella, often responded that some girls at Altavista were different and therefore worthy of their friendship. Apparently, most of their negative experiences with girlfriends had occurred during their middle school years. As will be noted in the next chapters, the "exceptionality" of their Altavista girlfriends might have been due to the antihegemonic space that the school afforded to young women in which the social pressures to conform to normative women's ways of being were released, and the girls were able to expand their interests, interrogate their world, and express their voices beyond stereotypical ways. Above all things, the girls valued trustworthiness in their friendships, even when their friends were different from them in many ways.

On Being a Woman

All the girls in this study perceived women to be socially positioned as fighters. Their ideas about empowerment were inevitably related to struggle and the need to stand up against oppression. They all admitted that women were in a disadvantaged position in society in comparison to men and that this often caused fear in their lives.

Fear, Containment, and Control

As discussed previously, the dangers posed by the city cast by not only the violent drug wars but also the never-ending shadow of the feminicides era in which these girls have grown up affected the ways in which they could carry out their daily lives. These girls, like most other young Juárez women, enjoyed less freedom to make decisions, to embark on any project of their choice, to move through various public spaces, or to pursue their individuation process. They had to monitor themselves, including how they dressed, with whom they talked, and what kind of information they shared about themselves. Having a car that could offer relative safety when traveling around the city was not an option for them, so they usually relied on public transportation for any activity they wished to pursue. Therefore, they also had to be constantly aware of their surroundings and the risks they faced by being out and about.

Things that people may take for granted when living in relatively safe cities or towns, such as going for a walk or riding a bike as a form of low-cost transportation or as a leisure activity, were out of the question for these young Juárez women. Even the idea of exercising could be challenging, since paying for a gym membership was obviously not feasible, and the size of their homes was limited. Thus, many of them did not have a chance to exercise beyond their daily walk to and from school. The things that many teenagers love to do, such as going to parties, attending events featuring local bands, or just hanging out with friends on the front porch, were considered risky activities in Juárez as assaults and drive-by shootings were on the rise. Therefore, fear was part of almost all the girls' lives. Karla explained how she felt during the incident presented in the introduction to this book, when she was being followed by a large white truck one day after school.

> I get afraid of what people may want to do to you simply for the fact that you are a woman. They want to . . . I don't know, that's how I felt at that moment, like "Oh my God, he's going to take me and rape me and I don't know what else." And that is the fear as a woman, that others may want to hurt me. Or sometimes just because girls are pretty . . . or I don't know, but just for being a

woman, I am afraid of something happening to me. Even when you just walk by and they harass you. For example, I used to walk by the store Electra, and the soldiers or federal police were patrolling there, and they would tell me, "From the waist and down *güerita* [blondie]." And whoa, I was so scared to hear them say that. They were too many against just me!

Marsella also shared similar feelings about what it meant to be a young woman in Juárez.

It's not that I have doubts about my sexuality, but sometimes it is exhausting to be a woman. Because sometimes, for example, I'm walking in the street, and the men go by and start yelling things at me, harassing me. And it really bothers me. Also in the morning when I'm coming to school, I'm all peacefully adjusting my backpack or whatever, and the soldiers that are standing right there start to say things. And I get so mad because instead of doing what they're supposed to—to protect people—there they are harassing you. There might be people getting robbed and they don't even notice because all they do is watch the girls that walk by.

While some people may naturalize street harassment, arguing that it is harmless and just a cultural trait, or that it is actually a form of chivalry, the reality is that it is a form of aggression that threatens women's safety, especially in a city with the background of Juárez's gendered violence. In this way, harassment effectively results in women's self-regulation of their own body and movement through public space.

Mónica: I know that as women we are many times at a disadvantage in that we face more dangers than men. I would like to get home at any time I want, but I can't because of the crime.

Iliana: For example, I can't go out, and I am very afraid of going out alone. I try to always be with somebody.

Several of the girls I interviewed resented the increased suppression of their freedom. "We have to keep on living," they would argue, and hence many of them abided by cultural norms that expected girls to remain in the protection of the home to a greater extent than is expected of boys, while simultaneously resisting the containment in which their parents attempted to keep them. Even those who liked to participate in school athletics had to limit their involvement. Although in some ways the school offered a relatively safe space to practice sports and visit with friends, parents were in a constant state of worry and urged their daughters to return home as soon as classes ended. Altavista's phone immediately began to ring when the girls took a little longer working on class projects in the library, participating in extracurricular activities, or practicing sports after school. All of this affected both their physical and mental health. Gabriela, one of the girls who had spent a lot of time in the streets, had a lot to say about how the perpetuators of crime and violence in the city had affected her life through a culture of fear.

> Now you can't be anywhere at night. It's like they're taking away your freedom; they are tying you up. First, they forced you to stop going to bars because they project it on TV, and you say, "No, hell no! I'm not going there! They're gonna kill me!" So then you're afraid of going to a bar. Then you say, "So I like to party, OK, I'll do it in my own house." But now they're coming to your house too! So what do you say, "I'm condemned to doing nothing. What am I going to do if I have to go out?" My grandfather tells me, "Stop roaming the streets!" And I tell him, "Grandpa I have to go out, I have to go to school, I have to get out there to sell things. I can't stay inside the house paralyzed because I think they're gonna kill me. We also need to think about our own needs. We can't stop living our lives just because of them."

Although sexual harassment and aggression were real dangers in the city for young women, and this definitely imposed fear on the girls, the macronarrative of danger and risk also served to increase parents' control over their daughters. Marsella explained:

> And it also bothers me that women are more repressed at home. You want to go out to dance, but "Oh no, you're a woman and there is more danger out there for you." Or you want to go to a concert: "Not you because you are a woman." Now the excuse is that because you're a woman everything is dangerous.

A combination of discourses of sexual control, danger, and social vulnerability, as well as gendered homemaking traditions, served as regulatory measures for young women's bodies, confining them to the home and naturalizing the constraint of feelings of competence and autonomy in the domestic sphere. While this is not atypical of many Latino families (see Hyams 2003), Juárez girls in this particular context were much more restrained than in past decades when the city was a much safer place to live.

Raising and Resisting Sexism

Despite the real threats that the young women experienced, some refused to naturalize the constraints that they faced and felt compelled to express their strength and counter the discourse of victimization. Some of them seemed to recognize that the macronarratives of danger and risk were also part of a larger patriarchal arrangement that positioned women as weak, inferior, and in need of control, and in order to resist their victimization they also had to resist the broader sexist ideologies that positioned them at a disadvantage. Take for example Diana's approach:

> Sometimes, not always, but sometimes in certain ways people perceive you as weaker, even if you are not. I mean in some ways they see you and make you believe that you are weaker. That makes me very angry, that society believes that because we are women we are more prone to all kinds of things, like violence. And I know that it can be true, but also, what I strive to show with my actions is that we are equal. I mean, men and women have the same capacities. We are not equal physically or sexually since there are differences in our organs, but we do have the same capacity, simply in our intellect, all of that.

For some, the idea of rising against this social position also had to do with the ability to recognize when they too were complicit in oppressive gender relations. Take for example Iliana's ideas about some women's internalized oppression:

> There are women that are repressed and that have a *machista* mentality. The worst thing is that many women have gotten used to be

treated like that, and that that's the way it is . . . so they get used to
their role. I think that's the worst.

Alejandra also acknowledged that sometimes women found themselves in
difficult positions, but it was important not to accept this as a natural and
permanent condition.

Some of my friends believe that women are naturally submissive.
But it doesn't have to be like that, even when that might be the case
for one reason or another, you know? Even if I'm living like that at
the moment, it doesn't have to be like that.

Karla also unpacked the ways in which the positioning of women as sacrificial and benevolent served to further their victimization through their
own consent.

Many remain silent. . . . Or there are times when in the middle of
sexual, physical, and moral violence some say, "I won't say anything
to not burden others." But you hurt yourself in the process because
you don't say what you feel.

This type of sacrificial behavior was something that Karla had learned to
overcome. While chapter 4 will explore her journey in detail, suffice it
to say that because of Karla's lived experience, it was not enough for her to
have overcome silence; she was also very interested in supporting other
young women to experience the same sense of liberation that she felt
today. Therefore, Karla had often organized singing and theater workshops,
not only because she enjoyed these activities but also because she found
them useful in supporting others, especially younger women, in coming
out of their shells.

I love it because the girls in their first year used to be so quiet and
repressed. And when they joined the singing workshop I started to
help them up. And you should see them today, dancing and
expressing themselves. You know what I mean? I like to give that
from myself.

Like Karla, Gabriela also made efforts to organize her female peers so that
they could get together, "de-stress and talk about topics of interest." Cristina

too expressed how much she liked helping others, but sometimes her hospitality could be easily misunderstood as subservience simply because she was a woman.

> Some think that just because we are women that they can treat us as if we were less. For example, I've had conflicts with some people because, like I tell you, I like to help others, and there I am helping with everything. So it makes me angry when people think I should be serving everyone, or that I'm only good at homemaking.

When I asked each girl individually about the attributes that they thought that every woman should possess, their responses were strikingly similar. For all, except Lizette, strength was perhaps the most common descriptor, followed by boldness, willpower, intelligence, confidence, and self-esteem. As they described each one of these attributes, they made references to the need to stand firm in the face of adversity, to be able to resist repression, to have the determination to leave an abusive partner, to have the intelligence to resist manipulation, and to value oneself in any circumstance. In their words:

> *Diana:* As women we need to be independent, or better said, to be self-sufficient—not look to depend on others. Also to have the curiosity to learn more. I mean it's not so much about being smart, but to seek more—to not just accept what others tell you, but rather to search for answers yourself to see what else you can find. And to be strong, to be brave because life is hard for us women. Maybe in other places it is different, but here and now I believe we need to be very brave because of all of the things we are living in this society. We need to be very brave to be able to face society, with all its implications, like violence, and all that. As well as to be able to tell society, "Look, I'm twenty years old, I am educated, I studied this and that, and I think this and that, and not for being a woman am I going to remain static."

> *Alejandra:* A woman needs to respect herself, to accept herself. And a woman should be able to reject manipulation. . . . I mean to not let herself be influenced by men. I mean, like just because I have a lot of male friends and they want to grab my ass, I'm like, "Hey

what's your problem!" and I don't let them. Because there are a lot of women that let that happen, and in that they're not respecting themselves. Just because they're pretty it doesn't give men the right to be grabbing their behinds. . . . It's like humiliating. To me, self-respect is like taking a shower every day. It shows that I hold myself in high regard. . . . Or like if I go to a party, I don't drink or smoke or anything. And just because others tell you, "Come on, what do you mean you're not going to smoke!" And you do it just because others around hear it. That also has to do with allowing yourself to be manipulated. If you think in a particular way . . . why are you going to do things just because of what others say?

Mónica: A woman must have a voice. Because sometimes people dismiss our opinions just because we are women. Yes, sometimes even within our own families.

Gabriela: The most important thing for a woman is to have confidence, strength, and willpower. I mean, sensitivity can overcome us, but we should still remain firm. Yes, maybe crying, but firm. Yes, because . . . for example, I met a girl. She lived with her husband and he would beat her up. So she would say, "I need to leave him; I want to leave him. But what do I do? I don't have money, I don't have a house, I don't have a family, and I'm not going to find a job, and I have two children." And I would tell her that she had to have willpower. That it was her strength against his. I mean, if she wants to do it, she can leave with her children and can go look for a job. So to me that was the first step, to have the willpower to leave. Once you've made the decision you can figure out what to do next.

It might sound naïve for Gabriela to say that the most important thing her friend needed was willpower and strength, as she did not have children herself. Perhaps she did not see clearly the obstacles that a single mother would face without the support of a husband or any other family members. On the other hand, it was perhaps because Gabriela had witnessed her mother's own struggles as a battered wife and then as a single parent that she could give her friend this advice. Perhaps she knew that given the constraints for young women in these circumstances, there would never be an ideal moment for her friend to stand up for herself. Therefore if she wanted things to change, she would have to gather all her strength, even when it appeared impossible, and do it anyway.

As this example reveals, in most cases the young women's home experiences helped them frame their notions of what being a woman entailed. Girls saw in their mothers', sisters', and friends' testimonies of oppression lessons for their own lives.

Iliana: I have friends who still think that the woman must stay home to take care of the children and that the man should be the breadwinner. They don't say it like that, but I see it. For example, I have a friend who spends the whole day at home, all bored, just taking care of her son and she never goes out. But I also ran into another friend who started high school with me, but she got pregnant and quit school. When I saw her, her baby was already a year old, and I was very happy to see her because she told me that she went back to school and that her boyfriend is going to nursing school. I was glad to see that both decided to *salir adelante* [keep going].

Cristina: I am young, but I've had to face guys that are awful! But that is the boldness that I have, to be able to tell them when things are not right and to stop that person. . . . But for example I have a friend who kept putting up with all kinds of things from her boyfriend. So when we became friends she left him because I would tell her, come on, don't be like that! Don't let him yell at you like that. And he also cheated on her and she would keep on begging him.

Iliana: I have seen the disadvantages that women have to face even in my own family! Like in the case of my mother. She used to work the third shift at a maquiladora . . . and thank God that she has a lot of daughters who can help her, right? While she went to work we would take care of my little sister, we cleaned the house, we took care of each other. . . . And my father also worked, but he would get home in the early evening. He would eat dinner and go to bed, like nothing. Instead my mother would leave to work at three in the afternoon and would get back at six in the morning. And she would cook breakfast for everyone, get us ready for school, take my little sister to school, and so she would get very little sleep. Imagine how exhausting it was for her?

Diana: I admire my mother very much. I mean, I don't want to be exactly like her, but I admire her for all that she's done. How she pulled us through, my brother and me. And I also admire my grandmother because she was in a way like my mother. She had her children very young and she had no support from anyone. When she told her mother that she was pregnant, her mother told her that she was going to get the baby out with a good beating, and she beat her up very badly. And so she left and had three children who she sustained all by herself. From my grandmother I get the strength to say, there is no reason for me to get pregnant right now. And from my mother, the strength that she had to leave my father and leave behind his support, as small as it might be, for our well-being.

Most talked about machismo as something from the past, yet they continued to see patriarchal arrangements and sexism in the present, impacting their own lives and the lives of other women around them. The difference, perhaps, was that they felt that they could stand up for themselves. They learned this from witnessing the consequences experienced by their mothers, grandmothers, sisters, or friends when they chose to either stand up for themselves or remain silent and endure their situation. Many also admired their mothers' or grandmothers' strength, even when they had endured a lot of adversity, and took this as a lesson and legacy for them.

Most of them rejected traditional gender roles in the family dominated by a patriarchal arrangement in which women had very little choice, but they viewed the path toward equity in the home as a long and difficult one. "In this society, the way it is right now, I don't see us going in that direction. And it makes me very sad to see many women trapped in that," Cristina confessed. Thus, far from a postfeminist position—that which assumes that feminism is no longer necessary—Diana expressed how we needed to dispel the myth that women had been liberated simply for entering the job market.

Diana: So OK, a woman may have her children, but her role should be together with the man. I mean that both of them should clean the house, work, take care of the children. This responsibility should not fall only on the woman. Because it is a heavy burden. And people may say, "Well today a woman can be independent and work, so hey we're done." But what about the kids? And what about the home? I mean the woman continues to be in charge of everything, and now in addition has to work. . . . And so I'm not saying, "Oh, poor women," but yeah, some say, "Stop nagging, women have all the rights to be independent and work now." But the domestic role is a very important one. I mean there shouldn't be a difference. No, no, no, not the least. The woman sometimes is the mother and that's it. Or the working mother. Or the caretaker of the children, nephews and nieces, and everyone. And the one taking care of the husband, even financially and everything. Yeah! That's the case for many women. And it is important to take care of others, but she should not carry the entire burden. The woman should not be the foundation; she should not be everything to everybody. Both men and women should be the foundation of the family.

In sum, these young women lived in far from ideal circumstances, but the interaction of their home experiences as well as school experiences and engagement in feminist and other collective efforts helped them frame their own social position as women, what they could expect from life, and their own role in changing the conditions that constrained their lives. Far from naïve, loose, or victimized, these young women cultivated their wisdom by learning from their own and other women's experiences.

Education and Aspirations

Adolescence is often considered a pivotal time for reflection about one's life prospects. Individuals evaluate themselves against their ideals, beliefs, and goals, as well as against society's standards, expectations, and opportunities afforded to them. Based on the perceptions of oneself and explorations of the options available to them, adolescents may develop commitments to aspirations for the future (Marcia 1980). Educational goals tend to receive particular attention during this time, given that schooling systems at the high school level allow relatively greater room for choice in terms of classes and academic tracks. Thus students can begin to reflect on their own interests and ideas about the future in order to make some major decisions and take more ownership of their education.

To the Altavista girls that I met, education was extremely important, as it represented the only vehicle available to them that could help them achieve some degree of social mobility or to fulfill the dreams that their mothers or other women in their lives had not had the opportunity to pursue. As such, all the girls in the study described themselves as good students, and all but one were, in fact, doing well academically. They ranged from average students to high achievers who attended their classes regularly, maintained high grades, and were very attentive and participatory in class. There were some who, despite being financially strained, were clearly more dedicated than others and thus had been awarded scholarships funded by individual teachers. Out of the ten girls, Cristina was the student who at the moment seemed to struggle the most academically. Most of this was due to the fact that she tended to miss class and instead spent much of her time hanging out with friends. Her teachers often worried about her and attempted, in various ways, to get her back on track. This, however, seemed to be part of the ups and downs that she would go through, as there were times that her high grades had also earned her a scholarship.

Some of the most academically oriented students, such as Karla, Diana, and Marsella, stressed that they were not fond of studying but considered themselves good students because they paid attention in class, asked many questions, interacted with the teachers, and completed their assignments. I also found that these girls defined "studying" differently from "learning." What they referred to as "studying" were drilling activities that led to memorization of information. Learning, on the other hand, involved the process of discovery and finding meaning. They all generally seemed to enjoy their classes, and several expressed great passion toward reading. Some, such as Diana, Gabriela, and Marsella, enjoyed conducting research on topics that interested them, working on group projects, writing, and even taking exams.

Some of the girls attributed their interest in books to the models and encouragement that their parents or some of their teachers had provided. Although only Diana had a college-educated parent, about half of them mentioned that they had grown up seeing their mothers reading. In fact, the girls at Altavista, and even the boys with whom I had an opportunity to talk, enjoyed conversing about books. This was an interesting trend at Altavista, which greatly contrasted with my experiences in other Mexican schools with mostly middle-class students, where reading was considered "uncool," "too nerdy," or not interesting enough to be a topic for informal conversation.

Despite the literacy that was promoted at home, about half of the girls in this group were to be the first ones in their family to complete high school. However, three of them, Gabriela, Alejandra, and Iliana, had sisters who had completed a bachelor's degree or were attending college. All the girls in the study indicated that they wanted to attend college, but they saw financial difficulties as a daunting challenge to overcome. Still, some were quite determined and thought of working for a year after their high school graduation to save for college. Others considered looking for scholarships. While I highly doubted that they would return to school after joining the workforce, I was proved wrong by a couple of them who returned to college after working at a maquiladora for a few years after high school.

Unfortunately, according to the principal, the reality was that of the girls who graduated from Altavista, less than 20 percent would go on to college. A significant challenge these young women faced in their pursuit of higher education, in addition to lack of financial resources, was the potential erosion of their dreams by life in the barrio. Only with great difficulty would they be able to continue their education if they were to commit to a boyfriend from their neighborhood. Armida, the principal, explained that in many cases, young women had to choose between leaving their partner to pursue their academic and professional goals and sacrificing their dreams in order to stay in the relationship. Navigating the two worlds, the barrio and school, was a thorny situation that brought feelings of displacement for those who wished to persevere in their educational objectives. Having had a similar experience, Armida revealed the difficulties of dealing with this dilemma.

When one goes to school, one is no longer from the barrio. You lose. There is no belonging. But you are not from the other side either. You're uprooted. So there is that social price to pay, and not all of us can do it. In the barrio, none of the guys will want to be your boyfriend. You go to school and they don't. You're not from there anymore. And neither are you from the other side because the other boys that you hang out with are middle and upper class and you don't belong there either. So you have to trace that path for yourself. It's not a tragedy either; it can be resolved. But to live it when you're eighteen years old is not the same as I see it today as an adult. You try to fit in with the boys that you went to elementary school with, and, like they often say, *"Ya nadie te pela"* [Nobody cares about you anymore].

Some of the girls were not naïve either about what to expect if they were able to go to college. Gabriela was very aware of the elitist nature of institutions of higher education. One day while I was talking with her and her group of friends about their ideas about college, she expressed how out of place the image of her sitting in a university classroom would seem.

College in Juárez is assumed and designed for middle- and upper-class students, to maintain social inequalities. I have a friend who is trying to convince me to go to UNAM[1] because he says that it's ridiculous that public universities here charge so much money. He laughs when he imagines me at the university here in the middle of all these *fresas*.

Gabriela used the word *fresas* to refer to the petit bourgeois or "preppy." Indeed, for girls like Gabriela, who held a working-class identity and had strong social-class consciousness, the social context promised a hostile and challenging transition from high school to college. However, I also found that for some of them, like Marsella, Karla, Diana, Nora, and Cristina, their motivation to complete their education was extremely strong because it was rooted in a commitment to their family and loved ones. In other words, this was not an individualist pursuit. Instead, they knew that their education had been a costly sacrifice for their entire family, not just financially but also in terms of emotional investment. Their educational success was something that had involved the work of many. Family members looked up to and had high hopes in them. Failing or giving up meant disappointing those who had supported their journey.

Marsella: I have to keep going, in part because I want to make my grandmother proud. Because although she is alone, she has sacrificed a lot for me. . . . She is very poor, but she has always made great efforts so that I can go to school. I was not going to go to middle school, but she found a scholarship and money to be able to put me in school. Also to be able to come here, she asked for help from all these political parties and governmental agencies, from everyone. She would do anything to get me the help I needed to be able to go to school.

After their high school graduation, I had the opportunity to witness the challenges of classism and sexism that some university contexts imposed on some of the women. Only with a lot of determination, confidence, and a strong support system would they be able navigate and overcome the psychological aggressions they received from many professors and peers, as well as the disdain on the part of some of their friends and family members from the barrio.

Coming of Age in a Digital World

In contrast to my own experience as a young woman in Juarez during the 1980s and 1990s, the girls of this study were coming of age in the technology and information era in which much of the formal and informal forms of communication was expected to be done through the use of computers and the Internet. Not only did their access to technology determine, to a large extent, their exposure to a global flow of ideas, languages, relationships, and popular culture, but it also affected the types of opportunities of which they could take advantage. The young women's use of technology was an interesting aspect of their lives that revealed not only the ways in which financial limitations affected them as students but also their agency and resourcefulness in the face of precariousness.

Several of them used the Internet as an important source of information for both their class projects and other areas of interest. However, computers with Internet access were extremely scarce in school and at the time, access to free Wi-Fi in public spaces or local business was not common. While a couple girls had cell phones that functioned on a prepaid basis, which they used as a way to store music and photos rather than to make calls, most could not afford this luxury, much less consistent access to the Internet. This lack of regular access to the Internet affected their ability to utilize technology for official business and was the reason for some missed opportunities. For example, the state offered scholarships for certain students from low socioeconomic backgrounds, but the entire application process had to be done online. Those with limited access to technology tended to forget their passwords or failed to check their e-mails, causing them to miss deadlines or important information. Preparing for their college admissions test was also a challenge, since the study guide was only available online. The digital divide, then, was a real barrier for these students, in that although they had enough exposure to technology to learn to use it, many were unable to make it a consistent or reliable resource.

Nevertheless, their precarious access to technology did not impede them from learning how to utilize it in resourceful and purposeful ways. Besides relying on the Internet to expand their academic knowledge, often in place of textbooks, many of the girls were able to search and upload videos onto YouTube and populate Myspace and Facebook profiles with bios, music, photos, and other images that allowed them to express their identities in creative ways, even when they were not able to maintain their sites very regularly. They also used the Internet and social media to connect with activists in remote places, learn about opportunities to join groups with similar interests, and get encouragement and help from allies, friends, and family who lived far away. This was crucial in a time when even hanging out with friends on the porch was a dangerous activity and when feelings of isolation, hopelessness, and fear pervaded families and youth. They also used social media as a tool to learn more about their boyfriends or other people, which in a couple of cases helped them make important decisions about their relationships or to protect their safety.

Crossing and Not Crossing Borders

As discussed in chapter 1, living on the border does not imply being a literal border crosser of international boundaries. El Paso's buildings and freeways, as well as UTEP and the shining star on top of the Franklin Mountain, could be seen from the school and from many of the neighborhoods where these girls lived. However, almost none of the girls in this group appeared to cross the international border on a regular basis for shopping or other activities, as girls from many middle-class Juárez families did. Most did not even have a border-crossing pass or visa, so life in the United States seemed distant and, for most, unappealing. Yet it was not completely unfamiliar. Several had relatives in the United States whom they had visited before, and a few others indicated having had a boyfriend in the past who had immigrated to the United States. Yet none of them had plans to migrate north.

While several indicated their desire to travel, they emphasized wanting to travel in México before exploring other countries. They viewed the

United States both with fascination and contempt. They were keenly aware of the imperialist position of the United States in the world, and while attending UTEP and visiting big cities like New York seemed like a dream to some of them, almost all of them expressed that American culture and lifestyle also appeared to be cold, materialistic, mechanical, and boring. The experiences of their relatives who worked low-wage and heavy laboring jobs in the United States gave them a window of understanding into what their life could be in the United States given their social location as Latinas from working-class families.

Girls' Images: Reimagining Self and Life in Juárez

As the discussion has revealed thus far, the girls experienced an era of great contradictions and instability. The mood in the city was of growing insecurity and, to some degree, of depression and learned hopelessness. The skyrocketing rates of unemployment and the economic decline, coupled with the unprecedented violence and prevalence of impunity, gave way to an understandably pessimistic outlook. Talking about the future raised feelings of anxiety, and in some cases it seemed almost like an insult.

Some might think that the conditions of the city as well as Altavista's emphasis on critical consciousness would result in even greater despair, yet these young women maintained their optimism, or rather a sense of critical hope (Duncan-Andrade 2009). Their views of the future were both bitter and sweet. They were idealistic about their aspirations and the type of life they wanted to have but were uncertain about how to accomplish their goals, given the limitations that their context imposed. While some of the women admitted that they often considered taking their families and moving to a safer place, they also knew that this was rather financially unrealistic and that finding ways to not just survive but also pursue their dreams in their current context was necessary.

In order to better capture the girls' perspectives, identities, and experiences in such a complex context, and drawing from auto-photography and photovoice methods, I asked them to participate in a photography activity. Wishing to represent a less bounded sense of the girls' identities, life experiences, and world views, I gave each girl from my selected group of informants a disposable camera and asked them to take photographs of anything they thought represented them or the things or people that were most important to them. My prompt to them was "If I were to tell someone about you and your life story, from your own point of view, using only images, what images would you want me to show?" There were no limits or guidelines on what kind of photographs I was looking for. The girls' photographs could be as creative, literal, or mundane as they wanted. Seven out of the nine girls that I asked to participate in the activity returned their camera to me. After processing the film, I had individual conversations with each informant to elicit their reflections about their images. In addition, each girl selected four or five images that were the most meaningful or representative and wrote a brief explanation on the back of the picture.

I should note that initially, the activity, as I explained it to them, involved solely an auto-photography strategy, meaning that I was mainly interested in their perceptions of self. However, when they turned in their photographs, I realized that the girls also followed a photo-voice approach in an organic way, by including photographs of their community with narratives about their interpretations of the social realities of the city. This highlights the girls' understandings of self as deeply rooted in their communities, as members of a collective, and as political subjects in a larger social and historical context. In fact, images where the girls revealed their identities as communal beings, observers, critics, and change agents were the most prominent in the entire collections of photographs as well as in their own selection of the most meaningful photos.

In my analysis of the images and the narratives of the most representative photographs that the women selected, I identified four salient themes that framed their perspectives on life in Juárez and concepts of self. These include: (1) Beyond the "wasteland": Images of injury, agency, and life in Ciudad Juárez; (2) *Resistir y salir adelante*: Images of school, family, and friends; (3) Nature as a mirror and as a source of spiritual renewal; (4) I'm still alive: Dreamers, thinkers, and creators. The following is a discussion of each theme and its respective images. I have also provided samples of these images, while omitting many photographs to preserve the anonymity of informants and their family and friends.

Beyond the "Wasteland": Images of
Injury, Agency, and Life in Ciudad Juárez

In contrast to the hopeless depictions of Juárez that abounded in the media especially during the drug war years, the girls in this study appeared to view their city in much more nuanced ways. Certainly they were not blind to the violence and distress in the city, but their interpretations went beyond that, instead indicating perceptions of other aspects that revealed the humanity and agency that exist in Juárez. All but one of the girls took photographs of Juárez, as an important aspect of their life. Yet none of them portrayed sensationalist images of the city. Instead, they had a very critical perspective on the militarization of their city, and stories of struggle, resistance, and even hope prevailed.

For instance, as one of her most important photographs, Marsella selected one that captured her barren neighborhood (Figure 4). On the back of the photograph, she wrote:

This is the place where I live. This is how several of the streets look in the city since the soldiers arrived. This street used to always have children playing and women talking, and today most of the houses that can be seen have been abandoned, and some are even at the point of collapsing because the people who used to live in them moved away because of the crime.

Alejandra included a similar photograph, but she wanted to reveal the everyday living conditions of her community. Her photograph showed the

Figure 4. Marsella's photograph of her neighborhood abandoned due to the exodus of people fleeing the city's violence.

muddy puddles that characterized the unpaved streets of her barrio, which would become more like swamps during heavy rains (Figure 5).

Iliana and Alejandra included a few photographs of the many military and federal police pickup trucks that patrolled the city, carrying armed troops ready to fire at any moment (Figure 6). These photos and narratives revealed, rather than a sense of safety, the increased feelings of stress, fear, and contempt that militarization brought to the city. Alejandra's photograph, which has been omitted here, shows that she tried to mask the fact that she was photographing the military truck, by having a friend pose in front of her. This revealed the careful strategies that the girls knew were necessary for their own protection. Mónica included a similar photograph taken at a march, where activists mocked the militarization of the city by mimicking the federal commando trucks (Figure 7). In this case the truck in Mónica's photo carried an oversize representation of a faceless military figure with fallen youth laying on his lap. This representation blamed the military and federal police for the exacerbation of violence and death in the city.

Gabriela and Mónica also revealed a sense of resistance in their photographs. They took very similar photographs at the activist march, which

Figure 5. Alejandra's photograph of her neighborhood revealing the unpaved roads that would flood during heavy rains and would cause difficulties in people's commutes.

Figure 6. Iliana's photograph of the recent militarization of her community that brought about a greater sense of restlessness and insecurity rather than safety.

Figure 7. Mónica's photograph of a city-wide march showing the representation of the military and its role in increasing the violence through abuse of authority.

called itself "Marcha del coraje, dolor y desagravio" (March of fury, sorrow, and atonement), in which hundreds of students denounced the impunity, ineptitude, and abuse on the part of the federal and state authorities as well as the military. Some of these photographs showed those participating in the march lying on, and blocking, the street leading to one of the international bridges. This was a striking representation of the thousands of deaths, particularly of innocent people, caused not only by the cartels but also by the military (Figure 8). Moreover, Gabriela's photograph shows a large sign that reads *"Somos estudiantes NO pandilleros"* (We are students not gang members), a statement that many of the activists tried to make to resist the discourse that stigmatized youth from the barrio and blamed the violence in their communities on the youth's gang activity.

These, however, were not the only depictions of the city. Some of the collections also humanized it by providing insight into everyday life in Juárez, including the cultural diversity of its residents. Gabriela and Alejandra included images that had little to do with the violence but exhibited the postmodern condition of the city, including a mixture of tradition and modernity and the everyday struggles of youth, the elderly, the poor, and

Figure 8. Gabriela's photograph of the "Marcha del coraje, dolor y desagravio" demonstration in which participants lay on the ground representing the many casualties of the drug wars and other acts of violence.

indigenous groups for dignity and survival within a capitalist society. Alejandra took pictures of the city's highways, a modern shopping mall—which she titled "Capitalism" (Figure 9), illustrating the major role that capitalism played in structuring the lives of Juárez residents, from consumption to work practices and policies. She also included photographs of a Tarahumara family crossing a large avenue, a high school soccer team, and the sign welcoming visitors to the historic park "El Chamizal," among others.[2]

Gabriela, on the other hand, took pictures in downtown Juárez, including the Catholic Cathedral with its surrounding plaza or square and the many vendors trying to make a living in the informal market (Figure 10). Given Gabriela's own participation in the informal market, she might have viewed herself as part of this community that is often marginalized, ignored, or viewed with disdain in more privileged circles. One of Gabriela's favorite photographs that was taken in this plaza was of a bronze statue of Germán Valdés, better known as Tin Tan. Tin Tan was an infamous Golden Age Mexican actor, singer, and comedian raised in Ciudad Juárez who displayed *Pachuco* dress and used *Pachuco* Spanglish in many of his movies, making the language and style of the Mexican American *Pachucos* famous in México (Figure 11). She also included a photo with a Mariachi band and one of a large group of bikers riding their motorcycles through town,

Figure 9. Alejandra's photograph titled "Capitalism," revealing a modern shopping center and symbolizing the central role of capitalism in organizing the lives of Juárez residents.

Figure 10. *Gabriela's photograph of street vendors in downtown Juárez, a generally marginalized sector of the population with which she identified given her own participation in the informal market as a means to earn some income.*

Figure 11. *Gabriela's photograph of Mexican Golden Age actor Tin Tan, who popularized the Pachuco style and use of Spanglish.*

whom she called *"mis compas"* (my friends) (Figure 12). Through these photographs, Gabriela revealed her sense of belonging to and appreciation of groups that are often viewed as deviant or unimportant by the dominant culture and elite groups. Gabriela's humanization of the city through her images also included a photograph taken inside the Mission of the Virgin of Guadalupe, where men and women kneeled down to pray and hundreds of candles and objects represented people's pleas and prayers. "This photograph represents faith," Gabriela explained. "I am constantly astonished and inspired by the faith that my people have despite the most difficult circumstances."

A similarly moving photo was included in Iliana's collection, and she chose it as one of the most important ones. It depicts a young girl sitting on top of a desert hill in a Juárez shantytown, contemplating the landscape framed by clear blue skies (Figure 13). Sadness, innocence, and hope all come together in this melancholic image revealing what was so close to Iliana's heart: celebration of the life of her little sister and worry about the life prospects that the city offered her. The image gives insight into both the limits that the girls' social context imposes as well as a glimpse of hope,

Figure 12. Gabriela's photograph "Mis compas" or "My buddies," which along with the previous two photographs reveals her identification with those often considered deviant by the Mexican elites.

Figure 13. Iliana's photograph of her sister contemplating her community—a melancholic portrayal of both struggle and hope.

and also the need for deliberate agency and determination to dream beyond what is at sight.

Finally, in contrast to the scorn and demonization of México by international mainstream media, Alejandra expressed her strong sense of Mexican identity by choosing the photograph of a Mexican flag waving high in the sky as one of her most representative images. "This photo represents me, with its tricolored flag, which is my city, my nationality, and my Mexican homeland," she proudly explained.

Resistir y Salir Adelante: *Images of School, Family, and Friends*

Images of loved ones were included in every girl's collection. More than just showcasing the people they loved, the girls spoke about them with a sense of admiration and gratitude. These individuals were those who inspired, supported, and taught the girls in their life journey of self-authorship. The girls who had parents and felt supported by them included their photographs. Karla, for example, wrote:

What can I say about my parents? I can only thank them for all these 18 years that they have been struggling to help me *salir adelante* and to not let me fall. And when I fall, I know that their hands will be there to lift me up. Plain and simple, I thank them for giving me life. I love them so much.

I have unsuccessfully tried to find an English phrase that can accurately represent what *"salir adelante"* means to Karla and to other girls who used the same expression. Dictionaries will translate it as "to succeed," but *salir adelante* has more to do with survival, with overcoming adversity, and with staying the course rather than achieving or arriving at a particular destination. Karla's sentiments express that *salir adelante* in her life was a collective effort, in which her parents helped her to rise above life's difficulties. Marsella also expressed this idea as she described the picture of her grandmother (Figure 14).

This lady is my maternal grandmother and I call her Mother because she raised me and took care of me since I was a baby. She is among the people that I love the most in the world. I respect her

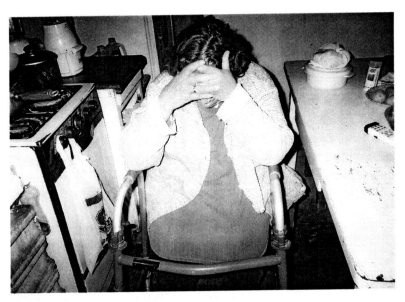

Figure 14. Photograph of Marsella's grandmother—the most important person in her life.

and I admire her because she has done everything she can to help me *salir adelante*, all by herself. . . . I live with her. She is 74 years old. She is all I have, and it could be said that I am all that she has.

Diana's photo of her mother also spoke of her admiration for this parent who had single-handedly raised her and taught her to be the person she is today. As a feminist, lesbian, and activist who had the determination to complete college and pursue a professional career as a psychologist as well as to raise her children after a painful divorce, Diana's mother embodied the strength, wisdom, and agency that inspired her to fight for her ideals, to not be silenced, and to be critical.

Friends, teachers, and, in a few cases, significant others were also part of every girl's photo collection. While I did not include most of these photographs for anonymity purposes, these important individuals were appreciated for the support and solidarity they offered through life struggles. "My friends are very important in my life because they don't leave me alone, and I know that when I need them they will be there to encourage me," Karla wrote. Diana also expressed that her best friends were young women with a lot of wisdom.

Without exception, every girl included photographs of Altavista and selected them as part of their most representative set of photos (Figure 15). "This represents my beloved school," Diana said. "I love everything about it, my classmates, teachers, everything." Alejandra chose her photo of Altavista as one of the most important ones in her collection and described it as "one of the best schools in Ciudad Juárez." And Karla called her class "my family" and her school "my home . . . to which I will always belong" (Figure 16). Like other girls, Karla referred to her teachers with much love and admiration, considering them to be not only intelligent but also wise and caring. In referring to a photo of one of her teachers, she said, "This is my psychology teacher, but more than that, she is like a mother because I know that if I asked her for advice, she would never refuse it. I love her a lot."

Without a doubt, Altavista had nurtured some of the girls' most treasured relationships, and it was also a space that inspired them and gave them open opportunities to forge new identities and a new worldview that challenged the criminalizing discourses about them and their community. This was evident in the photograph of Karla's best friends. She often talked about her embracement of and alliance with LGBTQ peers, even though

Figure 15. *Gabriela's photograph of Altavista as one of the most important things in her life. Different versions of this photograph appeared in all the girls' collections.*

Figure 16. *Karla's photograph of Armida, Altavista's principal and sociology teacher, lecturing during class. Karla titled this photograph "My family" to emphasize the crucial role of her school community in her life.*

she identified as heterosexual, and about how much she appreciated that Altavista did not police or criminalize the ways in which students dressed or the ways they expressed their gender identity. Karla and other girls were aware that other high schools in the city often had strict uniform policies and heteronormative expectations, and the photograph illustrates the freedom in gender identity, gender expression, and in general freedom of dress at Altavista that they recognized as unusual and quite empowering.

Almost every girl included photographs of the murals covering some of the school's walls, which had been created by students and had messages of social critique and a pursuit of truth (Figure 17). Several of the girls also included photographs of a festival that took place at Altavista, when various artists from the barrios came to perform and bring consciousness-raising messages in preparation for one of the largest student-led, city-wide marches against violence and impunity (Figure 18). While this image reveals mostly male MCs and artists, there was also an all-female band that participated. These images revealed the commitment of the girls, as well as of other people in their school and community, to activism, their solidarity with grassroots social justice struggles, and their determination to not be silenced by fear. The images represented the critical orientation that the

Figure 17. Mónica's photograph of a mural at Altavista with a message of social critique created by local community artists and Altavista students during Altavista Fest.

girls had gained at Altavista, but they also showed, in Karla's words, "the magic in my school, and how the artists that exist in it represent Juárez through their drawings." Or, in Gabriela's words, that "there is talent in the barrio."

Also demonstrating the spirit of freedom at Altavista and a counternarrative to the stigmatization of the school in the city was a photograph in Marsella's collection that captured a group of about ten students, sitting outside on a pile of landscaping chestnut-shells playing their instruments (Figure 19). She wrote:

> I love this photo. Others have always talked badly about the people at Altavista. They say that we are a bad influence, or that we are delinquents. But this photo shows a little bit about the beautiful people in this school, that most of them are very artistic and good people.

Marsella chose this photo as one of the most important ones in her collection. Her photograph and narrative show how crucial it was for her to emphasize that neither she nor her friends were criminals, as well as the

Figure 18. Alejandra's photograph of hip-hop artists performing raps of social critique during Altavista Fest.

Figure 19. Marsella's photograph of the "beautiful people in this school," revealing the common activity of making music during recess in which students frequently and organically engaged.

fact that talent is often overlooked in the midst of popular deficit discourses about the poor. What is important to note is that Marsella, and the other girls, also recognized that the talents in her community were not simply limited to individualistic pursuits for creativity and art but rather that the youth in the barrio aimed to raise critical consciousness and voice their resistance against injustice through their creative expressions of art.

Nature as a Mirror and as a Source of Spiritual Renewal

It would have never crossed my mind that nature was so telling of these girls' lives. Every girl included a photo of nature, in particular, of trees and plants, in her collection. While this may seem mundane, I learned that the girls felt strongly rooted in and truly inspired by nature. They saw nature as a metaphor of their own life and ideals, as the foundation of a wholesome self, and as a source of faith, critical thought, and spiritual regeneration. I also interpreted their emphasis on nature as their ability to appreciate life beyond the dusty concrete and the drying hopes of this desert city.

Gabriela, for example, included a photograph of a big tree behind a fence—its long leafy branches swinging freely with the wind (Figure 20). To her, this tree represented freedom, strength, and life. In contrast, Alejandra took a photo of a dry tall tree also behind a fence covered with graffiti, but she interpreted the image as a metaphor for the societal decay and constraints imposed on her and others in the city by the violence, social inequalities, militarization, and other factors that imprison people's lives and truncate their dreams and aspirations. Clearly, Alejandra's interpretation offered a critical view of her social context. Interestingly, the difference between Gabriela's and Alejandra's interpretations and choices of trees— while both being behind a graffiti-covered wall—reveal a difference in their perspective that might be possibly influenced by the way they felt about their personal lives. Gabriela seemed to openly challenge the repression that the violence in the city imposed on these youth. On the other hand, while Alejandra also attempted to resist this repression, she experienced an additional layer of threat by the presence of an aggressive boyfriend in her life—a relationship from which she struggled to escape.

Iliana, who often expressed her desire to maintain her roots with her indigenous background and her attachment to the natural world as a Mestiza,

Figure 20. Gabriela's photograph of a tree whose branches swing freely with the wind, representing freedom, strength, and life.

utilized nature in the majority of her photographs. She included a photo of her bare feet touching the desert, as well as her hand in the middle of the female Venus symbol made out of sand. These images represented her attachment to the land and her identification with the earth as a female being. A flower, flying birds, and even chopped vegetables in an artistic and colorful arrangement represented nature as the source of all good things in life including beauty, freedom, abundance, nourishment, and art. Finally, Iliana included an image displaying a hand mirror thrust into the sand and surrounded by plants, with the word "EQUIDAD" (equity) painted with lipstick on the mirror (Figure 21). This depiction illustrated social justice, including gender equity, which in her words "is the foundation of life."

Diana's photo of a dry tree standing alone in a bare field as a representa tion of her identity warrants special attention. This illustration brought together her past, present, and future affected by personal circumstances and also affirmed strength as a durable characteristic of her identity (Figure 22). Diana had recently survived one of the most dramatic experiences that took place during my year of fieldwork. One afternoon she and her mother took her cat to the veterinarian. While they waited for their pet's turn, a

Figure 21. Iliana's photograph of social justice and equity as represented by nature, "the foundation of life."

Figure 22. Diana's photograph representing herself after having been devastated by sexual violence: "I might look dead today, but I will be green and full of life again."

man, whom she thought "looked like a soldier without the uniform," asked to come in. As soon as the man entered the clinic, he pulled out a gun and ordered Diana's mother to close the door. He demanded that everyone give him what they had, threatening to kill the vet. Then he ordered Diana to go into a room in the back; threatening to kill her mother if she did not do as he said, he proceeded to rape her.

The man had left the site without killing anyone and without getting caught by any of the soldiers that patrolled through the neighborhood. But this assault had devastated this young woman both emotionally and physically. She felt enraged, humiliated, and hurt, and the incident took an additional toll on her family by sinking her mother into a deep depression and feelings of guilt.

After Diana was examined at the hospital and tested for HIV, she was told that she would have to wait three months to be retested, in order to receive accurate results. Because she developed other minor infections after the incident, she consulted with herbalists and homeopaths, who, after seeing her blood tests, determined that the possibilities of HIV were quite high and put her in an intensive treatment. Devastated, she shared with me the conversation she had with her friends, ironically only a few days before the incident.

> I remembered that we were talking about what would happen if someone told us, "Would you rather have me rape you or kill you?" And we all said, "Well let him kill me." I would prefer to die, you know? Rather than live with that.

Yet on the day that she shared her photographs with me, she bravely revealed that she had chosen to live, or rather to survive and overcome her victimization. Pointing at the picture of the small tree located in the middle of the school's backyard that faced the Rio Grande River, she explained:

> This tree represents me because though it seems like it doesn't have life, it's still extensive and its roots are firm. It also represents my spirituality and my love for Mother Earth. I might look dead today, but I will be green and full of life again.

And indeed this is exactly what happened. Still with an injured body and a distressed heart, Diana focused her energy on getting well, carefully following the instructions of her alternative medicine health care advisors, and engaging in as much activism as possible. Fortunately, when she was tested for HIV at the hospital at the end of the third month, the results came back negative. Without a doubt, her passion and soul were still alive when she told me, "My mother wants me to leave the city, but I told her, I would rather die on my feet than live on my knees. Whatever movement there is, I will be there."

Diana, like many of the other girls, often talked about finding refuge in nature. Clearly, Juárez is not known for having beautiful natural landscapes; rather, it is an industrial city in the middle of the desert. But the girls still found beauty and inspiration in its dry soil, scarce trees, and starry nights for social critique and social action, as well as for healing, strength, and personal renewal. Perhaps a better way to demonstrate the meaning of nature to these girls is through Gabriela's own words, the lyrics of a rap that she wrote on a bright spring day in 2010.

Amor Natural

Contemplando el verde resplandor
de la maleza creciendo,
puedo sentir el calor del sol
enredándose en mi piel.
Mi cuerpo cálido se llena de luz,
y mi espíritu se carga
de energía natural.
Es diferente este sentimiento
de contacto natural
al sentimiento de concreto.
Se podría decir que el concreto
ha hecho a las personas duras,
de piedra, sin sentir y grises de tristeza.
Carros, smog, muertes.
Delitos fronterizos en Ciudad Juárez,
delitos sexuales, delitos injustos,
y balas de corrupción,
balas de injusticia y cobardía.
Balas que atraviesan jóvenes con anhelos,
balas que se llevan niños inocentes

Adultos inconscientes llenos de maldad,
abundantes de desesperación,
atrapados en una gran dimensión de perdición.

[Natural Love]
[Contemplating the green glow of the
growing grass,
I can feel the sun's heat
wrapping around my skin.
My warm body is filled with light,
and my spirit is charged
with natural energy.
It is different
this feeling of contact with nature
from the feeling of concrete.
It could be said that concrete
has made people hard, of stone,
without feelings, and gray with sadness.
Because that's what happens in the city.
Cars, smog, and deaths.
Border crimes in Ciudad Juárez,
sexual crimes, unjust crimes,
and bullets of corruption,
bullets of injustice and cowardice.
Bullets that go through yearning
youth, bullets that take away innocent children
Senseless adults full of evil,
full of desperation,
trapped in a great dimension of perdition.]

I'm Still Alive: Dreamers, Thinkers, and Creators

The last set of photographs depicts the more intimate aspects of the girls'
notions of self. These include their own self-portraits, in some cases displaying their styles and physical characteristics, which give, at least, slight
reflections of their identities. The photographs with these representations
were the most diverse in their collections, demonstrating each girl's unique
sense of self.

In many cases, some of these photographs give some glimpse into the young women's past experiences as factors that helped determine their present feelings and sense of self. Marsella and Gabriela shared images that spoke of childhood memories. Marsella's photograph of an old doll represented her attachment to the last gift her father gave her as a little child before he was killed, and Gabriela's photo of an old shed brought back memories of an innocent childhood and free play.

Alejandra took a photo of a mural depicting indigenous women wearing long, white dresses and dancing in the desert under the sun. "This photo represents me because I am a woman, and I am free!" she wrote on the back. When I asked her if this feeling was at all related to the fact that she had just broken up with her aggressive and possessive boyfriend, she exclaimed, "Yes indeed! I am free!" The mural contrasted with a photo of her bedroom door. She explained that this door very much reflected her; not only did it display stickers and pictures of her favorite music and artists as well as her own drawings, but it also symbolized the many hours she spent alone in her bedroom accompanied by feelings of loneliness and sadness (Figure 23). These feelings were more specifically expressed by the poster of a crying young child at the very center of the door.

The girls also included photos of the things or symbolisms that they felt the most passionate about and that gave them encouragement in challenging moments, such as their faith and aspirations. Karla's photograph of plastic stars hanging from her ceiling and Marsella's photo of peace symbols represented their dreams and hopes of the future, which was what kept them going, even in difficult times. These representations were particularly related to pursuing their education, even when their economic situations were less than favorable.

Some photographs also represented the things that gave them strength and hope during difficult times. A photo of a massage bed represented one of Diana's passions and was selected as one of her most important images (Figure 24). "I love to give massages. It is what keeps me strong. In the worst moments it gives me strength to always keep on going with my head up high," she wrote. Karla represented her faith with a photo of a crucifix, which was also one of her most representative images. She wrote on the back: "This image means a lot to me because I am a strong believer, and I really know that he's always taking care of me and helping me."

Music and other art forms were important for all the girls. Marsella, Gabriela, and Iliana included photographs of musical instruments in their

Figure 23. Alejandra's photograph of her bedroom door, revealing her feelings of loneliness at home.

Figure 24. Diana's photograph of her massage bed at the spa where she worked, representing one of the activities that gave her hope and strength.

collections to demonstrate their passion for music. "I love this picture because this is what I do all day. I make music," Gabriela explained as she showed me the photo of herself playing the guitar (Figure 25). Karla, Mónica, and Alejandra also took pictures of murals that they had painted or figures they had made from broken mosaic around the school to represent their love for art. Diana included a photo that represented dance and explained that "dancing is what allows me to escape from my reality."

There were also photos that revealed the girls' unique personalities. For example, Diana included a photo of candy bars, illustrating the energy and passion with which she engaged in every activity in her life. And Mónica's introverted and quiet personality was represented by a photograph that brought together her favorite activities, such as retreating to her bedroom to read, listening to music, and drawing while drinking her favorite juice (Figure 26). Gabriela's thoughtfulness and fascination with the simple things in life, such as skateboarding, starry nights, and a proud-looking cat in the midst of a chaotic scene, were also evident in her photographs. She

Figure 25. Gabriela's photograph representing her passion for music and the time she often spent writing songs.

Figure 26. Mónica's photograph representing her introverted personality and the things she enjoyed doing in solitude, including reading her favorite pieces of literature.

captured an interesting image at a public restroom that depicted a girl using the toilet behind a closed door (Figure 27). Her explanation revealed her analytic eye.

> It's funny that you can always know when it's a woman because her pants and underpants are always on the floor. I think of how basic this difference is, but it represents so much of real life. Men don't have to take everything off to go to the bathroom. They can pee anywhere. But women have to take everything off and they can't just do it anywhere because they have to sit down. Everything is more complicated for women because of the rules that society imposes on us.

Finally, some of the photographs also allowed the girls to express attributes that are not often associated with images about girls from their barrio. An image of a tree with books hanging from its branches represented Diana's wisdom. "Although I might seem ignorant because of my young age, I know that there is a lot of wisdom in my spirit, soul, and mind," she

Figure 27. Gabriela's photograph representing the different constraints experienced by women, which also illustrates her contemplative and critical personality.

wrote. And Mónica's photo showing some of her favorite books, including Dostoyevsky's *Crime and Punishment,* spoke of her passion for reading (Figure 26).

Conclusion

The entire collection of the women's images depicts the people, places, objects, activities, and symbols of the things that gave meaning to their lives, and they are far from the stereotypical notions portrayed in popular media or the reductionist images of Juárez women as faceless maquiladora workers or as perpetually naïve prey of predatory violence.

A discourse of struggle was prevalent in the interviews with the young women in the study and in their descriptions of their photographs, but none of them perceived themselves as helpless victims or as ignorant, fragile, or mediocre. They talked about financial struggles, but this was not the prevalent topic of conversation. And while all of them did go through times of loneliness, difficulties, and sorrow, these experiences were conceived as part of the everyday life that gave them wisdom and deeper ways to understand the world rather than as an unavoidable state risk or crisis inherent in adolescence. Similarly, there were no images that depicted prevailing feelings of confusion or low self-esteem, as the common narrative about teenage girls would have it. Nor were there photographs revealing uncontrolled excesses of life on the border, hopelessly dragging their lives to perdition.

Although the women were far from living rosy lives, the photographs in the collections reveal that while much about their lives was determined by their social realities, they were not passive receptacles of power but active political subjects. They all had concrete and nuanced opinions of their social context and did not have a problem expressing them, and some even revealed the significance that engaging in social justice action had in their lives. In other words, the young women saw their identities as deeply rooted and committed to a collective. Just as Jessica Taft (2011) found in her study of activist girls across the Americas, the women in this study create, re-create, and perform their identities "through their stories of the self, through their political talk, and through their collective strategic actions" (180). And as Taft notes, this type of identity work in some ways conforms to but also challenges popular ideas about what it means to be a girl and a woman.

For example, despite widespread images of Juárez women as victimized maquiladora workers, popular culture in the United States and other Western countries has pushed a different message that has become well known: that girls can be and are powerful. These portrayals of "girl power" have, however, been consumed and used in very particular ways and have propagated around the world. As conceptualized by girl studies scholar Anita Harris (2004), the idealized empowered girl (or the "can-do girl," as Harris calls her) is one who is "flexible, individualized, resilient, self-driven, and self-made and who easily follows nonlinear trajectories to fulfillment and success" (16). All aspects of her life, including her sexuality, are characterized by confidence, powerfulness, and independence. The image of this empowered girl is one of diversity, inclusive of young women of many sizes and shapes and from various styles and walks of life. As such, this image of empowerment suggests that self-determination is all it takes to succeed and has been embraced and utilized by capitalist schemes to encourage the consumption of objects, media, styles, and images that depict certain role models and messages that challenge tradition. While some of these can-do girl traits were present in the girls' discourses, such as the desire to be confident and independent, this was not quite the type of "empowered girl" identity that I saw unfolding.

Rather than buying into the meritocratic and neoliberal myth that young women can do or become anything without seriously accounting for pervasive structures of injustice and inequality, allowing their identities to be completely defined by the marketplace, or remaining in paralysis in the face of loneliness, lack of opportunities, and a discourse of fear, these young women constructed their identities within a sense of struggle and commitment to their community and all while questioning the discourses and structures of power that oppressed their lives. In constructing their identities, they excavated from the narratives of their mothers, sisters, and friends, from the intimacy of their solitude, and from their lived experiences the healing, wisdom, and life lessons that they used as guides to read the world and to reinvent themselves.

Most girls were often candid in talking about their strengths but were also able to recognize their weaknesses and vulnerabilities. They were not always confident but were actively making and remaking themselves, not always independent but were critical thinkers, suspicious of the media and resistant to becoming naïve consumerist subjects. They were inquisitive, dissatisfied with the world as is, and bold in their activism yet grateful for the people who supported them. They were able to get up after tragedy struck their lives, and most important, they all found hope and reasons to live life to the fullest, even in the so-called murder capital of the world. Far from infantile, these women embodied *sabiduría*, a wisdom that stemmed from their own life experiences and from the lessons they learned in convivencia with other women (Trinidad Galván 2001). In other words, it was generated through the mundane and in "the intimate spaces where *mujer-to-mujer* conversations are whispered," teaching them lessons of *supervivencia*, boldness, resistance, and self-sufficiency (Villenas et al. 2006, 3). This type of womanist learning through convivencia thus constituted a critical pedagogy based on the relational aspect of the everyday life situated within the specific socioeconomic and political conditions of Ciudad Juárez. I should note, however, that it should not be assumed that all young women living in these conditions necessarily have the critical perspectives that the young women presented here had. As the women themselves have noted, they had many friends outside school whose perspectives were very different from theirs. What the following chapters show are the ways in which this type of mujerista pedagogy was also cultivated in great part by their school, Preparatoria Altavista, by fostering a space where the young women's convivencia could lead them to critical reflection and thus autogestión. In other words, Altavista served as a safe space where the young women could engage not only in the cultural production of "the strong woman" and the specific form of empowerment that was meaningful to them but also in actively self-authoring their own identities as Juárez women. The resulting identities were inevitably political and were connected to their own histories, as well as the struggles they witnessed in their families and larger community and unpacked in school.

Consequently, when the young women confronted painful experiences, these did not remain in the individual and in the intimate but rather resulted in efforts toward communal goals. As such, they often attempted to turn their knowledge production into actions for social justice, in solidarity with others. That is the reason why Diana, Marsella, Gabriela, and many other girls at Altavista did not tire of participating in activist struggles against militarization, feminicides, and other forms of social injustice, as these issues had affected their lives or those of their loved ones. It was in this political and activist aspect of their identities that their school, Preparatoria Altavista, played a crucial role, as will be demonstrated in the following chapters.

I would like to conclude with a poem that Diana wrote the year before I met her and read at a feminist convention in 2008. While this poem is an expression of the feelings of impotence at the oppression that Juárez women continue to experience, it is also an example of the solidarity and social action in which many girls at Altavista engaged—a collective form of self-empowerment.

Harta

Harta de la violencia
Harta de la impunidad
Harta de las mentiras
Harta de tener miedo a cualquier momento
Harta de no poder hace mi vida normal
Harta de recortar mi horario por temor
Harta de no poder alzar la voz y decir ¡Basta!
Harta de tener que acostumbrarme a esta vida
Harta de que me vean como consumidor
Harta de ser vistas como objeto sexual
Harta de ver a las personas con su indiferencia
Harta de ver llorar
Harta de llorar
Harta de tener esta impotencia dentro
Harta de oír lamentos
Harta de sentir que nos tienen controlados
Harta de ver tantas cifras de muerte y ver que día con día crecen
Harta de no poder soñar con un futuro
Harta de ser reprimida en pensamiento, mente y obra
Harta de ser clasificada
Harta de ser callada
Harta de ser sumisa
Harta de ser denigrada

[Tired]

[Tired of violence
Tired of impunity
Tired of lies
Tired of being scared at every moment

Tired of not being able to live my normal life
Tired of shortening my schedule because of fear
Tired of not being able to lift my voice and say Stop!
Tired of having to get used to this life
Tired of being seen as a consumer
Tired of being seen as a sexual object
Tired of seeing people's indifference
Tired of seeing people crying
Tired of crying
Tired of holding this impotence inside
Tired of hearing laments
Tired of feeling controlled
Tired of seeing so many numbers of deaths that grow every day
Tired of not being able to dream of a future
Tired of being repressed in thought, mind, and action
Tired of being classified
Tired of being silenced
Tired of being submissive
Tired of being denigrated]

CHAPTER 3

Enacting a Pedagogy of
Autogestión

We do not demand that you become leaders, or that you take part in the competition of a globalized world, or that you reach success. That is the popular rhetoric to convince us that we can be happy without others. We don't speak to you from a hegemonic discourse ... but rather from our ethic as educators, ... that which says that education is a means for emancipation, the achievement of freedom and happiness. We, your teachers, only want you to be educated, committed, and happy. Actually, I take my words back. Be whatever you want to be, we trust in your capacity to distinguish what is good for you and your world.

—Armida Valverde Cabral, Keynote address at Preparatoria Altavista's 2015 graduation ceremony (my translation)

HE HIGH SCHOOL YEARS are often remembered with nostalgia. Sometimes the way we feel when we look back does not accurately reflect the feelings experienced back then. But for many of the students I met at Altavista, their school had a very special meaning. Some of the girls viewed Altavista as a home, where they could find the connectedness and peace they needed, which was absent in their personal lives, and others saw it as a refuge from the repressions imposed by other social institutions. While it is natural for many kids to love their school, the fact that several of the students at Altavista had come from schools that had expelled them or rejected them or where they had a history of disciplinary or academic problems made their love for any type of schooling intriguing.

In this chapter my goal is to unpack the ways in which Altavista pursued its vision and implemented its own interpretation of critical pedagogy, which ultimately led to the promotion of the young women's autogestión. To better understand the interplay between pedagogy and autogestión, I focus on the unique aspects of Altavista that the women valued the most and that promoted the identities and agency they developed.

Before I proceed, I must confess that in coming from a feminist, social justice, and critical perspective, both as an academic and as an educator, I tend to view schools with suspicion, looking for a hidden curriculum that directly or indirectly hurts kids. But at Altavista, I was disarmed by both teachers and students, and it has been difficult to write without continuously questioning whether I am sugarcoating the story. In an effort to provide a more fair—though certainly not neutral—representation of what I have seen at Altavista, I try to include the voices of teachers and students, particularly the girls', as often as possible. This I do, however, while acknowledging that reality is in many ways experienced and interpreted differently by different people, including myself.

Altavista's implementation of critical pedagogy is neither perfect nor utopian, but it is authentic. It illustrates a deliberate effort to enact a revolutionary educational philosophy within the constraints imposed by the state and a dystopic city that clings to its capitalist dependency, as well as by the severe financial limitations of the school and the contradictions inherent in any social group. To be sure, while some classrooms were clearly counterhegemonic and are emphasized in this book, traditional, deficit-oriented, and banking (Freire 1970) approaches to curriculum and instruction were still evident and even prevalent in a few of the classrooms I observed. Therefore, I want to underscore that while critical pedagogy is nothing new, what makes Altavista's approach significant is not its novelty, originality, or faultlessness but the fact that it is unique in its context. Although critical pedagogy schools have existed in México for many years, according to the various academics, school principals, and educators I interviewed in the area, these are rare in northern urban centers, particularly in Juárez. A mixture of strict traditionalism, standardization, and neoliberal ideology guide the vision and mission of most public and private school systems in Juárez, aiming to prepare students for a global economy— which precisely drives the local economy—and often exerting strict control over students, teachers, school administrators, and the curriculum. In contrast, most Altavista teachers rejected the notion that schools should attempt to fit youth into the current conditions of society, and instead embraced the revolutionary mission to instill a desire to improve it.

Altavista's deliberate pursuit to offer students an education for the practice of freedom (Freire 1970) often endangered the very existence of the school in the midst of an educational environment highly restrained by the state, not to mention its stigma due to the communities and students it served. Yet despite all the challenges, Altavista's emancipatory ideals remained at the center of the teachers' work. Altavista had no rituals, no uniforms (though they were available if students wished to wear them), and no symbolisms imposed on students by the administration or the teachers to inculcate school patriotism. This did not mean that the school lacked a collective identity or distinct customs and rituals but rather that these were performed in untraditional ways and initiated and sustained by various people, including students and the community. What also warrants attention is that learning at Altavista took place in formal and informal settings, in the context of the classroom, at cultural activities organized collectively by teachers and students, during recess, or even outside the school. The young women often took the lead in organizing many of these activities, which revealed their creative agency.

Rather than a hierarchy, to a certain extent Altavista could be conceptualized as a *heterarchical* organization, in which power and privilege were more democratically distributed among its members, who in turn played various roles and connected to each other in different ways. This social network at Altavista was held together by a collective working-class identity produced, reproduced, and reinvented through cultural and pedagogical practices revolving around three major dimensions: (1) freedom and autonomy, (2) radical love and reciprocal caring relationships, and (3) critical discourse and activism. These core values were repeatedly articulated by both teachers and students, and it could be argued that without them, Altavista would no longer exist, for they gave the school community the impetus to fight for it during threatening times. Not only did the ways in which the three core values at Altavista were implemented shed light on the teachers' interpretation of critical pedagogy, but as the young women interacted with these interrelated dimensions, they began to enact their own forms of autogestión.

The following sections illustrate the ways in which the three interrelated dimensions were enacted and perceived by teachers and students, especially the women. While I will discuss each one of these aspects separately, it should be understood that none of these by themselves promoted the type of learning that Altavista teachers envisioned or the autogestión that the women embodied. Rather, all three dimensions were interrelated and dependent on each other.

I should also note that when I refer to teachers as a group, I am not implying that all educators at Altavista shared the same teaching philosophy or practices, or that I had the opportunity to observe or converse with everyone. In fact, Principal Armida often noted that at Altavista the teachers ranged from "the most conservative to the most liberal." Nonetheless, the ideas of critical pedagogy were predominant in the school and were in many ways contagious. This was evident in that students often expressed resistance toward more traditional practices by articulating the characteristics of the three identified dimensions.

Freedom and Autonomy

At Altavista, freedom was the goal, but it was also the fundamental means of critical pedagogy. Henry A. Giroux (1988) has emphasized that both a "language of critique" and a "language of possibility" are crucial to the pursuit of social justice. In this way, while it should be recognized that schools are often instruments for the reproduction of capitalist relations and dominant ideologies, they can also be sites of counterhegemonic practices. These practices allow learners to envision possibility as part of their development of critical consciousness by raising "ambitions, desires, and real hope for those who wish to take seriously the issue of educational struggle and social justice" (Giroux 1988, 177).

Altavista students enjoyed the possibilities inside and outside the classroom to define and shape their identities, aspirations, and interests as expressed by their dress styles and activities. For women this was particularly important, as the school offered a space to move beyond the hegemonic gendered and heteronormative expectations that constituted a significant source of oppression.

To some, the freedom that students enjoyed at Altavista might provoke suspicion, but research on the relation between teachers' perceptions and forms of control supports Altavista's approach. The degree of autonomy granted to students reflects teachers' confidence in students' ability to learn, without external motivation (Woolfolk, Rosoff, and Hoy 1990). These teachers may in turn display distinctively stimulating conversational and interpersonal behaviors that result in greater motivation (Reeve, Bolt, and Cai 1999).

Altavista teachers were idealistic but far from naïve. The freedom they offered to students was based on trust, as well as on the assumption that it was not possible to humanize each other on the basis of control, repression, surveillance, coercion, and punishment. Unless students experienced autonomy, they would not acquire the ability to think and act for themselves. Teachers often expressed that they understood students were going to make mistakes and make wrong choices, and they often did right before the teachers' eyes, but this was expected as part of the learning process. To be sure, not all students benefited equally, but my data and teachers' observations suggest that the longer students had been at Altavista, the more they learned how to use their freedom responsibly and in positive ways. While some would assume that at an urban school in the deadly city of Juárez, such a tolerant climate would lead to chaos and danger, Altavista was probably one of the most peaceful spaces that most of the girls in this study experienced—even as militarization, crime, and death devastated the city.

Freedom to Be

There was no bell at Altavista, but it was 11:10 in the morning, and as usual, students exited their classrooms into the warm and sunny school courtyard for recess. The ambiance was light and cheerful as students began to join their friends in small groups. For a moment, I forgot that I was in what was considered at the time one of the most violent cities in the world. Something that captured my attention almost immediately was the diversity of dress styles. While this might be a common practice in schools in the United States (with its limitations and restrictions) and other parts of the world and even in rural México, it was in direct contrast with most urban high schools in México, which generally have strict uniform, hair, and makeup policies that mandate not only the colors, patterns, and textures of clothing but also the length of a skirt, how tight and how loose pants should be, how stockings should be fashioned, what kind of haircut men should wear, and so forth. These policies are markedly gendered and heteronormative, and emphasize traditional middle-class, white, Western aesthetics.

Among the first- and second-year students, I was able to spot the few students who chose to wear uniforms and also had a more childish appearance, as well as other groups of students. There were those whom their peers called the *"fresas"*—who attempted a middle-class style and wore clothes found in American malls displaying a popular brand—and on the other side were the *"cholitos"* in their baggy clothes and hoodies. There were also the athletes who usually socialized with their women's or men's soccer teams, often wearing simple T-shirts and jeans or sports clothes. While all these groups tended to stick to their own apparent gender, there was a group of mixed ages and genders, which was highly noticeable due to some of the students' extravagant styles and overt expressions of gay identity expression. Some students called them *"los gays."*

It was those whom the students called *"los hippies,"* however, who usually took center stage. This was a mixed group of young men and women, generally in their last two years of high school. They sat around the courtyards playing their tambourines and guitars or could be seen trying skateboarding tricks in the parking lot. Oftentimes students from various groups joined them. While only a few of them resembled the typical hippie, what these students had in common was their passion for music, a relaxed and friendly demeanor, and a variety of dress styles.

As I looked around, students' styles seemed deliberate: from Goth, emo, and Rasta to grunge, punk, and Japanese fashion; from Walt Disney and Che Guevara bags to oversize and real-feather angel wings; from simple ponytails and clean haircuts to big Afros, dreadlocks, and asymmetrically sculptured hairdos. Considering that students often co-construct their identities on the basis of physical appearance (Matute-Bianchi 1986), that students used clothing and hair as their canvas for self-expression should not be trivialized.

Indeed, a major reason why many students chose Altavista over other public schools was their ability to display their taste and style through dress. While it may appear mundane, in a high school, especially in this Juárez neighborhood, the lack of uniforms or dress code was a significant challenge to explicit and implicit heteronormative, gendered, racist, and classist norms that attempted to normalize and discipline "deviant" students into hegemonic ideas of how a respectable person should look. In fact, Mexican uniform policies are so significant in many schools that students are often punished and even expelled or turned down when refusing to comply. Although supporters of uniform policies may argue that a standard form of dress reduces discriminatory practices and bullying among students, the reality is that it also silences one of the emerging ways in which adolescents can express their identities, represses their bodies to conform to normative constructions of how decency is displayed, and discourages many youth unwilling to comply from continuing their education.

In this way, through the freedom of dress, Altavista gave students who would otherwise be completely turned off academically an opportunity to continue their formal education. For example, Arturo, a third-year student with a big Afro who had been at Altavista for only one semester and who did not appear to be academically oriented, enrolled just because of the freedom that he was able to enjoy.

> At my previous high school . . . they kicked me out once for refusing to cut my hair and for wearing skinny jeans. When I heard about this school, I thought, Oh, that's cool, I don't have to wear a uniform and I don't have to get a haircut! I can try to finish high school.

The freedom of dress was particularly important for the women, as this is an area in which their bodies are often controlled. Unlike at other schools, young women did not have to wear skirts every day, nor were these and their stockings measured to ensure they covered their legs as much as possible. Considering that young Juárez women have to constantly watch how they occupy and move through public space for safety reasons, in addition to feeling sanctioned by hegemonic, heteronormative, and often contradictory ideas of beauty and decorum, the ability to dress and wear their hair in any way they wanted was quite liberating to some of them.

For example, Gabriela, who displayed a Rasta dress and hairstyle, had attended a middle school that had been extremely repressive of her racial identity and demanded a physical appearance that followed white normative attributes.

> In middle school, I had very curly and coarse hair and I would put it up in a ponytail and it would get all puffy, so they would pull me aside and ask me to do something to my hair. So I would tell them that my hair was naturally like that, Afro, and I could not style it any other way. I couldn't wear barrettes or anything like that. So they made me cut it very short and straighten it every day with the flat iron for a whole year. My mother didn't like that. She has an Afro because my whole family is very dark; we all have African features and heritage. Her hair was her inheritance to us. "How are you going to take off my curls that I'm giving you?" she would say, and I was also very bothered by that.

In fact, Gabriela had just gotten out of detention for wearing makeup and the wrong stockings the day that Armida and another Altavista teacher showed up at her middle school for a recruitment visit. "Armida started talking about Altavista, and as soon as she said that they didn't require uniforms, I thought, OK, that's the best school."

Moreover, at Altavista, the young women had the opportunity to use this freedom of dress to experiment with, construct, and reinvent their identities. Gabriela explained to me that her current dress style had not always been the same. She had changed her hard-core punk style, characteristic of her first year at Altavista, to her current Rasta style as a reflection of her own identity transformation.

Karla and Marsella had a similar experience. When Marsella began high school, she wore more *fresa* style clothing, trying to conform to hegemonic images and ideas of middle- and upper-class superiority she had learned in middle school. As she spent more time at Altavista, and realized that she would not be judged by her clothes, she began to dress in ways that reflected her own taste and stopped pretending that she belonged to the middle class. Karla, a curvy young woman who had entered Altavista as a very shy and insecure girl due to her being overweight, had left behind the clothes that mirrored her more *fresa* girlfriends from middle school who scrutinized her looks and that simultaneously hid her body. Her new confidence was evident in her current dress style, which varied from simple T-shirts and skinny jeans to revealing velvety dresses and high heels, depending on the occasion. And Diana, one of the younger girls, often changed styles, going from punk, to *fresa*, to sporty, to indigenous styles all in the same week.

The freedom to be was not limited to dress and style; it also implied the responsibility to let others be. It was not always easy because sometimes it was students and not teachers who had problems with this. For example, one time in conversing with teachers Gilberto and Jorge, a girl came in complaining about Diana, about how she was bothered by her assertiveness and outspokenness in class. She interpreted this as Diana's desire to make others feel inferior. She then critiqued Diana for not sticking to a single style. Gilberto and Jorge explained that while they understood how she felt, Diana had the right to wear any clothes she wished, and that it was absurd to judge her based on that. Moreover, Gilberto said, "Although you may not like her, it's not hard to recognize that when Diana speaks, she knows what she's talking about. You should try to get to know her better. You may just find out that she can be a great friend."

On another occasion, a group of girls in their first year at Altavista had gone to Armida, the principal, to request that a uniform policy be put in place and enforced.

"Yes, most definitely, you can wear your uniforms if you want. They are not forbidden," Armida had responded.

"But we want everyone to wear them."

"Oh, then you're not asking for uniforms, you are asking to control others; is that what you want?"

The girls left her office still puzzled by this question.

As students spent more time in school, they would slowly begin to understand and adapt to this new paradigm, that freedom had to be shared. For example, Alejandra, a second-year student who prided herself on her healthy habits, was an athlete, and detested smoking, once told me:

This school is so cool! It's totally different from others because here you can express yourself; you have all the rights to do what you want. Of course, as long as it's right, you know? You are free to create a workshop, to jump up and down, to smoke, to do many things that at other schools are forbidden.

When I asked her if she didn't mind that others smoked outside during recess, she responded that it was their choice, and she respected it.

Students who were lesbian, gay, bisexual, transgender, or questioning/queer (LGBTQ) also found a space of relative safety to express their gender identity. But this did not happen overnight and it was still an area with which some struggled. During one of our conversations, Armida recalled that in 2007 the students organized a school queen and king election. A queer male student had run and was elected school queen.[1] This caused a controversy that opened the door to discussions about freedom and the meaning of diversity.

I don't know if they elected this student because they were just joking around. But he won, and he was serious about it. A group of students then came to me in absolute indignation. "What now? Is he going to wear a dress at the crowning ball? That's crazy!" the kids would say. Some of the parents were also outraged. So I thought, OK, we have to talk about this and we had a meeting with everyone who wanted to come. It was an opportunity to talk about diversity. Yes, we say we like diversity and multiculturalism, but is it really true? What do we mean by diversity? To make the long story short, the boy was crowned as queen at the ball, and he did not wear a dress, but he did bring his boyfriend to the ball and he declared himself the queen of Altavista.

Jorge, the assistant principal, considered that while they had made progress, they still had a battle to fight because LGBTQ students did not yet receive the respect they deserved from all the kids, especially from heterosexual male students. It had also been difficult for some teachers to change their conservative perspectives. For example, Fito, the soccer coach, regretted that the previous year the girls' team had not done well mainly because they experienced serious internal conflicts that he admitted to have propagated.

> It was mostly my fault because there were two lesbian girls on the team and I didn't know how to handle it. I forbade them from holding hands or kissing in school and this created a lot of problems and divided the group. . . . Armida asked me if I had discriminated against the girls, and indeed I had. I should have tried to understand them and accept them.

The freedom that Altavista sought was then also about eliminating taboos, negative labels, and censorship directly related to gender issues experienced by women. For many years, the Mexican state, whose generally conservative and patriarchal ideology tended to dominate schools, had limited opportunities for young women who became pregnant. While allowing pregnant girls to attend regular high schools was a recent national policy, at Altavista pregnant girls had never been denied enrollment. So while pregnant girls continued to be stigmatized at other schools as a consequence of the traditional views inherited from past policies, at Altavista pregnancy and motherhood were not reasons for shame. This attitude was important even for those who did not get pregnant. To Marsella, one of the girls in her senior year, it represented a refreshing message that disrupted society's hypocrisy.

> I used to talk with my friends from El Parque High School, and they would tell me that if a girl gets pregnant there, she would get kicked out. Also at the CONALEP [National School of Professional Technical Education], a friend got pregnant and got kicked out. . . . But I love how here, pregnant girls come, and then all of a

sudden they bring their babies. And there we are, all the girls carrying the baby and stuff. So I don't know. They might say that in this school there's more *desmadre* [disorder] because "how can they allow pregnant girls?" But girls in every school get pregnant. It's just that here you see it because they give them the opportunity to study, and in other places they don't.

By admitting and refusing to stigmatize pregnant girls, Altavista gave students an important message. On the one hand, it spoke against the sexist constructions of female adolescence as a childish and innocent stage that must be protected and controlled, as well as against social constructions of who has the right to become a respectable mother. On the other hand, it showed that a child did not have to represent the end of a young woman's dreams or her ability to continue her education.

Freedom to Own One's Learning

Early in the fall semester, at 11:30 a.m., when recess was over, students were neither ushered to class nor policed about their whereabouts, but soon the crowd dissipated as they went into their classrooms. Contrary to many schools in México, which remain locked to prevent students from sneaking out, Altavista's school gates remained open the whole day, allowing students to come and go as they pleased. Students were allowed to move through almost any space they wanted. Aside from the one-on-one conversations with students to address individual problems and from the natural consequences of students' behaviors, severe disciplinary actions like expulsions or even detention were almost nonexistent. Armida explained that teachers had their own ways of handling things, but there were only two school rules: No arms and no drugs. "Some of us don't take attendance," Armida explained. The strong relationships that teachers had developed with students, rather than attendance rosters, helped them notice truancy problems. "If they are not coming to class then that tells me that my lessons are not relevant to them. So I should question what we're doing in the classroom instead."

At first, I was unsure about the benefits of this lack of pressure on students on the part of the teachers to attend class or perform academically. I feared that many students would abuse this relaxed attitude and would end up failing their classes. I also worried that the women, because of their more reserved behavior, would end up ignored and invisible to teachers, and due to the many pressures from outside of school would be easily discouraged from continuing their education. But I soon realized that these fears were based on my own perception of high school students as kids, and that by infantilizing them I assumed that they were in need of continuous guidance, extrinsic motivations, and forms of control. Further, I learned that although individual differences were clear, generally speaking, students also followed a somewhat predictable developmental process in their learning to be autonomous.

In the fall, first-year students would regularly attend their classes. It could be argued that they were still following self-regulation habits based on their previous schooling experiences, which made them expect punishment or some kind of external consequence for missing class. In the spring, after students realized that nobody would force them to go to class, many of them became more relaxed and truant. Although many teachers did not take attendance, students who missed too many classes were not ready to take the exams or submit quality work. This caused several of them to fail their classes, which required them to attend special courses at the end of the semester, either winter or summer, and to take an "extraordinary exam." This was extra work for the teachers, who would not get additional compensation. In the worst-case scenario, when students were unable to catch up and pass the test, they had to retake the course. This was indeed an expensive lesson, since they would have to repeat the entire semester.

However, the majority of those in their second and third years were aware of the risks of misusing this freedom. The young women in particular appreciated this autonomy, which had resulted in greater motivation and learning. Diana shared her perspective.

> There are many who don't know how to manage the freedom that they're granted. They think that because the men wear long hair, because we wear any clothes we want, or because we're not forced to go to class, that they know how to manage their freedom. But I like this education system a lot because if you want to, it's all on you, you are the one who is going to fail, not me, not the teacher. I think that's what helped me because in middle school, my average grade was roughly 74. And now, my average grade is 94. That's how much I like school now, yes, wow, I love it!

Although Diana was a very sharp young woman, she had continuously felt defensive in her previous schools, where she would get in trouble when she did not agree with a particular school policy. The opportunity to be autonomous at Altavista made her feel respected. As usual, there were a few who complained that they would like to receive more pressure from teachers. Among these exceptions were mostly boys, for example Arturo, who was in his first year at Altavista and relied on his girlfriends to get help with homework or even to figure out what class was next. "I'm lazy, so I need someone to nag me, I guess," he would say. But for most, and especially for the women, this autonomy was refreshing and empowering. As Gabriela put it:

We learn a lot, even if the teachers aren't constantly after us. Because if someone wants to be pushed and nagged, then there's plenty of other schools where they can go for that. There is no bell, so if you want to go to your class you look at the time and you go. Why wait for a bell to ring? I think that's just mechanized behavior.

Gabriela appreciated the opportunity to be liberated from bodily controls that came in the form of uniforms and bells. This was not insignificant considering the high degree of restraint and containment the young women experienced due to the discourse and realities of prevalent violence against young Juárez women, not to mention the increase of dangers that put the city in extreme distress. Thus the young women viewed the freedom that Altavista offered as a precious and unusual opportunity to take control of their own actions and their own learning, to explore possibilities about who they could be and what they were capable of in a safe space.

Among the favorite teachers were those who encouraged participation. Students, and the women in particular, expressed that what was appealing to them was the feeling of freedom to pursue their own interests in the learning process. They had the opportunity to select deadlines, assignments, and topics. They also enjoyed expressing themselves through artistic projects that students initiated on their own, like painting a mural in the back of the school or organizing a musical event. Others went beyond expression. For example, to Gabriela, this autonomy had more of a "social and cultural significance" that allowed her to project her social interests onto her school assignments and mobilize others for social action, "For example, if I want right now, I can create a forum right here, or a workshop."

And nobody is going to give me that opportunity to do it at another school."

Diego, a twelfth grade male student, had experienced this sense of autonomy firsthand. He had started high school at El Parque, a school with a high academic reputation in the city, but had transferred to Altavista after only a year. During a student meeting for an ecological committee that Diana organized, Diego summarized the meaning of freedom and autonomy at Altavista as he told the rest of his peers:

> This is a special school. I came from Preparatoria El Parque, but there, one can really feel the oppression. They don't let you express yourself and that's why I came here. Maybe those who come here directly from middle school don't feel it like that. They see it like any other school, but it isn't like that. I love the freedom and the quality of people is much better here. I know I can leave my things anywhere and nobody is going to take them. And we can propose projects and our school will support us. At El Parque they just tell us to go to hell.

After Diego spoke, several other students expressed their agreement with his statements, revealing how meaningful this freedom was for all students, and the significance it had not only in providing opportunities to create and speak but also in humanizing each other and fostering a sense of respect and community.

For the women, the ability to speak in class and share from their own lived experience had a special significance. In contrast to many of their homes and public spaces in the city, young women at Altavista were able to express their opinions and voice their knowledge, concerns, and desires much more freely. And in contrast to many schools where student discourse is extremely suppressed and controlled, the young women highly valued the type of critical thinking promoted at Altavista that elicited participation and action, and that gave them autonomy to make decisions about their own learning. Like Gabriela often said, "In these classes you can give your opinion and think. Not like in other high schools, where you just learn what and how the book says it." As will be evident in later sections, classroom discourse was heavily informed by personal experience, coming from both teachers and students. This validated women's experience and worldview as legitimate knowledge, and with this, they felt more empowered to take charge of their learning.

Freedom to Teach: Teachers as Intellectuals

Freedom at Altavista was not limited to students. Teachers also enjoyed a very high degree of autonomy. While the experiences of teachers at Altavista might appear at first sight as irrelevant to the school's impact on the young women, I found the role of teachers to be quite significant, as it gave the young women access to alternative ways of learning and seeing themselves. Teachers were the heart of Altavista, and they were among the most influential people in the young women's lives.

By experiencing a higher degree of freedom, teachers were humanized and in turn contributed to the humanization of their students as well. When it came to the faculty, there was no bureaucracy in place for teacher evaluation, nor constant supervision and monitoring of lesson plans. Instead, teachers met regularly during the year and spent a great deal of time in dialogue, self-reflection, and self-critique, their main forms of accountability. Some avoided it, but they still had the freedom to do that. In spite of the increased control of the state, teacher autonomy was one of the most protected rights. They preferred their limited budget over increased state funding or capitalist sponsorship that would cause them to follow somebody else's rules.

Juan, the instructional specialist, indicated that it was very important to keep their identities as teachers clear. "We're not saviors, and we're not nannies. We're teachers, and our craft and role should be respected as that." Autonomy, then, was essential to validate their role as teachers. This was evident in simple practices that revealed respect and trust in the teachers as professionals. Jorge, the assistant principal, explained:

I don't police the teachers to see who's present and who's absent. But we don't need bureaucratic approaches to prevent those problems because teachers are rarely ever absent. If they have to be out, it's always because they have a family emergency or they are truly very sick. Teachers see their colleagues and students as their friends and family, and they don't want to be abusive of them. They're here because they care.

The teachers' passion about their subject and craft made significant impact on the students and was one of the main reasons why students did not need external forms of control to keep them motivated to learn. Karla's green eyes sparkled as she explained why she loved her teachers: "You might say, today I don't feel like learning. But then the teacher says, 'Oh, but today we are learning about this or that topic,' and wow! It's so interesting! They transmit that energy to keep on going, to be learning about everything." Karla was already in her last year but dreaded the thought of ever leaving Altavista.

Considering Altavista's precarious financial situation, it was clear that money was not what motivated most teachers, old or young. Virtually all the teachers had additional jobs, and many of them had advanced degrees in other areas. What these educators had in common was not just a need for a job or a desire to teach but almost a philosophy of life. Students valued this and they spoke of their teachers with a mix of admiration, gratitude, and love. Diana described them as intelligent and wise: "I love the teachers here. Yes, they are so intelligent, so intelligent! My favorite class is history, with Rigoberto, a teacher who looks very serious. But I love it because that teacher knows so much! His wisdom is up to his elbows!"

It was not surprising that the teachers were regarded as extremely intelligent, for all of them were highly educated. Among the faculty, there were medical doctors, economists, sociologists, engineers, and lawyers. Juan had a PhD in the social sciences and was a professor at the Autonomous University of Ciudad Juárez (UACJ), and both Armida and Rigoberto were working on their doctoral dissertations. Several other teachers had master's degrees and were also lecturers at UACJ.

That educators found happiness at Altavista was important for the students. It communicated to them that they were not a burden but rather were an important part of teachers' lives, and that school could be a space of fulfillment and freedom for both teachers and students. For Juárez youth from the barrio, and especially for girls, who have often been regarded as worthless and disposable, this passion and dedication carried great significance. As Gabriela explained:

There are teachers here who teach classes at the university, and I know that that is a higher level. But in some way they also enjoy their freedom here. They come and feel happy, and I know that in many ways they prefer to be at Altavista. I know that it is also important for them to teach here.

In sum, freedom was undeniably the hallmark of Altavista. It represented the skeleton that kept the school standing and distinguished it from other schools. It gave teachers the ability to keep their idealism and their passion alive. While teaching at Altavista implied many sacrifices, and teachers' economic conditions did not improve dramatically, they had the opportunity to be happy. Students, on the other hand, explored new possibilities, and as they did, they took their freedom to various levels. Some were bothered by it, feeling that more control was in order. Others misused and suffered the consequences. But most were able to take advantage of it to express their identities, discover and share their talents, define and pursue their learning in their own ways, and, as will be discussed in the next sections, question and critique, or mobilize, create, and engage in transformative social action.

Radical Love and Reciprocal Caring Relationships

During recess and after school, the big trees in the courtyard offered a refreshing shade, and various teachers stood underneath them or sat on the benches taking their break. Some students passing by joked around with them and some of the girls stopped to greet them with a kiss on the cheek. Pretty soon, there were small groups of students gathered around teachers here and there. Teachers and students conversed together, joked, played the guitar, or took a cigarette break.

I could not help to compare this image to my experience as a teacher in the United States. Typically, teachers went through their days rushing and stressing out about the next assignment, the next meeting, the standardized tests, and paperwork that had to be completed. Unless one made substantial effort, there was never such a thing as just "hanging out," and much less with students.

Though open and laid back, interactions between students and teachers at Altavista were quite opposite to the common relations in American schools (Rippberger and Staudt 2003). But at least in Altavista's case, this type of relationships was more than a cultural pattern or an accident. It was a reflection of the deliberate democratic philosophy of schooling held by many of the teachers and consequently the students. What stood out to me as well was that although not all teachers engaged in this type of interaction, those who did continued the same pattern inside the classroom. There was no such thing as leaving emotion or expressions of caring at the door. Instead, it was evident that this human aspect was part of the pedagogy inside and outside the classroom. While at first sight these expressions and interactions could be reduced to mere cultural forms, I posit that on closer examination, they are surface-level evidence of *radical love*—that is, of a deeper political project enacted by teachers and reciprocated by students aiming to alter the context of oppression that often frames schooling as well as the lives of both teachers and students from the barrio. Antonia Darder explains that this is

> a political and radicalized form of love that is never about absolute consensus, or unconditional acceptance, or unceasing words of sweetness, or endless streams of kisses. Instead, it is a love [that is] unconstricted, rooted in a committed willingness to struggle persistently with purpose in our life and to intimately connect that purpose with what Freire called our "true vocation"—to be human. (2003, 497–98)

Radical love is the second pillar in the critical pedagogy enacted by Altavista's teachers and students, manifested through mutual humanization, the transgression of borders of power relations and gendered expectations, and a commitment to a collective struggle for justice. To bell hooks (1994a), the political dimension of this love is "without an ethic of love shaping the direction of our political vision and our radical aspiration, we are often seduced, in one way or another, into continued allegiance to systems of domination" (243). The following sections offer some examples and analysis of such a type of love that was key in the building of collective agency and solidarity.

Altering Power Relations

At Altavista the relationships formed outside of class laid the foundation for what was learned in the classroom. Freire's critical pedagogy is based to a great extent on the notion of love and commitment to other people and to their liberation, which is fundamental in developing democratic dialogue with students. Freire's (1997) view of the teacher as a cultural worker implies that the teacher not only speaks to the learners but also speaks with them, listens to them, and is heard by them. While apparently simple, the radical love enacted at Altavista was characterized by mutual demonstrations of authentic caring between teachers and students. Angela Valenzuela (1999) argues that there are at least two different kinds of caring that may characterize teacher-student relations. On the one hand, *aesthetic caring* involves the behaviors that teachers expect students to exhibit to demonstrate that they "care about" school, even before they feel cared for. This kind of caring focuses on whether students follow rules, schedules, and academic objectives as well as on student demeanor and appearance. Valenzuela posits that aesthetic caring positions students as passive objects expected to receive instruction and learn the dominant curriculum through detached, formal, and bureaucratic approaches. In contrast, Valenzuela defines *authentic caring* as the relations formed with students that are culturally bound and constitute the foundation of pedagogy. As such, authentically caring teachers are sincerely invested in their students and in their interests and concerns.

Altavista's administrators as well as the core group of critical teachers understood the crucial role of schools as socializing agents, which instill specific values and norms. They considered that most institutions in which the youth participate instill values that emphasize authoritarian behavior, subordination, conformity, and obedience. As stated by Stanley Aronowitz (1992):

> The child learns that the teacher is the authoritative person in the classroom, but that she is subordinate to a principal. Thus the structure of society can be learned through understanding the hierarchy of power within the structure of the school. Similarly, the working-class child learns its role in society. (75)

In part, Altavista teachers' efforts to disrupt this cycle of institutional arrangements involved reshaping the power structure with a new set of values. Teachers attempted—albeit with varying degrees of success—to reduce traditional hierarchies and develop authentically caring, collaborative, and horizontal relationships of power with students and colleagues. It was not that authority did not exist in these heterarchical relationships but rather it was determined by knowledge, purpose, and authentic demonstrations of caring. In this way, knowledge and caring, rather than just technical or instrumental concerns, constituted a foundational value that guided the very structures and culture of the school.

After having the opportunity to observe the interactions between teachers and students at Altavista, it was not surprising to me that almost every girl I spoke with saw the relationships with their teachers as one of the most significant attributes of their school. Teachers at Altavista strived to eliminate that "me versus you" type of teacher-student relationships that students had been exposed to for many years. They sought to earn student respect on the basis of knowledge and authentic caring. The teachers' knowledge would not be as important to the students if it were not for the teachers' eagerness to share it with them. In fact, much of the learning took place outside the classroom while teachers conversed with students, shared stories, and answered questions. Students repeatedly emphasized how much they valued these interactions, which to Diana expressed a balance in power relationships "They aren't stuck up, like 'I'm your teacher only, so you can't talk to me, you have no right to talk with me about anything.'"

Karla considered it an honor to be able to have a closer relationship with her teachers.

> Armida is so intelligent; she's a great principal and she's so good at so many things. But what I love the most is that she is so open and sincere and is always willing to talk to you. And so are Rigoberto, Jorge, and Paula [the counselor]. Their intelligence is so great that I can't believe I can have a teacher like that, that they aren't just like teachers, that you can know them beyond that. And they let you get to know them. You can talk with them about anything you want.

This *authentic* form of caring stresses reciprocal relationships between students and teachers in which both parties are seen as subjects (Valenzuela 1999) and is reinforced by the freedom and affirmation of identities that the general school climate fostered. Rather than judging students as "not caring about" education, teachers *cared for them* by trying to understand the root underneath youth's expressions of academic disengagement. In addition, as evident in Karla's description of her teachers, they also *cared for* their students by demonstrating unconditional acceptance (Valenzuela 1999).

Contrary to the social separation between teachers and students that is typically found in many schools, teacher-student relationships outside the classroom were the foundation of Altavista's pedagogy. This reciprocal receptivity revealed teachers' and students' "fighting for the restoration of [our] humanity ... [through] the restoration of true generosity" (Freire 1970, 45). Many students were attracted to their teachers' real-life knowledge and often approached them outside the classroom. In some cases, these interactions served as important teaching moments that were more effective and fruitful than actual classroom instruction, as illustrated by Diana's learning process.

> This is what gave birth to my interest in Cuba. It was when I took the language arts class with *profe* Juan. He didn't take roll or force us to come to class, but I used to talk with him after class all the time. He would share stories about his travels and he told me about Cuba. I kept on asking him more and more. He even brought a guest speaker from Cuba who shared about the education system there. . . . It sparked my interest so much that I started my own research and now you can find all these essays, summaries, and syntheses that I have written about Cuba. I don't do this type of research on just anything, only on what really sparks my interest.

Branches of the Same Tree

Armida attributed teachers' ability to interact so closely with students to the fact that they shared a common background. The teachers also had a working-class background, which helped them identify with the students' experiences. Moreover, they made it a point to remain rooted in the community. Armida explained:

> What makes our work easier is the identity that we share with the students. We come from the same place, we have the same cultural codes, we understand each other. Our socialization is very similar. Many of us teachers got here very young. I've been working here for twenty-three years, and the majority have been here for twenty, fifteen years. We know the area very well. So we go out into the colonias to hand out flyers, to visit with the kids, and to just roam around. *Andamos de vagos* [we cruise around], we buy some beers and sodas, we hide them and we go to the colonia to hang out for a little while, just to be in touch with what is going on out there. For example, we noticed that from one year to the next, most of the small businesses in Anapra, like the tortilla factories and pharmacies, don't open their doors anymore. They have metal

bars. We see what's going on in the city, live and in full color. We talk with the people, and they say, "I was assaulted, I was robbed, that guy too."

Armida revealed that the relationships that teachers formed with the students had a foundation that was formed even before the kids entered the classroom. It is this personal history and firsthand knowledge of the community that helped them connect in natural ways. In Freire's words (1997):

> Our relationship with the learners demands that we respect them and demands equally that we be aware of the concrete conditions of their world, the conditions that shape them. . . . Without this, we have no access to the way they think, so only with great difficulty can we perceive what and how they know. (58)

The social background that teachers shared with their students not only gave them a deeper knowledge about each one of their students but also increased their sense of responsibility. They understood that parents had to make sacrifices to send their children to school, so Armida noted that those teachers whose salaries were mostly funded by students' tuition tended to be the most responsive and committed to the students' learning and liberation. On the other hand, teachers who were there only a few hours a week and whose salaries were paid by the state were much less involved in the students' lives and were the ones who occasionally displayed opposition to the vision of the school.

Armida also indicated that teachers knew almost every student in the school by name, and each teacher had students that he or she mentored. Rather than formal assignments of mentors and mentees, these relationships emerged organically. Students often came to teachers for *consejos* or advice about dilemmas they encountered in their personal lives. In some occasions, these interactions served to break taboos or disrupt hegemonic and oppressive discourses.

For example, students approached Chuy—one of the youngest teachers—for more than academics. It was not unusual for both female and male students to come to him with questions about their sexuality, such as a boy asking for advice on safe sex, a girl who came to borrow money to buy a morning-after pill, and beyond.

I remember a student who came to me because he was in doubt about his sexual orientation. We talked about it for a while and I told him that whatever he found it to be, what mattered the most was to stay true to himself. Ultimately, the decision to come out of the closet was his, and many people would reject him and mistreat him. It wouldn't be easy, but that was something that nobody else could impose on him.

Chuy thought that perhaps students came to him with these questions because he was the health teacher, but there was another health teacher and students rarely went to her. According to some teacher and student accounts, she was much more authoritarian and rigid, while Chuy tended to build relationships with students and was much more willing to openly discuss the topics that mattered to his students in everyday life rather than limiting their relations to academic discourse. "Students at this age are always concerned about sex. We all know that, so if they want and need the information, it is my responsibility to give it to them, not to judge them and keep it as a secret."

The disruption of taboos was also important in destabilizing traditional gender roles. Marsella, who was in her last year at Altavista, also went to her female teachers for advice on romantic relationships.

They talk to you like they are your friends. For example, I have been talking to some *maestras* about how to approach the guy that I like. They have told me about their experiences when they were my age, and they give me advice. So right now I'm writing a list of pros and cons about declaring my crush to this guy.

While the question appeared simple, considering that in Mexican culture women are not generally expected to initiate romantic relationships, this interaction assumed a mutual unconventional understanding of gender roles on the part of both the teachers and the student. Moreover, Marsella's application of analytical thinking to a personal issue was quite remarkable. Clearly, at times teachers took the role of advisors and at other times they were more like friends.

Iliana, who had transferred to Altavista from a very traditional and repressive high school, also noted the way in which the closeness that students enjoyed with their teachers disrupted traditional teacher-student power relations.

> I really like that this is not a hierarchical school. There aren't too many norms, we don't wear uniforms, there aren't detention slips, or punishments. There is a lot of freedom. I like the atmosphere, the students, the teachers. I don't know, I feel that there is a very close relationship between teachers and students, more like friends. I like everything here.

The antihierarchical stance was also reflected in the language both teachers and students utilized with each other. Students referred to and called their teachers by their first name or simply by *"profe,"* an informal abbreviation of professor or teacher. Some students even used the informal singular second-person pronoun *"tú,"* which conveys closeness and informality, instead of the formal *"usted"* when talking to some of their teachers, particularly the younger ones. Occasionally I observed some girls addressing some of their male teachers with nicknames, ranging from *abuelo* (grandfather) to *panzón* (potbellied). Though sarcastic, they were not utilized in an offensive or hurtful way and teachers seemed to take them as part of the natural playful language utilized in their interactions.

While the power relations were altered in some ways by the caring relationships, it would be naïve to think that teachers' power over students was eliminated. Teachers were still in charge of the students' grades and many other curricular decisions. George W. Noblit (1993) points out the importance of assessing the role of power in an ethic of caring. This requires differentiating between power used for the sake of domination and that used for the benefit and moral service of others. What is important to note, then, is how power is being used, and whether it truly benefits both parties.

Students continued to view their teachers as having some degree of authority over them, but this authority was framed by a profound sense of respect stemming from the admiration students felt for their teachers as well as their sense that their teachers truly cared for them as human beings. Some of the young women then viewed this authority as that of a parent. Marsella, for example, referred to Rigoberto as *"mi Papá"* (my Dad) because he gave her a scholarship and took the time to talk with her. Having lost her father at a young age, Marsella evidently felt that Rigoberto filled this void in some way. Mónica, who was an orphan, also expressed a similar feeling. "Gabriela and I were talking about how cool it would be to build a house here in the back of the school. Armida could be like our mother and Jorge like our father," she said.

Teachers also utilized their authority in minimal but deliberate ways to help students get back on track. Some of the girls expressed their appreciation of teachers who once in a while would get their attention when they were skipping too many classes or were getting, in Karla's words, "too crazy." "I like it when Paula gets on my case because she does it with love, like if she were my mother," Karla confessed.

Cristina, who often struggled with truancy, also felt cared for when teachers watched over her.

> For example, the history teacher [Rigoberto], when I missed one of his classes, he would have this grim expression on his face. But I knew he did it in a good way. Here, it is up to you to go to class or not. But, for example, when the teachers see that I'm getting too loose, they call me out. All the teachers here know me, they all know who Cristina is. Jorge, for example, one time called my mother and told her I was a good student, but I was really getting out of line, skipping classes and what not. So the three of us sat down to solve that problem, and that was it. And with the history teacher, all I need is one of those grim looks.

While many teachers rejected traditional punishments and tried to give students many opportunities to learn, sometimes they found it was necessary to intervene. As Chuy's example illustrates, this was also guided by authentic caring.

> Last year there were two girls who started messing around too much. You would see them hanging out with their boyfriends, and skipping most of their classes. Armida was worried, so she asked me to talk to them since I had a good relationship with them. So one day I took them aside and had a conversation. "So what do your parents do for a living?" "Oh, my dad is a carpenter" or "My mom works at the *maquila* [maquiladora]." So I asked them, "Do you think your parents would be happy to see that you're wasting their hard work by just hanging around and failing your classes?"

"You are right," they told me, please forgive us. "Oh, don't ask me to forgive you. You've done nothing to me. Rather, forgive yourselves and apologize to your parents because the consequences are on you and your family, not on me." The girls started crying. "I'm sorry," they said, "we are going to change." I wasn't mean to them, but I wanted them to reflect on their behavior. And it actually helped.

In this way, teachers used these relationships as a resource to teach students important lessons and foster reflection. The fact that these forms of disciplinary action took place in a context of freedom gave them more validity. Because these were an exception to the rule, rather than the regular type of interactions, students often interpreted them as authentic demonstrations of caring.

Disrupting the Patriarchal Economy of Emotion

Beyond the friendly and antihierarchical interactions, advice, and sporadic admonitions that teachers offered, the dynamics between teachers and students led to much more profound relationships of caring that compelled and freed students to reciprocate. In other words, students felt responsible to respond to these relationships as they began to view their teachers as human beings and as being with and not against them. Authentic caring in this sense was not reduced to one single form of affect but to a set of actions, behaviors, and the expression of multiple emotions. For the young women (as I assumed would be the case for the young men), this was liberating, in that they were able to be themselves as their values and ways of being were affirmed. In other words, it was not expected of them to exclude affect, emotional expression, and investment in personal concerns from the learning experience. Thus they were able to build fruitful caring relationships with many teachers—even those who were not as charismatic or friendly—with whom they took the initiative.

For example, there were teachers like Jorge, Armida, and Gilberto, who seemed naturally extrovert and were very popular among all students. Rigoberto, the history teacher, on the other hand, had a more stoic demeanor and invited a different kind of relationship. During my first month of fieldwork I heard a couple of boys in their first year complain about Rigoberto. They thought he was too strict and that his classes were boring. But when I interviewed the girls, I was puzzled by the fact that most of them appeared to love him dearly. Karla explained to me why there were so many misconceptions about him, especially among the young men.

> We cover a lot of theory in his class, but he explains it very well. There are some who, because of laziness, don't like it. They think he's too stern. And I understand because I used to say the same thing my first year here. Because as soon as I walked into the classroom, I was like, damn! I'm scared! So I talked with Armida and she encouraged me to try to get to know him, to open myself up to him. "Get to know him as a person and as a teacher, and you will see that he's wonderful," she said, and she was so right. I adore him now! He's wonderful because, yes there is a lot of theory, but he teaches it well, and you can tell that he loves being a teacher. He is never late, he doesn't miss classes, and he does what he says.

Although Karla's narrative seems to focus on Rigoberto's attributes as instructor, her perspective appears to be heavily influenced by her willingness to initiate the relationship. She did not settle for an arrangement of disconnection and decided to follow Armida's advice. Her investment allowed her to appreciate Rigoberto's efforts and his more quiet demonstrations of caring, such as dedication to his classes. She saw in his dedication what Freire (1997) considers to be an embodiment of the necessary quality of lovingness. Karla again emphasized Rigoberto's qualities as a good teacher when she compared him to Toño, the world history teacher.

> Toño is a good person and he also explains his lessons well. But he is absent a lot and when he gets back he might want to move ahead really fast, but it's hard when he's been out so much. Rigoberto, on the other hand, is always on time, he never misses class, and not only does he explain the concepts well, he also teaches you to analyze every point, and wow!

Similarly, the young women's ability to humanize their learning experience contributed to their own development of academic identities. Take for example Marsella's perspective about her self-perception as a "good student."

> I consider myself a good student. I do my homework and complete my projects. But it's not just about that. Like I tell you, I interact

with the teachers, I talk with them. Not just about school subjects but about what I'm concerned about. What good does it do to say, *profe,* here is my homework; I did what I had to do and I got a 100, but there was no relationship, everything was cold.

Unlike at many other schools, this notion of the "good student" is not based on competition to get to the top in the academic achievement hierarchy. Instead, it could be argued that students learned from their teachers' modeling of not only responsibility but also the importance of building caring relationships. In this way, to Marsella and others, the notion of the "good student" was related to the broader and culturally situated concept of *educación,* which, according to Valenzuela (1999), "is a conceptually broader term than its English language cognate. It refers to the family's role of inculcating in children a sense of moral, social, and personal responsibility and serves as the foundation for all other learning. Though inclusive of formal academic training, educación additionally refers to competence in the social world, wherein one respects the dignity and individuality of others" (23). In this way, for Marsella and other girls, developing an academic identity was also related to their ability to form humanizing relationships with their teachers.

On another note, I should emphasize that it should not be assumed that the young women at Altavista had a more natural tendency—even if culturally induced—to reciprocate or be caring toward their teachers merely for being women. I simply do not have data to analyze the type of caring relationships that developed between male teachers and male students aside from the narratives that teachers shared about their closeness with some of the young men and my observations of male teacher-student interactions. My point here is that the learning process was broadened for the young women I got to know—as it probably did for other students of any gender—by naturalizing the value of deep connections with their teachers. In a context where fragmentation, policing of youth, and distrust pervaded social relations, this human connection offered a new experience that other schools with traditional separations between teachers and students were not able to provide.

Take for example Diana, a girl to whom the premise of caring as a stereotypically natural characteristic of women did not apply (Belenky et al. 1986). Diana confessed that she had changed significantly since she started attending Altavista. Her strong temperament, perfectionism, and impatience had caused her many problems in middle school with her peers and had made her develop a constant defiant behavior against all her teachers, who often exasperated her with what she considered absurd demands. Both the lack of connection with teachers and the stigma carried by young women who expressed anger had made her middle school experience a negative one, promoting an aberration against schooling.

> Being here has helped me relate much better to my teachers because I used to have a different concept of them. I never thought of them as people who existed outside the classroom, never tried to build relationships with them. So with the exception of history teachers, with whom I've always [gotten along], I used to complain about every one of them. But here, that changed. I don't know if you've seen me, but I laugh a lot with them, with Rigoberto, Gilberto, Jorge. I play around with them a lot. I see them as humans now, like they too can laugh and joke around.

Diana reveals that as simple as a joke can be, it speaks to the interest in getting to know and relate to each other as people. Love and caring thus become a mutual process of humanization in which both students and teachers of any gender can participate and benefit.

Moreover, the undoing of gendered emotions that students were allowed to express, such as countering the idea that it is appropriate for women to express love, peace, and happiness but not anger, impotence, or desire, was also part of the type of radical love that existed at Altavista and that young women demanded. For example, Diana, after having suffered the violent rape during the winter break, went to Jorge, one of her favorite teachers, to confide this experience, expecting some kind of consolation and sympathy. In turn, he responded with absolute silence, which deeply disappointed and hurt Diana. While she understood that perhaps he was in shock, she was very upset about his response. Therefore, a few weeks later, she confronted him, expressing her anger at his lack of support.

While clearly Jorge was an imperfect human being who failed at giving Diana the support she needed during an extremely vulnerable time, the relationship that they had developed allowed Diana to speak up, confront him, express anger, and demand an answer. Diana never explained fully how this conversation happened, but in the end, they were able to talk it out and their relationship remained as strong as before. This demonstrates that the radical love built at Altavista did not necessarily mean that nurturing was its only characteristic but that there was trust that students could express a range of feelings and emotions, even when teachers failed them.

The same was true for some of the teachers. According to hooks (1994b), *engaged pedagogy* is a reciprocal process in that not only students are empowered or are asked to share or confess. Teachers can also be empowered and grow as they are willing to take risks and be vulnerable in sharing their own narratives. Although the relaxed attitude of many teachers to simply engage socially with students by conversing, playing songs on the guitar, or taking a cigarette break with them gave students the message that they did not take themselves too seriously—that they were all at the same level, humanly speaking— nothing made more of a statement to students than teachers' willingness to be vulnerable with them. As will be illustrated below, a common trend I observed in the classroom among many of the teachers was their emphasis on narratives and personal stories that confessed intimate feelings and difficult personal experiences as valuable knowledge. For teachers like Rigoberto, this was about sharing real life as it happened, being fully human with one's students. While it should not be interpreted that the sharing of emotions and vulnerability happened constantly in the classroom, when it did, the school became an oasis in tough times for both parties.

One cloudy morning in March, I heard the terrible news that Rigoberto's son-in-law had been killed. According to teachers' accounts, he had just left the maquiladora where he worked and was walking home when suddenly he found himself in the middle of a cartel battle and was shot to death. Rigoberto was out that morning, but the next day he showed up to his twelfth-grade history class looking weary and with his eyes red and swollen from crying. When students saw him they immediately took their seats. He also sat at the teacher's desk—something that he rarely did—and, looking down, slowly and softly began to speak.

Last Sunday, something terrible happened to my family. My son-in-law was murdered. He was only twenty-six and was just trying to make a living, like many of you. So I thought of you.... He was married to my twenty-three-year-old daughter and had a fifteen-month-old baby girl.

Rigoberto told the students the entire story of how he found out and what his family had done about it. As he spoke, he tried to find a reason for the tragedy.

My daughter is an activist. She was not in town that weekend. She was in México City denouncing the feminicides with the victims' mothers and other human rights activists. . . . Some think he was killed as a message to my daughter, so that she will calm down and subside her activism. But I don't think so. It was just a matter of being in the wrong place at the wrong time. The same thing that's happened to so many others. My daughter has already informed the national and international media, but I don't know what else can be done.

When he finished the story, he sat silent for a few seconds. Devastated, he sobbed. The students remained quiet and attentive, and tears rolled down some of the girls' cheeks. Seeing such a beloved teacher go through so much pain was excruciating. He then asked the students to forgive him because he was not all there. He had come to class to tell them the reason why he had been absent the day before and to apologize for not being there for them in the next few days. He then told me, "Claudia, I'm sorry, I can't help you today."

Some of the girls got up and surrounded him; a few of the boys then followed. He talked for a few more minutes, venting his sorrow, his impotence. He talked about his daughter, about her pain, and about the strength she had. "I thought about you. So many of you have lost loved ones in the same way, and I'm so sorry. I wished no one would have to go through something like this. Be careful."

Then students around him came up to him and one by one embraced him, in a silent but sincere attempt to console him. I followed the students' lead and joined their embrace of him, feeling both the impotence at such a loss as well as the expression of love that, through vulnerability, melted down titles and the delineation of borders between teacher, student, and researcher categories. Through witnessing vulnerability, sorrow, and outrage, the students not only empathized with their teacher's experience but were also compelled to act toward human connection, to break through social boundaries and hierarchies.

This is then how it did not matter that Rigoberto was often perceived as reserved or stern. Those who got to know him realized that as a teacher, he was "wholly present in mind, body, and spirit" (hooks 1994b, 31). Students, particularly the young women, were able to build meaningful relationships with him such that these significantly enriched and deepened the learning experience. In turn, Rigoberto also found in his students the support that he needed in some way. When I mentioned that I admired his strength to show up to class, he responded to me, "It helps me. Because we have to say it, we have to say how we feel."

As these examples illustrate, the type of radical love and authentic caring that characterized the teacher-student relationships at Altavista went beyond one single feeling. It involved tangible actions, including the expression of emotions that often disrupted gendered stereotypes and hierarchies. It was not inappropriate for students to initiate relationships with their teachers, or to confront them about their behavior. Teachers were able to express humor, love, and vulnerability. Young women were able to express anger and men were able to express sorrow.

I thus posit that these relationships had a liberating potential for all students, especially the women, whose expressions of emotion and care can easily relegate them to the realm of irrationality, objectification, and subservience as if the emotional and the intellectual were necessarily separate or in opposition. In order to understand the potential impact on the young women, it is necessary to take a look, even if briefly, at the ways in which caring and emotions have been theorized in education research.

Aside from test anxiety and other negative feelings, the analysis of a broader set of emotions has only taken place in more recent decades within the field of education (Schutz and Pekrun 2007). Much of this research, however, has come from the fields of medicine, cognitive science, and behavioral psychology, which tend to position their claims under positivistic traditions that assume objectivity. In this sense, although emotions and affect are considered an important aspect of the learning process, they are viewed as separate from cognition, and as external factors often with the potential of either disturbing or motivating learning. Thus, through constructs like emotional literacy or emotional intelligence, feelings are often viewed as something that should be tamed and disciplined by the power of reason (Zembylas and Fendler 2007). Nonetheless, these constructs are far from natural and are rather situated within a historical context of power relations. The Cartesian dichotomy that views the mind and the body as two separate entities, and thus views reason as belonging to the mind and feelings to the body, has left a legacy in traditional research that exalts rationality over emotion in the production of knowledge (Cruz 2001). Considering the androcentric, racist, and colonialist ideologies as well as the Protestant ethic that have historically added to this perspective, women and people of color and those in the Third World have traditionally been perceived as savages more prone to follow corporeal urges, and hence they are viewed as emotional and irrational people, whose bodies are in need of control (Saldaña-Portillo 2003). These ideas not only have permeated research and the production of knowledge (including which knowledge is recognized and who produces it) but have also contributed to normalized ideas of femininity and masculinity.

On the other hand, the feminist scholarship on caring in education that emerged in the 1980s (e.g., Noddings 1988) has attempted to bring to the fore the emotions and nurturing characteristics that have been traditionally devalued in educational research for being in the dominion of women to highlight their importance in the learning process. Nonetheless, this body of work has tended to reinforce assumptions that associate emotion with femininity and reason with masculinity, as their argument is that we need both without disrupting the idea that caring, nurturing, and emotion are inevitably or naturally characteristic of women.

Cultural studies and ethnographic scholarship have only recently begun to theorize on the cultural meanings of emotional practices in educational settings. This critical perspective has interrupted both the positivistic and Cartesian as well as the gendered assumptions about knowledge, rationality, and emotion by conceptualizing emotion in novel ways such as "emotional capital" (Nowotny 1981; Zembylas 2007) or "self-care" (Zembylas and Fendler 2007). These theories are important in that they shed light on how emotions can become a resource that stems from the consciousness of the body and social relations. They also highlight the agency that is generated through the expression of emotions, and offer historically and politically situated analyses of the limitations, delimitations, and exclusionary and surveillance power that social contexts pose by determining and naturalizing certain emotions as acceptable or expected.

Nonetheless, these theorizations also have their own limitations. What I find most dangerous, especially when theorizing about the type of love at a school like Altavista, is the potential to draw on utilitarian, androcentric, and capitalistic language to explain the purposes of the types of emotional expressions that occurred. While I do not suggest that this is the intention or foundation of the alleged theories, I am wary of, for example, utilizing the term "emotional capital" to theorize the vulnerability and caring that I observed at Altavista. This term suggests an overemphasis on functional purposes, as well as a capitalistic approach that views expressions of caring as simply the transaction of emotional resources to obtain personal benefit. I also find that the notion of emotional expression as a form of self-care (Zembylas and Fendler 2007), while coming from a critical Foucauldian perspective and emphasizing agency and speaking one's own truth, fails to explain the collectivity promoted by the radical love at Altavista. While teachers and students clearly benefited from expressing their emotions, this occurred for and within the development of relationships that fostered a sense of the common good, human connection, shared solidarity and kindness, and a higher and collective purpose in educational pursuits rather than mere individual advancement.

By sharing their experiences, joys, and pain, teachers gave students the message that their relationships with the students were valuable to them and that they were not superior or unreachable. As Karla put it, "They let us into their world of teachers." Also, the transparency that they conveyed was not just a strategy to control them, nor even a mere technique to support students' learning (though it clearly served this purpose). Rather, it was a mutual process of humanization, where while all were not the same, all were important, and where teachers also recognized their need of students' validation and love and the need to work together toward collective goals.

In this way, while Altavista still promoted a particular "emotional economy" (Zembylas 2007) or a particular set of acceptable expressions of emotion, it was often organic rather than simply instrumental, it emphasized a type of authentic caring that in some way interrupted masculinistic frameworks of intellectualism, and, as will be seen in the next section, it contributed to the other aspects of Altavista's critical pedagogy—freedom and critical discourse and action—to affirm subaltern knowledges. As Freire (1997) noted, this is an "armed love—the fighting love of those convinced of the right and the duty to fight, to denounce, and to announce" (42).

As will also be discussed in the next section, the expression of women's voice through testimonio played an important role in shaping the women's identities and agency. In turn, the young women began to voice their concerns and develop forms of action within their classes, with the collaborations that were done with other community members in which students actively participated or even led within the informal discourse that occurred among the young women. It is highly possible that without the support and validation they received from their teachers at a personal level, many of these and the examples that will be provided later would not have taken place. Valenzuela (1999) notes that authentic caring by itself is not enough to overcome a "subtracting schooling" process and turn it into empowering education. She underscores the potential of overemphasizing the emotional dimension of authentic caring while neglecting its political and ideological connotations. For this reason, the authentic caring I observed at Altavista, rather than a single emotion or affect, involved the expressions of a range of emotions as well as actions. Love and caring for students can still be oppressive, for these are not neutral entities (Bartolomé 2008), and when they are assumed as politically neutral, complacency and inequality can be reproduced. In contrast, this radical love is characterized by *politically aware authentic caring* (Valenzuela 2008), an investment in students' welfare that is necessarily attached to political awareness and that offers students and teachers tangible tools to have agency over their world. Radical love requires an explicit critical pedagogy orientation, in which students are able to discuss openly and in-depth the issues that concern them and the societal structures and power dimensions that oppress them. The relationships founded in radical love through experiences and interactions inside and outside the classroom and based on teachers' firsthand knowledge of the students' realities, affirmation of identities, trust, reciprocity, and fostering of independent learning were crucial in creating a pathway for true dialogue and critical literacy at Altavista. This dialogue is one step in the process of humanization, as those who have been silenced are able to reclaim their right to speak and could not exist in a context of antagonism, the imposition of "truth," or the banking model of education where ideas are deposited and consumed. This takes me to the third dimension that characterizes Altavista, the emphasis on raising critical consciousness.

Critical Discourse and Activism

Before starting my fieldwork at Altavista, I had not sat in a Mexican high school classroom in seventeen years, but I certainly did not remember my high school classes ever sounding or looking like Armida Valverde's. Besides being the school principal, Armida taught a twelfth-grade sociology class of about thirty students in the humanities and social sciences cohort. The students were sitting in old, individual desks positioned in a semicircle with a few desks scattered in the front of the room, facing the teacher. There were not enough desks, so one boy stood against the wall and about six other students sat on the floor, as well as myself. Armida had key terms on "social Darwinism" written on the board with arrows indicating their relationship as she reviewed the concepts previously covered. Her lecture consisted of a question-and-answer format, continuously attempting to engage the students.

"So who survives?" Armida asked as she concluded one of the class discussions.

"The strongest and the fittest," responded several students almost chorally.

"This can also be seen in school, if you are not strong and fit for it. . . . Any questions?"

Armida transitioned to her next topic: the capitalistic and socialist foundations of industrial society and the search for utopia. She wrote another set of key terms on the board and explained their connection. Then she continued the dialogue with the students.

"So what do you think? Was a utopia achieved?" inquired Armida.

Two boys and one girl pointed out that it was but only to a very limited extent. One of the boys sitting on the floor in the center of the room replied, "The rules are made for those in power who wish to help the people, but only insofar as they can satisfy their own interests. For example, I wanted to study music at the university, but they will only admit you if you have friends there in power."

"Not all knowledge is recognized by science or by universities. For example, which universities grant degrees in alternative medicine?" Armida asked.

A couple of girls and a boy responded that almost none because they do not recognize homeopathy as real knowledge.

"What would happen to pharmaceuticals? It's important to also pay attention to power relations." Armida continued her lecture in this dialogical format. At one point, she noticed that boys began to dominate the conversation, and she deliberately asked questions encouraging girls to participate. As they did, their responses were mostly of social critique. They talked about how the "real medical" world has positioned itself above any other forms of medicine, "even though our ancestors have been curing people using alternative medicine for ages." Armida's demeanor was friendly and candid, and, as usual, her eloquence captivating. At times I forgot that I was there as an ethnographer and not as a student. Like me, most students were attentive. But I soon realized that the building could be an obstacle. The hallways produced a loud echo that sometimes made it hard to hear the teacher. Due to swelling, the classroom door did not shut completely, and the noise outside the room got some students distracted. A couple of students often whispered to each other, and even one of the most participative boys fidgeted with a soccer ball. The traditional teacher in me suddenly came out and I began to feel irritated, but Armida did not seem bothered by the distractions, nor did she demand students' absolute attention. She neither corrected behavior nor used condescending language. She just continued lecturing in what sounded more like a conversation with other adults. Soon the distractions dissipated and students were attentive again.

Despite Armida's use of scholarly vocabulary, students appeared to follow the lesson quite well. However, she did not make assumptions and utilized some literacy strategies to attempt to scaffold the lesson. The students had a handout and she asked them to skim it and identify difficult words. When they did, she helped them figure out their meaning.

"Empirical, what does that mean?" a girl asked.

"Anything you can relate this word to?"

"Maybe something that has to do with practical. There are *'músicos empíricos'* [empirical musicians]," a boy added.

"Empirical means observable. In the example that you gave us, that type of musician is the one who learns by observing." Armida continued to explain the meaning of the word "empirical" as knowledge based on evidence. She then proceeded to respond to other questions the students had. As I looked at the patterns in her discourse, I noticed that she continuously connected complex concepts to events or phenomena that were familiar to the students.

We are in a process of transition in which production will be digitalized. The industrial society changed the structure of the family, from meals' schedules to family roles. What have the new forms of communication and technology done? Sometimes I see you all together but some are on the cell phone, and some have their headphones on. Are you really together? We don't live in an industrial society anymore, but in an era of knowledge and information, the postindustrial society.

"I needed some word definitions and it never crossed my mind to look for them in the regular dictionary. I went directly to the Internet," a boy pointed out.

"Yes, we are now socializing ourselves to be dependent on technology. Some would call it a postmodern society."

"Sometimes my mother and I are at home and I prefer to browse the Web, chat, or listen to music rather than to talk with her," Nora added.

"It's more comfortable not to communicate with your mother and escape into your Barbie world," a boy replied. Nora appeared bothered by this comment. She turned to him and the two and a few others around began to have a side conversation about what he meant by escaping into "your Barbie world." The class conversation then continued about the ways in which technology may affect the structure of society.

This snapshot captures the type of discourse that Armida fostered in her class. While her teaching style was unique to her personality, it was similar in many ways to the style of several other teachers at Altavista. Most of the teachers I observed acknowledged that teaching was a political act and they were not interested in appearing neutral. Their lectures were characterized by a combination of explicit instruction and a dialogical approach with a clear emphasis on critical discourse.

Teachers attempted to facilitate understanding of complex terms in different ways, from providing explanations through examples and the use of student vernacular to teaching them metacognitive strategies to find the answers on their own. A common practice was a process of persistent questioning that allowed students to connect simple and familiar ideas to more abstract concepts. Students appreciated when teachers took the time to provide clear instruction, but, more important, when they taught them to become independent learners, which was the empowering aspect of their lessons. As Iliana put it:

> *La maestra* Armida is my favorite one because she explains every-
> thing extremely well and in different ways until we understand it per-
> fectly. But it's not like she teaches us with little apples and pears; she
> also helps us in that she teaches us to be reflexive about the readings.

At the heart of critical pedagogy is the notion of *conscientization,* or the development of critical awareness, in which both students and teachers learn to recognize social, political, and economic forms of oppression and take part in transforming their reality. Teachers also structured instruction by combining lectures with whole-class dialogue and small-group discussions. Freire (1970) insisted that students' reality should be used as the basis of literacy, and that the educator must begin with the students' language. Teaching "academic language" was pointless when it failed to transcend the classroom walls. Therefore, a common approach was to have students develop projects related to the theory covered in the classroom but illustrated by examples of topics of interest.

To Altavista teachers, it was imperative to blur the boundaries between school and students' daily lives. Some of the teachers utilized the students' slang or vernacular as a vehicle for instruction, as they progressively infused new academic terms. In this way, "academic language" and concepts were not exclusive to the classroom and students' experiences and "vernacular" were not exclusive to the streets. "I don't care if you think your writing isn't good, but I want to hear your voice and your own words coming from your own chest as I read your papers," Armida would tell the students.

Teachers like Jorge, Gilberto, and Armida illustrated hooks's (1994b) idea of the performative aspect of teaching, which compels educators to engage the audience and seek reciprocity, giving way to reinvention, spontaneity, and change. Karla could not quite put a finger on what it was when she tried to describe why her teachers made learning so enticing.

It's how they speak, how they move, I don't know, the way they relate to us. Like Jorge when he calls us *"chavalillo"* [kiddo]. . . . What I mean is that they don't act all rigid when they speak to you, they are so enthusiastic about what they want to teach! And they let you have an opinion, even if it's not correct, or if it's only halfway right. I like them because they express themselves with us.

When education is the practice of freedom, teachers do not perform for the sake of entertainment but rather to stimulate students to take charge of their learning, making dialogue ever changing and evolving. Rather than engaging in a mechanical process of decoding words and sentences or in simple retelling of innocent stories, Altavista's pedagogy insisted that students engage in opportunities to reevaluate the history they were told in contrast with the histories they had lived. Mónica explained to me that she enjoyed her teachers' teaching style because they did not just lecture; they also helped students apply the concepts by utilizing their own realities to illustrate them: "you learn it because you live it." Thus, a salient aspect of the instruction I observed was the direct linking to students' realities. Issues of violence, crime, impunity, feminicides, sexism, poverty, social inequalities, repression, globalization, and local, state, and national policy were brought up in almost every class I observed. The chemistry teacher discussed the impact of neoliberal policies on the Rio Grande River. And in the accounting class, students discussed the labor policies that continued to benefit the wealthy at the expense of the middle and working classes. Students also organized panels on topics such as the hunger crisis, global warming, and violence. In one class, a group of girls, Gabriela included, investigated the reasons for prostitution in Latin America, and they even went to downtown Juárez to interview a sex worker.

Diana also expressed how some teachers promoted students' desire to think critically.

> I love Rigoberto's history class because he doesn't tell you the story of Pancho Villa [an infamous Mexican revolutionary] the hero. I mean, he tells you that he was human like everyone else, or that he raped women in his trajectory. Or like Benito Juárez, who stole land. He doesn't tell you what the textbooks or what SEP [Secretariat of Public Education] say, like oh these are the heroes of our independence. No, he tells you the way it really was.

Although teachers had to abide by the federal standardized curriculum, they found ways to adapt it to their students' interests and encourage critical thought. They also involved students in the decision-making of these projects and some assigned group projects that were open enough for students to apply the content to issues they cared about. Take for example Jorge's communication studies class. One of the first lessons analyzed the notion of media functionalism. Students studied how the media fulfilled an instrumental role in society by providing information about products, encouraging consumption that benefits the market economy, and reinforcing status quo values. Students worked in groups to develop skits that illustrated these three areas of focus. After explaining the instructions for the project, Jorge asked the class to come to consensus on a deadline for pre-sentations. The groups then worked for about two weeks, conducting their research, planning, and practicing their skits. Jorge met with each group individually every class period to monitor their progress and offer advice. On the designated day, students presented their projects. Their analyses explored the media roles assigned to women, gays, people of color, people of various age groups, and people with disabilities. One group, for example, examined the use of women's bodies to promote and sexualize alcoholic drinks, but by incorporating different female and gay characters, they emphasized how this objectification of women's bodies and the portrayal of homosexuality as deviant capitalized on heteronormative and sexist ideologies in society to sell their products, all while perpetuating an ideal body type, sensuality as the only source of power for women, heteronormativity, and the use of alcohol to define masculinity. Other groups also provided other examples of gender roles, family values, and ideas of normalcy reflected in commercials that, while aiming to sell a product, also fulfilled a latent function of indoctrinating the viewers.

After each presentation, students had a whole-class discussion, which provided additional opportunities for analysis and critique. What kind of information is provided explicitly and implicitly? What products, behaviors, values, or views does it promote? Who benefits from this? These were the types of questions that guided students' reflections. This project proved to be highly engaging, gave the students the tools to analyze the media they were exposed to on a daily basis, and required that they use their creativity and problem-solving skills.

Jorge followed a similar approach in his literature classes, which he strived to make relevant to his students' lives. He taught various genres by drawing from authors who wrote about topics that concerned his students, from violence to sexism. As opposed to most schools, where only the classics in Spanish literature are read, Jorge utilized a variety of contemporary Mexican and other Latin American writers. He also included works by women and queer authors, and would give students the opportunity to choose the books they wanted to read. Students did skits, or wrote essays, and on occasion used multimedia as their final presentations.[2] Sometimes they would adapt a legend or a fable to represent the realities they lived, such as the current conditions of violence in the city.

At times, what I perceived to be a lack of structure made me somewhat uncomfortable in Jorge's classes. In a couple of instances, I sat in the empty classroom waiting for a while for class to start, and just when I assumed that Jorge was late or had canceled class, I would be informed that students were working on their projects at the library, or practicing their skits somewhere in the school, or holding class outside in the courtyard. His spontaneity and untraditional approach appeared to confuse some of his tenth graders, who, like me, were unaccustomed to this teaching style. Yet all the students I spoke with pointed to him as one of their favorite teachers and to his classes as the most productive ones. Much of that, I believe, was due to the fact that students did most of the work, even when it appeared at first sight that they were not doing anything.

Similarly, what made Armida one of the favorite teachers was not only the clarity of her instruction but also her ability to help students see complex concepts reflected in their daily lives, as well as to help them question their current reality. Interrupting hegemonic notions of knowledge was fundamental in her instruction. Not only did it promote students' critical thinking about how certain knowledges were legitimized and others subjugated, but it also allowed students to view themselves as producers of knowledge.

One Monday morning in April, Armida offered one of the most poignant lessons during her sociology class. The students sat around Armida's chair while she lectured in a Socratic style.

"A colleague did a sociological study of why students don't speak, both before and after 1968. And I was wondering about you, why don't you speak?" Armida asked.

"Because we are listening," Diego responded.

"Because we are used to listening," Karla replied.

"Because we are embarrassed of not knowing," Marsella added.

"We think that maybe the teacher knows more," Diego offered again.

"So you're saying that legit knowledge belongs to the teacher. But no, there are many knowledges that for example I don't have," Armida explains. "You also have knowledges." They talked about the many things in which they were more proficient than the teachers themselves.

"It's the way in which we've been educated, 'don't talk,' 'don't say anything,' 'you don't know,'" Diego responded. "It is the correct way to be in school."

"But it's not only at school. It's also at home, and at church," another boy pointed out.

"Yes, they teach you not to talk, to feel ashamed," Nora agreed.

"They ask you questions that you can't answer," Marsella added. "That's how they implicitly tell you not to talk."

"One time at church, the priest asked me something and I answered," a girl said, "but I didn't know that I was not supposed to do that."

Armida asked whether church was different from school.

"It's like the teacher represents the priest and the students represent the churchgoers," Diego replied.

"That is a sociological structure," Armida explained. "The way in which we interact with other people is a structure of society. In school, the teacher talks and the students are silent. School has its origins in ecclesiastic instruction." Armida illustrated this by pointing to the closed doors and the confinement typical of most schools: "a principle that comes from the church." "The prefects," she said, "those who usher students into the classrooms, originated in the church." She then explained that this particular structure in which one was assumed to know and the other was not was called an "asymmetric structure."

"I had a history teacher who didn't know much, and he would ask me questions to embarrass me," Diego replied. "So I began to study a lot until I knew more than him. At the end he failed me."

The students and Armida continued to talk about examples of when students' knowledges and languages were subjugated through forms of authoritarian control. "I don't believe in grades," she said, explaining that it was not through coercion and external pressures that she wanted them to learn but through autogestión, a process of self-creation based on their own interests, concerns, methods, and goals.

Autogestión means that you organize, you search your own topics, you decide your order. That's what we are going to do the rest of the semester. But I'm interested in knowing if you can do it. . . . There are some people who think that learning is voluntary. Others believe that the teacher must motivate students as if she or he were a clown. But what I believe is that learning is an intrinsic desire. So that is my question, what do you want to learn? I can support you with materials, with guidance, but can we do it or not?

During the rest of the class the students proposed doing research on social movements and they organized in groups to choose their topic and the approach they would follow.

To most students, this critical thinking was what appeared to trigger their desire to learn. They repeatedly expressed that at Altavista they really learned because they were taught to dig deeper, to analyze the foundations of everything, and that real knowledge did not consist of sterile, neutral, and shallow versions of academic content. Marsella elaborated on how this was different from her friends' schools.

> Take for example the massacre of 1968 in Tlatelolco. Many schools hardly ever talk about it. But here you learn about what really happened, whose fault it was and why. And when I talk with my friends from El Parque High School, they didn't even know anything about it, much less that thanks to those struggles we have the IMSS [Mexican Institute of Social Security] and all that, because it was a pivotal event. . . . I can't believe they don't know anything when they go to those schools of supposedly high academic levels. But the thing is that those schools are so conservative, students don't have real relationships with their teachers, and they only talk positively about the government; they would never critique it. If the government stole something you're not supposed to care; you're supposed to learn about history, geography, and math, and that's it.

Students also engaged in critical discourse outside the school through the partnerships and opportunities that Altavista developed with community members and NGOs. One afternoon early in the fall, students attended a play presented by Telón de Arena, a nonprofit association dedicated to the production and promotion of shows that seek to foster a culture of appreciation for the arts. Every year, Perla de la Rosa, a local actress, director, and founder of Telón de Arena, invited Altavista students to one of the shows, offering transportation and free tickets. About one hundred students signed up and were taken on a bus to a local theater. As we took our seats, I realized that Altavista students had not been the only ones invited.

The play was titled *Getting Divorced without Dying in the Attempt*. It was a melodramatic and comic satire of the typical Mexican telenovela (soap opera) with scenes that included suicide attempts, passionate encounters, jealousy and affairs, desperate phone calls, an unexpected pregnancy, and a robbery that culminated in a dramatic slap to the face.

At the end of the show, the actors came back to the stage and had a dialogue with the audience that invited a reflection on the culture of telenovelas. Altavista students asked questions and participated in the dialogue. De la Rosa explained that they wanted to show the oppressive consequences that telenovelas can have on women. The discussion also focused on the victimization narratives in which women get socialized from an early age. In a culture of telenovelas, "women do nothing important, they don't study, they don't create anything, they just fall in love," De la Rosa noted. The dialogue was definitely insightful and provocative, but I noticed that it was only Altavista students participating. Students from the other high schools were completely quiet.

After the play, a few of the girls, including Gabriela, Karla, and Iliana, stayed to say hi to De la Rosa, who apparently knew them personally. Later I found out that in the past she had brought to Altavista theater workshops through which some of the students learned to act and became involved with the organization.

When I mentioned to Jorge, the assistant principal, that I was impressed by the level of engagement on the part of Altavista students, he explained that this was one reason why they were always invited: "People in the community know that our students are not afraid to ask questions, engage in dialogue, and be critical." He recalled an occasion when other schools had been invited, including the infamous Preparatoria El Parque: "It was embarrassing. The El Parque teachers were walking up and down the isles policing and shushing their students. No wonder why the kids never asked a single question. They are taught to shut up."

In addition to critical discourse, Altavista fostered an environment in which students felt encouraged to participate and even initiate their own cultural activities, often with political purposes. Cultural activities at the school level sometimes stemmed from the critical discourse that took place inside of class, but most often, these were organized organically and generated by the politically aware authentic caring relationships between teachers and students. Students and teachers then had the opportunity to draw on their social relations in the barrio to bring up the concerns of their community, as well as to tap on and strengthen their relationships with various NGOs and activists outside of school. These grassroots and cultural activities were one of the main sources of student enjoyment and participation and served to raise critical consciousness and promote activism.

For example, during the first week of March, the students organized a cultural event called Altavista Fest. This event was in part fueled by a massacre that took place in January when gunmen murdered a group of eighteen high school and college students who were having a birthday party, causing great outrage. Consequently community members and university students organized a march to demonstrate solidarity with families of the victims and to raise consciousness and demand attention and action against the violence and impunity that were devastating the city.

Some Altavista students, including Gabriela, Iliana, Mónica, and Marsella, were very interested in not only attending the march but also contributing to this movement. With the support of teachers, especially Lolo— one of the youngest teachers, who was also an activist and former Altavista student—a group of students began to organize Altavista Fest. The goal of Altavista Fest was to open up a space for students to reflect and voice their pain and anger, and to raise consciousness about the need to demand justice and get involved in the march. "We talked about organizing a gig somewhere else, but then we thought that we needed to start at home, for many of the students needed it too," Lolo explained.

On the day of the event, all kinds of artists and activists from the barrio showed up. A group of female hip-hop artists performed their raps, which eloquently expressed the impotence and distress they felt at seeing injustice prevail, and encouraged others to rise up and fight for what they believed in. With the help of the local artists, students created a mural on the wall of the main building in the center of the school that represented the current condition of the city: from the hypocrisy of politicians and the military invasion of their city to the growing number of tombs and the loss of innocence and future offered to children. Others worked on creating banners to be used at the march. Although the number of students who were present at the march was relatively small, the mural they created was an important reminder of what they stood for.

This is only one example in which critical discourse did not remain contained in the classroom. Instead, it was followed by autogestión and collective action, and it was connected to the larger community. Of course, not all these activities affected everyone equally. Some of the students found the discussions interesting and some took cultural activities like this as just a fun distraction from their classes. But others began to reflect at deeper levels about their own positionings and issues that they had not considered before, and those who were already concerned about social justice issues or had an inclination to activism like Gabriela and Diana found a space where they could act on it.

The consistent critical discourse embedded in the cultural activities at Altavista also filled the gaps created by the limitations of working with a state-imposed standardized curriculum, or the practices of more traditional teachers. This predominant and deliberate discourse is important, as Mohanty (2003) writes:

> Resistance lies in self-conscious engagement with dominant normative discourses and representations and in the active creation of oppositional analytic cultural spaces. Resistance that is random and isolated is clearly not as effective as that which is mobilized through systemic politicized practice of teaching and learning. (196)

The critical dialogue that was promoted in the classroom and nurtured by the freedom and radical love experienced and enacted in school turned into critical action that trespassed the school walls and became part of how the students approached the multiple worlds they inhabited. While we cannot necessarily determine the effectiveness of students' forms of resistance against oppression in producing actual change in the policies and social structures in the community, what was observable was that Altavista's practice of teaching and learning, broadly speaking, had an impact on the ways in which the young women self-authored their identities and saw their place and role in society.

Conclusion

The hallmarks of Altavista's critical pedagogy, freedom and autonomy, radical love, and critical discourse and activism, worked in unison to promote a space of liberation for women and the development of autogestión, as articulated by students and teachers. For the young women, as for everyone else, to be autogestivas meant to have the will and embrace the possibility to develop their own mission, to undertake their own project of life. It included developing one's own methods, abilities, and strategies through which individuals and groups could autonomously work toward the achievement of their own purposes and the production of their own knowledge.

Autogestión was most necessary for Altavista youth, considering their precarious living conditions. Most did not have a social network to rely on for climbing the social ladder, nor could they depend on their family's economic resources. Autogestión was necessary to be able to not only dream but also pursue their goals with little external support, particularly the young women who often faced obstacles within their own homes. This is an ultimate form of agency, the most empowering result of the students' education, which may help them overcome or mitigate the conflicts, contradictions, peer pressure, and challenges posed by life in the barrio and everywhere else.

Altavista's pedagogy illustrates what Antwi Akom, Julio Cammarota, and Shawn Ginwright (2008) have termed a "youthtopia" for its students where young people, and in this case also adults, "depend on one another's skills, perspectives, and experiential knowledge, to generate original, multi-textual, youth-driven cultural products that embody a critique of oppression, a desire for social justice, and ultimately lay the foundation for community empowerment and social change" (3). Needless to say, the project of autogestión that the school sought to promote was both supported and countered by a multitude of other factors. Students' lives were also influenced by their life history, family dynamics, socioeconomic and political contexts, and the views they had acquired throughout the years. But attending high school at Altavista was certainly an experience that they would hardly find in any other school and that marked their last adolescent years in transformative ways.

CHAPTER 4

Building a *Mujerista* Space
at Altavista

In our dreams we have seen another world, an honest world, a world decidedly more fair than the one in which we now live. We saw that in this world there was no need for armies; peace, justice and liberty were so common that no one talked about them as far-off concepts, but as things such as bread, birds, air, water, like book and voice.

—Subcomandante Insurgente Marcos,
"In Our Dreams We Have Seen Another World"

HE IDEA OF YOUNG WOMEN'S empowerment through formal education has often taken center stage in discussions of economic development and gender equity in the Third World. However, the question of "education for what" or what it means to be empowered through education remains both ubiquitous and obscure, as the answer is highly dependent on the sociopolitical, cultural, and economic contexts that frame gender relations for young women (Adely 2012). For example, while a focus on economic development and a neoliberal vision has guided educational initiatives in Ciudad Juárez (Silva 2006), the young women I had the opportunity to get to know were not naïve about the limited financial benefits of their education. Given the economic challenges in the city and in the country in general, as well as imposed gendered constraints, the young women knew quite well that receiving a high school diploma was not necessarily going to significantly improve their economic situation, or at least not immediately. Three of the girls had female family members who were college educated; nonetheless, they had witnessed how not only the economic recession of the past several years but also patriarchy and sexism that pervaded institutions added a multitude of challenges to their careers. High school graduation, then, was only one step out of the many difficult ones inherent in the ambiguous road that would give them better chances for social mobility. Therefore, both teachers and the students I got to know at Altavista understood that education had to mean something more than a tool to achieve social mobility.

The women in this study sought in their formal education the ability to acquire some tools to help them cope with and if possible confront and challenge the very social structures and ideologies that shaped their daily realities. This chapter aims to illustrate some of the ways in which the women interacted with Altavista's pedagogy to experience a type of empowerment that was significant to them and to develop their own forms of autogestión. The autogestión that the women began to embody became evident externally through their actions in the school, but it was also a process that the women experienced internally. In this way, much of the impact of the school's pedagogy is more evident in the intimate lives of the women that may or may not be as visible during school hours. While chapter 5 will explore these innermost aspects of the women's lives, this chapter will illustrate four major ways in which the women co-constructed with their teachers and their peers a space for their own purposes and for empowerment in their own terms: (1) challenging patriarchy and sexism: a necessary struggle, (2) looking for peace: Altavista as a place of refuge, (3) politicized girl discourse: testimonio as a mujerista pedagogical tool, and (4) activism at the heart of learning: young women taking action. These practices, whether enacted by teachers or by the girls and their peers, created a space where young women could engage in a type of education that helped them expand the vision for their lives, practice autogestión, and take part in a process toward individual and collective healing.

Challenging Patriarchy and Sexism: A Necessary Struggle

While it might be true that, because of the many sociocultural factors that shape gendered behaviors and ways of being, many girls tended to be more docile than boys, the girls' commitment to their education at Altavista offered insight on what school represented to them. Obtaining a high school diploma obviously supported the young women's pursuit of a professional or academic career. But what is more, at Altavista, their education also offered them elements for their own liberation as they experienced freedom and opportunities to engage in critical discourse, name and interrogate the oppressors in their lives, and initiate their own forms of action. Thus, for those who experienced more restrictions at home, their school offered new possibilities to participate, make decisions, and become autogestivas.

This, however, did not come without challenges. The young women's growing awareness of their rights and an engagement in critical discourse also resulted in an increased reclamation of a critical voice, agency, and self-authorship, which sometimes put them at odds with their own parents, particularly their fathers, and others in society. Principal Armida noted that some of the parents sometimes complained that ever since their daughters started attending Altavista, they had become more "*hociconas*," or feisty and outspoken. In fact, according to Armida, there were girls at Altavista whose fathers would prefer that their daughters did not go to school, so it was the mother who paid the entire tuition. Some fathers found little value in giving their daughters an education, considering the expectation and assumption that girls would ultimately get married and devote themselves completely to the domestic sphere.

Some of the girls also complained that they had less time to study than their brothers. According to Principal Armida and to most of the young women I got to know more closely, including Lizette, Marsella, Cristina, Mónica, Iliana, Karla, and Nora, girls tended to be responsible for household chores, babysitting younger siblings or cousins, and feeding their fathers when they got back from work. Their brothers, on the other hand, could relax, watch TV, or hang out with their friends. These family structures sometimes put girls at a severe disadvantage, yet many of them continued to do better academically than their brothers. Armida also revealed that some of the girls attended school against their entire family's will.

> We had a girl from Oaxaca and she would come to school without permission. Sometimes she would be absent for days because her brothers would beat her up. But she would come back. Of course nobody would help her with her tuition or to buy supplies or anything. So she is one of our scholarship girls. So you will find those extremes, from those whose parents sacrifice everything to provide an education to their children, to the girls who come against their family's will.

Needless to say, patriarchal ideologies and gendered social arrangements infiltrate in every school system—especially considering that most teachers at the high school and college level are males compared to a majority of female teachers in the early childhood, elementary, and middle school grades. But Principal Armida believed that the evidence of gender inequalities in school and in society granted opportunities to reflect upon and openly discuss the issues the young women faced with both teachers and students. This discussion, she thought, gave way to a greater understanding of the meaning of school and education for women.

While Altavista's teachers and administrators tried to be intentional about furthering women's rights, that women did not experience oppression or aversion on the part of male classmates was not the case. Sexist behaviors on the part of students were not prominent as they were mostly generated outside of school, but students still brought with them their own patriarchal views and learned behaviors into the school. Principal Armida recalls:

> I have seen instances of boys that like to bully women. We had a situation once in which a very petite girl in her first semester, who was also very shy, finally got the guts to let me know that a big boy in her class would grab her from the back of her head and push her to keep her head down. We can't be blinded and pretend that our school is perfect. To think that those things don't happen would be naïve.

Considering then that freedom did not come without challenges, particularly when students' inherited patriarchal and sexist views resulted in oppressive behavior, it was important that students did not confuse freedom with lack of accountability. Thus when instances of abusive behavior against girls were brought up, teachers tried to take action. Some teachers, like Chuy, took strong measures against sexism.

> Students know that I only have one rule, that everyone must respect women. One sign of disrespect and I kick them out of the class. That's it. There are no second chances. I am very strict about that. One time I heard two boys bullying girls as they walked by, "Hey you fatty!" and this and that, they yelled, and I could see the girls feeling humiliated and enraged. So the next day I sat with the boys and I asked, "Isn't Ms. such and such your mother?" "Yes, she is," one of the boys answered. "Man she's freaking ugly and fat, haven't you asked her to get on a diet?" I asked. The boy was so

angry at me. "Come on, Chuy, why are you talking like that about my mother? You should show some respect!" "Well, I'm talking like that because I heard you say the same thing to a girl yesterday. She felt exactly the same rage that you felt right now, but she probably felt worse because she knew she couldn't confront you because you're a man and you could physically hurt her." We talked for a while. I wanted him to understand how women feel. He apologized to me, and I said, "Apologize to her instead, and stop that bullshit."

Surely other teachers, particularly the women, took additional measures that went beyond protective, paternalistic, or authoritarian forms of action. They communicated regularly about the girls' needs and the issues that arose. Feeling a double layer of responsibility, female teachers were prompt to address cases of abuse that occurred even outside the school, serving as counselors and advocates.   *how to prevent this?*

Issues of patriarchy and machismo were most prominent for students in their first year. The first time I went to observe a first-year class, a group of about six or seven boys stood by the door and began walking toward me in a threatening demeanor. This was the only time I felt intimidated, but I kept on walking with my head high and cut right through the middle of the group. When I shared this with Rigoberto, the history teacher, he explained that without a doubt, first-year students took a while to evolve out of the insistence on male domination. He recalled that only a few weeks earlier, boys and girls would completely segregate from each other in the classroom, mainly because the boys were so aggressive toward the girls. I also observed the same behavior in the first-year classrooms, in addition to a different body posture and ways in which boys and girls occupied space. Boys would spread their legs and lay back on their chairs, banding up together, acting loudly, and performing an overconfidence and owner-ship of the space. On the other hand, girls would sit close to each other and communicated in a much more quiet and reserved way. The girls' bodies were also much more constrained; they tended to immediately exit the classroom when the class was over or waited in their seat until the boys had left. But according to Rigoberto, slowly and gradually during their first year at Altavista, the boys tended to change their ways and girls appeared to feel less threatened and to execute more agency over the space. Rather than constantly policing the young men, the freedom that the school offered, along with the other philosophical pillars of the school, critical consciousness and politically aware reciprocal caring, contributed to this transformation. "I have seen a similar pattern every year. The boys begin to realize that they don't have to be defensive, that nobody here is against them," Rigoberto explained. "So now there are some girls and boys that begin to mix in the middle of the room." At the same time, it was possible that the young women also came to realize that instances of oppression did not have to go unquestioned and that they too could speak up. Time and interaction with the discourse and philosophy at Altavista contributed to a gradual evolution on the part of the students. The socialization process was powerful and the students themselves did much of it. The longer students had been at Altavista, the more open they became and the more fluid the groups were.

Given the strong ties between teachers and students, teachers also participated in critical dialogue about their own ideologies, discourses, and actions, as they were not exempt from sexist, deeply entrenched patriarchal views and sexist behaviors. As Principal Armida explained, female teachers in particular felt responsible to stand up against these issues even when this meant confronting their own colleagues.

> So we will argue with our colleagues. One time we had a new teacher. She was an Altavista graduate, and very good looking and young. So the men began to say, "Oh, she's so beautiful, the students won't want to get out of her class!" and what not. So when I heard them I told them, "Hey, why don't you say, 'We have a new teacher who is finishing her master's degree, a very capable and brilliant woman'? There is no doubt that she is beautiful, but she did not come because of her looks, she came to do serious work, and when you say those things, and your students listen to you, they will say the same thing: 'I won't miss class because the teacher's hot.' And you are reinforcing what the boys say. An intelligent and hardworking woman has joined us; she did not come to show you her legs or how her jeans look on her." There they are, defending women and what not, but that type of gaze toward women is still strongly rooted among our colleagues. So I tell them, "Stop your emancipatory gender discourse. Examine yourselves first and then you can talk, because discourse and practice are two very different things."

Moreover, and quite important to the women, teachers gained the confidence to disrupt traditional and hegemonic ideas of schooling and learning, allowing the intimate aspects of students' lives to play an important role in their education process. As such, they interrupted masculinistic perspectives of knowledge and learning, which was key for the women to develop a sense of knowledge, authority and autogestión.

Looking for Peace: Altavista as a Place of Refuge

Seeking gender equity and making Altavista a safe place for women were not trivial goals. In fact, it was the essential foundation to cultivate young women's autogestión. While chapter 5 will detail the ways in which Altavista fostered dramatic transformation as well as various pathways toward autogestión among some of the protagonists of this book, here I highlight the role of the school in those whom I call the *Refugees*. For this group of women, the school served as a space of refuge where they could temporarily escape from a life of sorrow, loneliness, or fear, or where they could engage in activities and pursuits that offered them hope. While big changes in the lives of this group of women might not have taken place during their time at Altavista, the school offered a crucial space where they could begin to envision alternative possibilities for their lives. In fact, I posit that without such a space of immediate peace, the possibilities for many of the women who experienced the most dramatic transformations (see chapter 5) to enact their autogestión in the ways they did would be hampered. Virtually all the young women I met expressed in various ways the liberating effect that the peace and freedom at Altavista had in their lives, and both teachers and peers took part in building such a space that was so significant to women experiencing great distress. Below I present portraits of two young women for whom Altavista's most significant role was providing refuge.

Fortrait of a Refugee: Alejandra

Alejandra was Gabriela's younger sister and was sixteen years old when I met her. She was a practical and talkative young woman with a strong personality. Alejandra characterized herself as frank, cheerful, and with very few friends. Definitely not as popular as her sister, Alejandra felt that she did not get along well with her classmates. Her direct way of talking to people would sometimes offend others. Nonetheless, Alejandra got plenty of attention from boys. Medium tall, slender, and athletic, she was a member of the soccer team and a former track and field athlete. She also liked to save money and mend her clothes, and dreamed of traveling and getting a college degree in tourism.

Although Gabriela and Alejandra grew up in the same household, they were very different from each other. Alejandra had always been critical of Gabriela's drug consumption and was not as interested in activism or in living outside the capitalist system as Gabriela was. But Alejandra also expressed feelings of profound loneliness. She spent most of her days home alone waiting for her mother and sister.

> I don't really like being at home. When I get home I watch TV, do homework, take a nap, listen to the radio, make my bed, and that's what I do every day. When Gabriela gets home at around 8:00 p.m., we don't talk very much, we just say hi, and that's it. . . . I get on her nerves when I talk too much. And then my mother gets home and goes to bed. . . . Only when we eat together do we get to spend time together. When I leave school late, and my mother has to work in the afternoon, I don't get to see her until like in a week when she gets a break. That's why I feel like this. . . . I feel lonely.

From a young age, Alejandra felt the need to develop a strong character that would bring order and a voice of reason to her troubled home. One of the greatest conflicts was with her mother's partner, whom she hated. "When I was little, my mother and her partner would fight and I would get in the middle of it . . . and I would throw whatever I could find to calm them down," Alejandra confessed. "I was only seven years old, and I think that that experience marked me. I wouldn't want my children to grow up like that."

Alejandra was also the one who would get on Gabriela's case when she came home intoxicated. She was very offended by Gabriela's behavior and would even get into arguments with her mother for not disciplining her enough. Feeling that Gabriela could not be trusted with money, when their mother gave them an allowance, she would administer it for both of them. "I never have to ask my mother for more money during the week because I know how to save." When she worked for a month at an auto parts shop, she would buy food for her mother and sister or take them out to eat.

As a young woman, Alejandra was very conscientious of the way in which a patriarchal society oppressed women, and she had seen it in her own family.

> Machismo puts many women at a disadvantage. My mother and
> my grandmother are examples of that because in those times
> machismo was at 100 percent, and the beatings and abuse were
> nonstop. Like I tell you, my mother was one of them. My father
> took her to the United States, he got her all excited and everything,
> and at the end he broke her nose and sent her to hell.

Like Gabriela, Alejandra had also participated in feminist workshops, and she even traveled to New York City in 2008 to present a performance on gender issues. She believed that every woman should respect and accept herself and not let men manipulate her. Ironically, as strong as her convictions and character were, Alejandra found herself trapped in a situation that seemed to contradict her principles.

> I'm in a new relationship. I have a boyfriend, but I don't like it . . .
> because my boyfriend is very arrogant, dominant, and *machista*.
> I've been with him for nine months, but I myself cannot explain
> why, if I've always been to feminist workshops and things like that,
> today I don't know how to get out of this. It sucks.

Alejandra's boyfriend, Rafael, was twenty-one years old, and she met him at Altavista when he was still a student there. They were friends for a while and used to spend a lot of time together. After he graduated, they started dating. Three months into the relationship, Rafael began to pressure Alejandra to have sex with him. At first she refused because she did not feel ready, but then she gave in. This not only went against what she wanted for herself but also changed the relationship for the worse.

> It was my first time because I really like to take care of myself . . .
> because I'm scared that something might happen to me and that it
> will prevent me from ever having children. But I started having sex
> with him, and then . . . from that moment on he was like "You're
> mine, and you will do what I say."

Going out with friends on the weekends as she used to became a problem
and led to many fights. Not only would he try to control her whereabouts
but he also criticized the way she dressed and manipulated her mind by
bragging about the many women who desired him. Her strategy against his
controlling behavior was to be passive aggressive and pretend that she did
not care about his threats. But she felt hurt.

What made matters worse was that Alejandra felt unprotected because
Rafael had almost immediately gained the trust of Alejandra's mother, who
had failed to set boundaries or rules for him. Instead, she hoped for Alejandra to marry him one day. Rafael took advantage of this to exert even more
control over her.

> My mother says that I will end up marrying him, but no, no, not
> even joking! Imagine getting pregnant, no, no, no! In the summer,
> he would visit me every day, and one night it got really late. "Stay
> here," my mother told him, and he went and stayed in my room.
> "What are you thinking?" I told him, "I don't want to sleep with
> you!" So he slept on the couch and I slept in my bed. But in the
> morning, he was already laying in my bed with me. And I was like
> oh no! And my mother saw us and all she said was "Damn kid!"
> and that was it! And I was like "Mother, tell him something!"
> Because if I told him, he was going to say, "Oh, you don't love me"
> and whatnot. But I still told him that I didn't like it, and he said,
> "I don't care, I'm going to stay with you whenever I want." . . . And
> I get mad at my mom because instead of telling him, "I want you
> to respect my daughter," she'll be like "and when are you going to
> get married?" And I feel like she throws me under the bus.

Rafael did not have a good reputation at Altavista. When Jorge, the assis-
tant principal, learned that Rafael was Alejandra's boyfriend, he cautioned
Alejandra that Rafael had been a drug dealer while he was a student there.
Alejandra acknowledged:

> That's how he started making a lot of money, and got all popular,
> and that inflated his ego like crazy. Now he doesn't have any
> money, but I hate it because he tries to humiliate me because I've
> never had money. Most of my family don't like him because he's all
> pretentious and *fresa*.

What caused Alejandra to try to bring the relationship to an end was
that she realized he was flirting with other girls through Myspace, an online
social network, and she suspected that he had cheated on her. Rafael again
tried to manipulate her by reminding her about all the things he had done
for her, all his "sacrifices," and even started stalking her. Although it was not
clear what these sacrifices were and Alejandra resisted for a few months,
she was in love, so after a while she gave in again.

> I miss you, he told me, and I want to get back with you, no matter
> the price. I've changed a lot, and blah, blah, blah. I already know
> that line, I told him. You men always say that, and it's like I've
> memorized it. I've heard it too many times, and it's stupid women
> like me who fall for it because of love. And I told him, it's not true,
> people don't change. But OK, I'll come back with you if you do
> this, this, and that. And I listed all of my conditions. And yeah,
> sure, the first few weeks were very nice, but after that, oh no.

Alejandra confessed that she still loved him, and that at first she really
cared when he got angry, but said that her love was waning. She felt captive
in a relationship that did not let her live her life freely, and admitted that
she knew that as long as she stayed tied to him, she would never be able to
live her life.

Her sister Gabriela and other people around her advised her to break
up with him, but she was afraid. Rafael was very aggressive, and he seemed
to undermine all the women in his life; he would even physically fight with
his mother and hit his younger sister. He had never hit Alejandra, but he
would insult her, laugh at her, and threaten her.

> I still don't know how to talk to him. He's very aggressive. I told
> him from the beginning that if he ever dare hit me, he would never
> see me again. "What are you gonna do to me? You're gonna kill
> me? I'll kill you first," he said. . . . He always tells me that if I ever
> cheat on him, that he will kill me because he says that betrayal can
> only be paid by death.

Alejandra agonized about how to end the relationship. She lived in constant fear of his threats and forms of control, and in some ways she felt
hopeless. This fear, I suspected, also had to do with the fact that he still had

relationships with the drug dealing world, in which violence and impunity were a way of life, not to mention her awareness of how common violence against women was in the city and about how the police often protect criminals for money. She sobbed as she told me how she felt.

> He already told me that he wants to be with me forever, that he will never leave me. And I don't know what I'm going to do. I think, what if I cheat on him, but then I'll get other people in trouble and he might just kill me. One day I was at a party and a guy who has a crush on me suddenly kissed me, and Rafael's friends saw me, and I started crying uncontrollably because I was so afraid. . . . I know that I can't go to the police because of course not. Like I tell you, I do confront him, but then I step back because I know how he is, and I fear for my family. Because the ones who would be affected would be my mother and Gabriela, and I don't want that, I don't. . . . If he wants to hurt someone, then he can hurt me. Who cares, right? So I let him say and do whatever he wants, so that hopefully he will eventually get bored of me.

Not only was Alejandra tortured by fear but she also felt incredibly lonely as she tried to keep her problems secret in order to protect her family and friends. Moreover, Alejandra felt disappointed in herself. She found it ironic and frustrating that while she had wanted to make different choices from her mother's and hated her mother's partner, she ended up with a boyfriend who was just like him.

What role did Altavista play for women like Alejandra? Certainly, the school did not help Alejandra break up with Rafael, nor did it help her overcome her fears. It had supported her development of critical consciousness, but clearly, this had not been enough to help her get out of this difficult situation, at least not yet. What Alejandra found in Altavista was a space where she could escape from her troubles, in both the literal and the metaphorical sense. At Altavista, Alejandra felt safe, confident, loved, and free. While Rafael had been a student there, he hardly ever visited the school, for he did not get along with the soccer coach or the teachers, and most of his friends had already graduated, so Alejandra felt sheltered from his surveillance. Her teachers gave her a sense of security and reliability that she could not find at home. "What I love the most about this school is the teachers, especially Rigoberto," she said. "I tell him about my problems and he always listens to me and gives me advice. I can also just talk and joke with him. I even call him grandpa."

In addition, at Altavista, Alejandra was able to live as if she did not feel lonely, scared, or disappointed in herself. She could pretend that she did not have a big problem, and that she could start her life anew, if only for a few hours a day. She expressed that her time at Altavista was the highlight of her days.

> Many people here don't know the way I am outside of school.
> Because here I am a completely different person from the one I am
> at home. When I'm here, I'm always happy. That's why I love this
> school, because I'm always happy, and at home I'm not. At home I
> feel lonely. I love being here. I don't care what I'm doing, even if
> there's no one around. I can just talk to the trees.

Altavista offered Alejandra the freedom that she could not have with Rafael. "Here I have all the rights," she said. Although Alejandra could talk to the trees, she could also talk to other boys. I often saw her socializing with young men and looking completely peaceful. She also stayed after school almost every day to practice soccer, or just to spend time with friends. She actively participated in most of the cultural and activist events, and organized fund-raisers for her soccer team. While Alejandra's actions outside of school did not match her beliefs about what she wanted for herself and the type of woman she wanted to be, her agency was still evident as she tapped the resources provided by the school to author the self at least temporarily in ways more congruent to her ideals.

Another Refugee: Lizette

Lizette was very different from the rest of the young women in this book. Because she had been at Altavista for only one semester, her discourse was not as critical as the rest, and she seemed content with some of the gender roles that society assumed were for women, such as cooking and cleaning. Lizette had many friends and seemed confident and cheerful all the time. Lizette wanted to improve her living conditions by finishing her high school education. However, she had moved to Juárez from another town in Chihuahua in order to help her father recover from alcoholism. He had, in exchange, offered to pay for school and all her expenses. But after a few months of living with him, it became clear that she had to move out. Annoyed by her insistence that he get help, he began to get aggressive and reproached her for wanting him to change. Thus, she had to move in with her paternal grandmother. Every day she rushed home to help her grandmother cook and complete all the household chores. She then would rush to visit her father, as she constantly worried about his illness and feared that something terrible could happen to him. Nevertheless, her father only seemed to get worse. He had already been laid off from a couple of jobs, and it was difficult for him to find employment, even temporarily, due to the fact that he was always drunk. He threatened to stop his financial support if she kept pushing him, and there were many times when she did not even have money to eat or pay for her basic necessities.

Clearly, there was nothing that Altavista could really do to help Lizette overcome this problem. But in school she was able to find a moment where she could be at peace and spend time with positive people who did not judge her. While at home she felt like a burden and intruder, in school she felt that she belonged. She was also able to experience some degree of success, which helped her feel some sense of achievement despite the constant setbacks from the situation with her father.

Although Alejandra and Lizette were very different from each other, they converged in the fact that both of them were experiencing difficulties that seemed inescapable in their personal lives, and that kept them feeling repressed, anxious, or hopeless. While they did not find a permanent solution to their problems in school, the freedom and caring that Altavista offered allowed them to temporarily forget about their troubles and engage in an autogestión that allowed them to at least envision who they wanted to be, even if they felt powerless in a particular situation or were unable to change it. At Altavista they found a space where they could temporarily enjoy the peace and human connection they lacked in their other social contexts and engage in a temporary process of self-authorship without being overwhelmed by the many burdens that afflicted their lives.

Politicized Girl Discourse: Testimonio as a *Mujerista* Pedagogical Tool

At Altavista, it was not surprising that young women appeared to be more academically oriented than their male counterparts. The space of peace, trust, freedom, and critical discourse that Altavista offered represented for women, perhaps more so than for men, a space for liberation that though not complete was more appreciated because of their everyday gendered experiences. The young women had the opportunity to unpack in their classes issues of sexism and patriarchy by connecting the academic concepts to their own life experiences. Furthermore, this context allowed the young women to expose their vulnerabilities and reclaim their voices as they engaged in their own pedagogical practices inside and outside the classroom.

For example, one morning during the economics class, a conversation about the job market turned into an analysis of gender relations and expectations. Several of the young women, including Gabriela and Nora, discussed the barriers they confronted when they went to look for jobs, such as the objectification of women and an emphasis on certain beauty standards and gender performances that are not expected of men. "I don't get jobs because of my hair. They probably want us to wear miniskirts. They don't wait to get to know whether you are intelligent but rather make their decision based on physical appearance. So all I can do is sell the bracelets that I make," Gabriela shared with the class.

Gabriela's illustration of social dynamics through lived experience was a typical way in which students engaged with the content of their classes. As I have noted earlier, and evident in the narratives that inform and are presented throughout this book, one way in which Altavista teachers deliberately promoted the legitimization of students' voices and critical dialogue was through the sharing of stories. Teachers took these stories seriously and offered ample time and space for them in their critical discussions. Both teachers' and students' narratives of lived experiences became part of the everyday curriculum and were considered a legitimate and valuable knowledge for critically applying and analyzing theory, often substituting for the scarce resources and lack of access to textbooks. Perhaps this was one reason why some of the young women were so eager to participate in this study.

Beyond offering relevance to the content learned in class, this type of personal engagement in critical discourse was crucial for the young women as they shaped Altavista into their own space of agency. The critical discourse at Altavista was neither limited to the classroom nor always initiated by teachers. In particular, in the case of the young women, the naturalization of politically aware, authentic caring and the expression of emotions and experiences that characterized the school, combined with the critical discourse promoted in the classroom and within these relationships, allowed the women to excavate and draw upon subaltern ways of knowing and heuristic learning processes that had been silenced in past schooling con texts. These aspects that were part of Altavista's philosophical foundation also opened up a space for young women to expose more deliberately the issues that were of concern to them and to explore their own ways to address them.

In reflecting upon the young women's narratives (most of which are provided in chapter 5), as well as in observing the types of conversations in which they engaged outside of class and in their class and activist projects, and even in their writing of poetry, raps, and songs, I realized that their discourse went beyond the sharing of stories. Their critical stance often turned common girl talk into a political endeavor that exposed the knowl edge and wisdom they had gained through their emotional, bodily, intellec tual, and social struggles for freedom, dignity, and life. The young women's engagement in these forms of discourse—whether through organic con versations, their participation in this study or in grassroots activities, or their artistic writing—revealed its epistemological and pedagogical nature. Therefore, in analyzing the young women's discourse, I have found the notion of testimonio from a Chicana feminist perspective in education to be very useful. As Dolores Delgado Bernal, Rebeca Burciaga, and Judith Flores Carmona (2012, 363) explain:

> While the genre of *testimonio* has deep roots in oral cultures and in Latin American human rights struggles, the publication and subsequent adoption of *This Bridge Called My Back* (Moraga & Anzaldúa, 1983) and, more recently, *Telling to Live: Latina Feminist Testimonios* (Latina Feminist Group, 2001) by Chicanas and Latinas, have demonstrated the power of *testimonio* as a genre that exposes brutality, disrupts silencing, and builds solidarity among women of color (Anzaldúa, 1990). Within the field of education, scholars are increasingly taking up *testimonio* as a pedagogical, methodological, and activist approach to social justice that transgresses traditional paradigms in academia. Unlike the more common training of researchers to produce unbiased knowledge, *testimonio* challenges objectivity by situating the individual in communion with a collective experience marked by marginaliza tion, oppression, or resistance. These approaches have resulted in

new understandings about how marginalized communities build solidarity and respond to and resist dominant culture, laws, and policies that perpetuate inequity.

On the other hand, a common characteristic in the use of testimonio in this way is a sense of political urgency. It is here where Cherríe Moraga and Gloria Anzaldúa's (1983) notion of "theory in the flesh" (23) becomes evident. By invoking this organic theory that emerges in urgency and privileges the real experiences, voices, and knowledge of subaltern women of color demanding attention and action, we are able to unveil the epistemological processes present in the young women's testimonial discourse that could potentially be trivialized by traditional or androcentric analyses. The notion of "theory in the flesh" highlights the "struggle of the flesh, and struggle of borders, an inner war" (Anzaldúa 1987, 100) in which women's brown bodies become the mediums, witnesses, and agents (Cruz 2001). The young women's bodies thus comprise the very sites where the First and Third Worlds collide (Anzaldúa 1987), where the personal becomes political, where identities are negotiated, and where knowledge and theory are generated and materialized through experience.

As the mind and body become one in this organically generated theory in the flesh (Cruz 2001), the personal narrative becomes the very means for agency and dissemination of knowledge. Testimonios offer the opportunity to develop and expose theory in the flesh and urge the audience to action as "the voice that speaks . . . in the form of an 'I' . . . that demands to be recognized" (Beverley 2000, 548). Thus, as young women testify about their own politically, economically, and socioculturally situated experiences, they break the silence and negotiate new identities that might help them better overcome shame and heal the wounds brought about by colonization, violence, patriarchy, and other forms of oppression (Moraga 1993). At the same time, those who witness also engage in their own identity negotiations and learn from other young women's experiences. In this way, the theory in the flesh that the young women generate is turned into *sabiduría* or lessons for life and for self-transformation.

The testimonial discourse among the young women at Altavista exemplifies the possibilities of mujerista pedagogical and epistemological theory (Villenas et al. 2006) by serving as counternarratives, confessions, and *consejos* (words of wisdom or advice) based on their own life experiences (Cervantes-Soon 2012). Illustrations of the young women's testimonial discourse are evident everywhere in this book. Many examples are provided in chapter 2, in the description of their photographs, which offered some insight into not only their intimate expressions and definitions of self but also their critical perspectives about their community, the authorities, and the militarization of the city, among other things, in the form of images and counternarratives. Chapter 5 also provides many other illustrations of this testimonial discourse. However, below, I offer two examples that might help the reader better capture the young women's politicized talk.

Diana's Testimonio: A Counternarrative

My name is Diana Blanco Corona [pseudonym]. I am sixteen years old, and I am a student at Preparatoria Altavista.... Since December 14, some things have happened that have changed me. On that day, I went with my mother to the veterinary clinic and we got assaulted, and the man who assaulted us raped me. The veterinary clinic is on a corner of a major avenue where the military are patrolling every five minutes. But, what good does that do anyway, right?... The man did not beat me, but I realized how people can manipulate your mind. Before the man raped me, he told me, "Don't say anything, and don't do anything because I'll kill your mother." We went to take our cat and were waiting for our turn. A man then arrived with a dog. I remember thinking how odd it was that it looked like a stray dog wearing a new leash. The clinic was about to close. "Open the door," he demanded. "Yes, let's open," said the vet. "He will be the last one." As soon as he got in, he ordered my mother to close the door, pulled out his gun, and said, "This is an assault." And that's where everything started. We didn't know ... well, I had no idea of how long it all lasted because from that moment I lost any notion of time. He made me take off my shoelaces and tie up the vet, and then sent me to a little room in the back, ordering me to look for I don't know what. He then went to the room with me and told me, "Look, don't freak out, right now I'm going to kill the vet, but if you don't want anything to happen to your mother, don't say anything." He said, "Pull down your pants," but I wasn't registering anything; I was in a nervous shock, gone. Then as he began to take off his pants, he put his gun on the table. I tell my mother that I wouldn't have hesitated to grab it, but he saw me looking at it, and he took it back.... And then that was it. He raped me and then sent me back to the main room. I just sat on the floor and put my face between my knees. I bowed my head so that my mother would do the same and wouldn't look at the scene if he ended up killing the vet. . . . What enrages me is that he thinks that he did us a favor for not having killed us. He would refer to us as "señora" [Mrs.] and "señorita" [Miss] and would say "Excuse me" and I don't know what. You see? Like if he was doing us a favor by treating us like that. Then he said, "They're picking me up. Don't leave the clinic in the next fifteen minutes." He then told the vet, "I'm going to say that I beat you up, and that I didn't kill you because there were two women." Again, as if we should thank him, you know what I mean? . . .

. . . My mother asked me if I wanted to report him to the authorities, and I said, "Yes." He had the appearance of a soldier 100 percent. He was wearing military boots, was dark skinned, had a birthmark on his face, sounded like a Veracruzano [a native resident of the southern Mexican state of Veracruz], and seemed southern. I reported him, and it was very denigrating having to declare twenty-five times and being examined in front of I don't know how many people. It was very traumatic. They asked me for my undergarments to get the DNA, but I know they won't do anything—as usual they won't do anything. And I am sure there was DNA everywhere.

. . . Before, I used to tell the story and cry, but the therapy from a civil association has helped me. . . . Although sometimes I get attacks of rage, not fear, but rage, I hope to transform this rage into boldness. That's why I'm getting involved in all these marches against violence. This experience changed my perspective completely. . . . But from then on, only good things have happened. I got a job, and my friends here at Altavista, and all the new people I have met, have helped me heal.

—Diana

When I invited Diana to participate in this study, she immediately and enthusiastically said yes. "I want others to know that we aren't silent victims," she asserted, and several times she expressed that she viewed her participation in this study as an opportunity to share with others outside her community the realities of young Juárez women and dispel some of the stereotypes prevalent in the mainstream media. At the time, she had not gone through this devastating experience. However, when I interviewed her the second time, it was this testimonio that took center stage as if she was anxious to share it despite the intimate and painful feelings that it would expose.

By testifying, even just to me—but with the awareness that her words would be shared with a larger audience—Diana wanted to demonstrate that violence against women was not the consequence of a life of excesses or reckless rebellion. Her testimonio speaks against the images of young border women as being too loose, too silent, or too passive and sheds light on the layers of patriarchy and impunity that pervade the city. But her testimonio is also a counternarrative that highlights the significance of the agency through collective action and knowledge among many Juárez residents who have chosen not to run away but rather to stand firm for themselves and others, healing the wounds and reclaiming the humanity of those suffering injustice. Rather than a victim, Diana saw herself as a fighter and survivor who, despite any situation, would rise again with courage and hope. However, her hope was not in the hands of the authorities, whom she viewed as incompetent and indifferent. Instead, her healing came from her community: her friends at Altavista, civic agencies, and women healers, as well as from her own struggle. By sharing her testimonio, Diana was able to pick up the scattered pieces of a painful experience in a new way that generates wisdom and consciousness. In Anzaldúa's words:

> You've chosen to compose a new history and self—to rewrite your *autohistoria* [self-story]. You want to be transformed again; you want a keener mind, a stronger spirit, a wiser soul. Your ailing body is no longer a hindrance but an asset, witnessing pain, speaking to you, demanding touch. *Es tu cuerpo que busca conocimiento* [It's your body that seeks knowledge]; along with dreams your body's the royal road to consciousness. (2002, 558–59)

Sharing Sabiduría through Testimonio

While Diana's testimonio was shared with me in the intimacy of our interviews, the young women often engaged in testimonial discourse in natural ways when conversing with their friends. This was, in a way, no different from the conversations that occurred between mothers and daughters, between sisters and girlfriends, at the kitchen table, at the Laundromat, or while riding the bus. They occurred during the mundane and in their everyday contexts. Nevertheless, the pedagogical nature of their testimonios was evident in that the goal was to share wisdom and the theories for self-transformation that had been generated in their own flesh. Through this testimonial discourse, the women shared confessions about their own lives and experiences, making themselves vulnerable to the listeners— particularly when these involved even shameful or regretful behaviors. But they did this intentionally, believing that their experiences carried a lesson of wisdom for life, a *consejo* that was worth sharing with others.

For example, I witnessed an informal conversation among girlfriends one warm afternoon in the school's courtyard. Margarita, a twelfth grader, shared with Gabriela, Karla, and me her story about how she had become very aggressive and even a violent bully after having joined a female gang in middle school. She had engaged in these activities and behaviors, she explained, as a response to the repression that she had felt at home simply for being a girl, and as a consequence of the rejection she had experienced in middle school by various girl cliques due to her looks not fitting the norm.

> That's how I became a bully. I had to hit and physically hurt other
> girls, even if they didn't do anything to me, just to prove that I was
> in. And I had to act aggressive like them. People couldn't look at
> me without me yelling "what the fuck are you looking at!" But I did
> it just to fit in the group. . . . But in a way I enjoyed it because I
> found a way to please them, and at the same time people were
> scared of me, and I knew my friends would back me up if anybody
> did anything to me.

Margarita continued to express how she still felt resentful against most girls, particularly the *"fresas"* and others who made her feel ugly or inadequate, and these feelings continued to fuel her aggressive and antisocial tendencies, even if she did not engage in these behaviors to the same extent as before.

After Margarita shared her story, I witnessed an exchange of testimonial nature through which Gabriela, in particular, sought to offer Margarita an alternative for her life. Gabriela explained that she too, influenced by drugs, alcohol, and friends, had become extremely aggressive, very different from the way she was today.

> Once I even started a fight with this one *chota* [police officer] at a
> bar. I beat the crap out of her, and she was real skinny so I was

stronger. . . . I ended up in jail. . . . I got my mother sick and tired of having to get me out of jail. It was awful; I had never beat up someone like that. . . . Yeah, like Karla says, when I first got here, I was different. I used to listen to hard-core rock and punk music, and I dressed in that same style. I wore dark eye makeup, tight dark clothes, and chains, do you remember? . . . I didn't talk to anyone, I didn't like anyone, and I would treat everyone badly. I was evil, evil. I would tell them, "Hey güey, what do you want? Fuck off!" I was strong, but I wasn't a bully. I just didn't care about anyone. And everyone was afraid of talking to me. Sometimes I didn't want to be like that, but I was too prideful and I didn't want to get rid of that image that I had made for myself; I didn't want to appear weak.

While this account may have helped Margarita identify with Gabriela, Gabriela was interested in a conversation that would not lead simply to commiserating together or to glamorizing stories of aggression but rather would lead to unpacking the reasons for that kind of behavior and the consequences to their lives. Therefore, Gabriela did not stop there but instead began to also share about her own process of reflection that had incited a 180-degree turn in her life. She incited a conversation in which the young women shared stories about the pain that that lifestyle brought to their families, and about the futility of that kind of resistance against the authorities' injustice and hypocrisy. As Gabriela put it, the lesson she learned was that "it's better to fight with the mind than with fists."

The testimonios shared by Margarita and Gabriela started off as confessions, but they soon revealed their pedagogical nature as they learned from each other lessons about critical reflection and agency. In this way, the young women engaged in a self-authorship process by affirming similarities or differences and provoking new constructions of self—hence negotiating new identities: "I am not the way I used to be anymore either. I dress the same way, but I don't fight anymore," Margarita told us after listening to Gabriela.

Beyond this type of conversations, Gabriela engaged in testimonial discourse in various ways. In addition to the stories she shared with her friends through informal conversations, Gabriela's poetry and raps also involved this type of discourse. The following testimonio was one of the many raps Gabriela wrote spontaneously during her free time as one of her hobbies through which she shares her experiences and those of her friends in the barrio. Exhibiting the necessary understanding of power dimensions and the role of spirituality in the search for healing, the goal of her rap was to advise the audience to reject the life of drug dealing and addictions and find spiritual peace:

I was fifteen years old when cocaine got to my hands
What's the situation here in the barrio?
There're no more basketball or soccer games
We all saw how Carlitos was devoured by the barrio
When a shooting burst out in the middle of the crowd
And Carlitos remained dead on the ground . . .
I know you're tired,
I can see it in your eyes
It's been a while since the coke won't do it anymore
The effect fades away and the sorrow continues
You look weary and old
Listen to these words
They bring a message of peace for your soul
It's not a bunch of lies,
Jah points at my mouth, and I speak the truth
Listen to the words of life.
This is the only way out
This one will forgive you and heal your hurt,
Will erase the pain, fill in the void,
The memory of your friend broken on the ground
Or the time when you had to tell your girl good-bye . . .
Did you listen, my friend?
Do you know I'm with you?
I don't force you, but I give you these words
So you can think of your decision
To choose between life or remain between the blocks

Represented by Carlitos were the many children from the barrio who used to enjoy sports and create barrio hip-hop but, having spent so much time in the streets, ended up trapped in the vicious cycle of drug dealing and addictions. Finally, Gabriela noted that the line about choosing life or the blocks represented not only a personal decision to improve one's lifestyle but also the choice between taking a stand and continuing to be manipulated by world powers that fueled the drug business—the United States in particular.

In sum, the *sabiduría* shared through these testimonios embodies mujerista pedagogies as they lead the audience to examine and question their lives within an understanding of power dimensions, all while offering a language of hope and agency generated from their own life experiences (Hernández 1997; Elenes et al. 2001; Cervantes-Soon 2012). By engaging in the practice of testimonio, an inherently political yet naturalized form of girl discourse, the young women drew on their daily realities to speak against oppression, confess intimate and difficult experiences, share wisdom and advice with their peers, and ultimately generate a collaborative process toward healing.

Activism at the Heart of Learning: Young Women Taking Action

As has been discussed, the space that Altavista offered for critical thought and the legitimization of personal experience and narratives as valid sources of knowledge allowed the young women to cultivate their own forms of autogestión through testimonial discourse. But there were other forms of critical action and external manifestations of agency. The young women took ownership of their space at Altavista by taking the lead in organizing and participating in various forms of critical action that, while imperfect, gave them opportunities to enact their critical voice, make decisions, and experience activist organizing for social change. The collaborative and dialectical process that these activities involved constituted forms of mujerista pedagogies through which the young women contributed to the cultural production and socialization at Altavista.

For example, as has been noted before, in addition to speaking about the ways in which patriarchy affected her and other women, Gabriela began to organize a women's group to talk about issues of concern that situated their own experiences as working-class young women in Juárez and developed class projects related to the objectification of women's bodies. Gabriela also helped organize marches and other school activities, like Altavista Fest, to which the entire community was invited and where local activists and artists would also share their testimonios and raise critical consciousness through their music and art. Diana also often shared her poetry in school and in women's conferences taking place in the community, which expressed the anger and impotence about sexual harassment, feminicide, and the objectification of women. In preparation for these events, the women engaged in critical dialogue with peers and teachers about the issues they were attempting to address and what their message should be. Moreover, the entire process contributed to the development of their own identities as educated women and the potential to be agents of change. While both male and female students engaged in these cultural and grassroots activities, it was quite noticeable that young women were often the main initiators. The two examples below may better illustrate their autogestión and their role in promoting activism among their peers.

"La Marcha del 2 de Octubre"

The revolutionary background and orientation of Altavista was not a secret, and students sometimes took it upon themselves to continue the tradition and build on the legacy of activism from previous generations. In the fall, students organized a march to commemorate the massacre of Tlatelolco, which took place on October 2, 1968. This infamous and atrocious event was significant, not only because it took place precisely in the year when the school was founded but also because the founders of Altavista had participated in and led student movements themselves. The march was perhaps a way to remember the school's vision and extend it to the new generations.

When I asked who was organizing this march, there was never a clear answer, but I learned that this had been organized by students in previous generations and had turned now into a tradition that was usually carried on every year by the new generation of senior students. Nonetheless, it was clear that it was mostly the young women, particularly the twelfth graders, such as Gabriela, Marsella, Karla, and Iliana, leading the movement. They were the ones who more deliberately took charge of creating the banners, communicating with teachers, getting the materials, and planning the activities for the event. The teachers would support them by providing resources for banners, helping them coordinate and communicate the schedule to the rest of the school, and providing information during class or making videos available to show to those who were not familiar with the historical event. Some students wrote or did their own research, found poetry on the topic, and posted it on the bulletin board, and others went to each classroom to announce the event. Everything was planned in a matter of a few days.

On October 2, students dedicated the whole day to the march. Two students, Gabriela and Diego, were selected as spokespersons, just in case the media asked questions. Students spent a couple of hours creating large banners with messages that read "We were all born on October 2," "Give peace a chance," "The struggle is not for war or peace, but for the right to a decent life," and "Not one minute of silence, rather an entire life of struggle." Clearly, this march was not only a commemoration of what had happened over forty years ago. Considering the conditions of violence and impunity in the city, their demands for peace and their statements of struggle were more a projection of their current reality than a reference to the Tlatelolco incident.

About two hundred students, followed by approximately fifteen teachers, walked out of Altavista on the morning of October 2 and marched along the boulevard that parallels the Río Bravo or Rio Grande River. Gabriela, Karla, Marsella, and other young women led students in chanting revolutionary slogans such as *"¡Dos de Octubre, no se olvida!"* (October 2nd is not forgotten!), *"¡El pueblo unido jamás será vencido!"* (The people, united, will never be overcome!), and *"¡Zapata vive, la lucha sigue y sigue!"* (Zapata lives, the struggle continues!). They also chanted messages that invoked their ideals as students, including:

> *Porque somos estudiantes,*
> *estudiantes de primera,*
> *y no somos criminales.*
> *Como dijo el Comandante,*
> *Comandante Che Guevara,*
> *¡hasta la victoria siempre!*

> [Because we are students,
> top-of-the-line type of students,
> and we are not criminals.
> Like the Commander said,
> Commander Che Guevara,
> Always all the way to victory!]

and

¡Educación primero al hijo del obrero!
¡Educación después al hijo del burgués!

[Education first to the child of the worker!
Education later for the child of the bourgeois!]

The march also served as an outlet to respond to the current dystopia of the city from their position as working-class students. As they marched right in front of the government buildings and military and federal police troops, they chanted ever more loudly: *"¡A estudiar y aprender para chota nunca ser!"* (Let's study and learn so that we may never be cops!), *"¡Esos son, esos son, los que chingan la nación!"* (It is they, it is they who fuck up the nation!), and *"¡Juárez, Juárez, no es cuartel, fuera ejército de él!"* (Juárez, Juárez is not a military base, get the army out of here!).

City buses and cars would pass them by and honk in support. They arrived at their final destination, a park where the *mega-bandera* stood—an oversized Mexican flag that can be seen from both sides of the border. The plan was that some students would give a speech and others would perform a skit to illustrate the historical event. Usually, at that point the media and vendors who were used to Altavista's tradition would be expecting them, but this time the park was empty. Only a dozen federal police officers wearing their black uniforms, masks, and heavy boots and carrying their big riffles were at the park. The officers told one of the teachers that the park could not be used because the governor was expected to land there in his private helicopter in a few minutes. The teachers informed the students and asked them to remain calm, which they did, and after taking a break and chanting for a few more minutes they returned to the school.

Although the event culminated in an unexpected way, it still served its purpose to some extent. Given that the historical event is almost never mentioned in the teaching of Mexican history in schools, it was a perfect opportunity to raise consciousness about the legacy of activist repression and the violation of civil liberties and human rights that had been committed against youth by those in power for many years. Some of the girls, like Marsella, Cristina, Alejandra, and Mónica, expressed to me that they learned the most from experiences like this, even when other people in the city criticized it as irrelevant.

In addition, because this march took place at the beginning of the semester, it served as a socializing moment that helped frame the school's culture and political orientation for the new students and give momentum to other student-initiated forms of activism and expression. Initially, the degree of commitment varied among students, and about one-third of them did not attend the march. But for those who chose to attend, it was certainly a poignant moment. It also gave students an opportunity to denounce the injustices they experienced in the current reality of the city. This was perhaps the first time that most of the new students ever participated in any form of protest, and witnessing them passionately express their discontent with the current Juárez situation was rather moving.

The young women were aware that the school was ostracized because of their leftist expressions, but most of them shaped their own identities by inserting themselves in the collective identity of the school. Cristina, for example, explained that the school constantly battled repression from the authorities.

> There was a Zapatista mural on that wall in the back of the school, and the government had it stained. So we have always had problems with them. For example, the October march, it's the same thing. I was surprised that we didn't have problems this year, but last year there were many journalists and media reporters and soldiers. And I think they don't like us because we are very *grilleros* [feisty]. For example, a journalist asked me why we marched if we hadn't been there: "Why do you care?" So I responded, "Well, then why do we celebrate El Grito [Cry of Independence] if we weren't there?[1] We haven't been anywhere, but there we are, yelling, '¡Viva México!' and all that, why not this then?" He just stood there in silence.

Although Cristina was one of the least visibly vocal girls in class among the group of young women I got to know, she still engaged in critical discourse in her own spaces. She also saw herself as belonging to the movements at Altavista and in that way engaged in her own identity self-authorship as someone who was outspoken and ready to defend her critical perspective when necessary.

The Ecological Committee

One of the clearest ways in which autogestión was enacted by one of the young women is the creating of an ecological committee. Initiated and led by Diana in collaboration with a small group of peers, the ecological committee was created to raise consciousness within the school to take better care of the environment and, in doing so, make an effort to beautify the school grounds. Diana was passionate about ecological issues as well as about her school, and she found a way to bring these two interests together and mobilize her peers to take action. Diana requested support from the administration and teachers, who not only encouraged her but also offered tangible supports, such as a small budget for supplies and the possibility for those who got involved to earn credit for the community service requirement that all high school students in the state had to fulfill.

Diana and her group of friends called a first meeting at the library, inviting everyone who would like to participate. The goal of this meeting was to build community, explain the vision of the committee, and determine goals and steps for action. About twenty-five students from various grades joined the meeting.

Diana started the meeting by asking everyone to introduce themselves and engaging everyone in community-building activities and games. After about thirty minutes of these activities, she asked everyone why they had chosen to participate. It seemed that the younger students were attracted by the opportunity to receive credit for community service. In contrast, most of the older students were there because of the love they had for their school and their desire to give back.

Diana then described the purpose of the committee and began a conversation about the vision and foundational principles of the group. For one, things would be done in a democratic way. "I am not here to impose what I want to do, but rather I would like for all of us to do this together and make decisions collectively," she told the group, explaining that the main goal was to raise consciousness about environmental issues and promote ownership and responsibility for taking care of their school. As such, the next hour was spent in dialogue about what they envisioned as their long- and short-term goals. They determined that raising consciousness and instilling new behaviors that were more ecologically friendly while doing it in a way that was meaningful to Altavista students was one of their first priorities. Therefore, one of their short-term goals was to promote garbage reduction by separating trash so that they could begin to develop recycling and composting practices. As a side benefit, they thought this would also help students keep their school clean.

One of the activities they came up with in order to address this goal was to paint trash cans to encourage the rest of the school to classify their trash and deposit it in the appropriate color-coded trash can. It was through this discussion that the impact of cultivating critical discourse was evident in Diana's approach to enact and promote autogestión. When deciding on the steps they would take to promote ecological consciousness and encourage students to separate their trash, one of the students in his first semester at Altavista, Armando, suggested they should have some form of competition or a system of penalties for those who did not follow the rules. Diana strongly rejected these ideas, for they went against the philosophy of the school. "We want our peers to understand the reasons why they are doing this, not to do it because they will win a prize or feel threatened," she argued. Armando and a few others insisted on the implementation of rewards and penalties, arguing that it was a common practice in other schools, and others continued to explain why this would lead to the results they wanted.

"Well, if you want to just try to convince them all that they should do this because it's the right thing, it's going to take you forever. You may never see results," Armando argued.

"I disagree because that is the very point of this activity, but I also believe in making democratic decisions. So let's put it to a vote," Diana responded.

Armando was used to top-down decision-making, which was a lot more efficient. He wanted to set short-term, measurable goals and get them done in a specific time frame, but Diana, who believed it was impossible to define how long it would take for students to embrace this way of life, insisted on a longer-term vision. After a long time of deliberation, most students voted against Armando's proposal and it was rejected.

As they moved into a discussion of how to raise consciousness among the students, Diana argued that they needed to have a theory to frame and give cohesiveness to their project. Diana proposed the idea of *permaculture,* a holistic approach to ecological ethics and sustainability.[2] "This goes beyond recycling and conserving water. We are an element in the ecosystem, so it includes not just purifying the earth, but also ourselves, our own minds and bodies, before we can think of the environment."

The discussion led to a range of topics that concerned them, including issues of violence, malnutrition, alternative and natural medicine, and even gender roles and teen pregnancy. When they brainstormed ideas for a slogan, Armando suggested "Without Borders." "I like your idea, Armando," Diana responded, "because this is precisely what we want, to transgress borders of many kinds."

Unfortunately, the initiative was not completely successful, as the committee was ultimately unable to sustain itself and the enthusiasm eventually eroded for many of the students, especially those in their first year. Nevertheless, Diana's leadership revealed her own autogestión. Through the process, she learned about obstacles and challenges in engaging in collective action, and she also experienced what it was like to lead and undertake her own initiatives in ways that were meaningful to her. Diana admitted to me at the end of the school year:

> I don't regret the experience. I struggled in trying to help some of my peers see that what matters is the intrinsic desire to make things better and in overcoming apathy. But I learned a lot from this experience. I cannot change others, but I can change myself.

For others, witnessing Diana's autogestión was also a learning experience. This was the first opportunity for many of the first-year students to create something on their own and break through old paradigms of top-down initiatives. Moreover, it provided opportunities for student-directed dialogue, where many of the new students' traditional views were challenged in dialogue by their peers for the first time or where they saw a young female peer take the lead.

Conclusion

In this chapter I have tried to unpack the specific ways in which women found and contributed to the co-creation of a space that addressed their unique needs, tapped into their own ways of knowing, and allowed them to engage in creative and authentic action and cultural production. By offering first and foremost a space of peace, safety, and trust, Altavista functioned as a *sanctuary school* (Antrop-González 2006) characterized by caring relations between students and their teachers, a place where students viewed their peers and teachers as family, and where they felt safe from psychological and physical harm.

For the young women, Altavista was a co-created space that promoted their ways of knowing, validated their experiences, nurtured pride in their community, and privileged their sociopolitical and heuristic knowledge in its curriculum, instruction, and cultural practices. The women participated in the dialectical process of building and shaping this space as they organically enacted their own pedagogical practices through their habitual testimonial discourse and activism. The learning that resulted was based on more than rationality, as other ways of knowing that are traditionally ignored, discouraged, or stigmatized even in critical pedagogy (Ellsworth 1989) took center stage. The autogestión that the women developed, even if at various degrees, allowed them to generate and validate their own community-situated cultural and social capital, as well as acquire a language of critique and boldness for social action, while maintaining the hope and vision to forge their own futures.

In explaining the elements that characterize critical hope, Jeff Duncan-Andrade (2009), drawing from Tupac Shakur, refers to young urban people who overcome socially poisonous environments as the "roses that grow from concrete." To Duncan-Andrade, in order for these roses to emerge, there have to be cracks in the concrete—spaces of possibility. Altavista offered such spaces in which women could envision, create, build, interrogate, speak up, take action, and collectively take steps toward healing. As the young women learned and grew in this relatively protected space, they embraced the material justification to hope in the midst of pain and engaged in autogestión—a form of action stemming from freedom, critical reflection, and collective and politicized identities. In sum, Altavista's enactment of critical pedagogy equipped them to carve out and shape their own space for reflection, action, self-authorship, and the co-construction of empowered identities.

CHAPTER 5

Mujeres Autogestivas

Young Women Authoring Their Identities

Without a sense of identity, there can be no real struggle.

—Paulo Freire, *Pedagogy of the Oppressed*

ACCORDING TO LUIS URRIETA (2007), identity is the basis for agency. That is, beliefs and concepts of self often serve as a guide to the actions and direction that we give to our lives. In this chapter, my intention is to uncover some of the ways in which schooling at Altavista impacted the intimate worlds of the young women and hence fostered the self-authorship and political identities characteristic of their autogestión. As has been previously discussed, the interaction of Altavista's core dimensions—freedom and autonomy, politically aware authentic caring relationships, and the promotion of critical discourse—served to socialize students into a collective subaltern identity and provided a space that fostered autogestión. While the young women were autogestivas in initiating their own projects and forms of activism, it was in their intimate lives where their autogestión was negotiated and crafted. Through the self-authoring of their identities, the young women's agency became more evident, as in many cases this self-authoring challenged the social determinism that may assume them as victims or a lost cause given the realities of their social context. On the other hand, and as previously noted, their autogestión also challenged postfeminist and neoliberal ideas of "girl power" (Harris 2004; Taft 2004; Ringrose 2007) as well as definitions of women's empowerment that tend to focus on economic development as the main and most important result. It is this intimate aspect of these women's autogestión that this chapter will attempt to reveal.

In chapter 4, I offered insight into the role Altavista played in the lives of a group of women whom I call the *Refugees*. This chapter presents three different journeys that the rest of the protagonists of this book followed in their identity construction: the *Redirectors*, the *Reinventors*, and the *Redefiners*.

These girls are different from the Refugees presented in chapter 4 in that in addition to finding a space of peace at Altavista, they appeared to have experienced significant transformations during their high school years. Each one of the three journeys in this typology involves various degrees of influence from the school as well as various degrees and forms of self-authorship and agency. This typology is based mostly on the young women's life history narratives and testimonios shared during interviews, but it also includes the informal conversations that I witnessed or had with them, field notes, and the debriefing of the photography activity.

In the following sections, I provide a description of each one of these three pathways as well as portraits of four different young women, Gabriela, Diana, Karla, and Marsella, whose journeys appeared to be the most representative. As has been noted before, not all the women participated in all the activities or to the same degree. Therefore, the women whom I have selected to illustrate these journeys are those with whom I spent the most time and/or those who shared the most information and thus I got to know better. However, I also provide a brief discussion of the other women who may fall in each typology at least to some extent. These additional illustrations may be briefer, in part to avoid redundancy as their stories might have already been shared in another chapter or simply because they might not have participated in all the data collection activities, and thus my knowledge of them is more limited.

My analysis involved the identification of salient themes across the data, as well as an analysis of the continuity in the narratives that gave insights into the individual trajectory of each woman (Polkinghorne 1995). In particular, I paid attention to the ways in which the women discursively constructed and made sense of their lives through their narratives, gave meaning to seemingly random or chaotic events, and interpreted how Altavista, as well as particular experiences, people, and other factors, gave way to a change in their trajectory or strengthened their perspectives (Bruner 1985).

An important aspect of my analysis included capturing how lived experiences, as mundane as they might seem, shaped their intimate concepts of self and thus their agency in the various realms they inhabited—including those collective spaces of cultural practices and social relations (Cain 1998; Holland et al. 1998; Urrieta 2007). In particular, I paid attention to how gendered experiences as young women at the intersection of race and class contributed to the formation of their *self* consciousness, and how this moved them into a *collective* consciousness through a "'womanist' sensibility or approach to power, knowledge, and relationships rooted in convictions for community uplift" (Villenas et al. 2006, 7).

The typology I propose illustrates three different journeys, but they are not always mutually exclusive, nor are they the only existing ones. In some cases these pathways could be seen as phases, as they overlap in some ways and/or build on each other. The extent of the women's agency in orchestrating the messages from their own life history as well as those from the multiple worlds they inhabited was diverse and complex, and without a doubt, much of the influence that Altavista had on the girls' development of autogestión was contingent on other heuristic tools they brought with them. Therefore, each one of the women and their stories were unique, even when fitting into the same category. Moreover, not all of them fit the typology perfectly, and I do not claim that these pathways to self-authoring are the only ones possible at Altavista or elsewhere; I am sure there are other possibilities that did not clearly emerge in my data. However, the three pathways I present are the most salient patterns that emerged in my analysis, which shed light on the girls' agency and can be useful in understanding the development of autogestión and the empowering role that a school with a critical and social-justice orientation can have in the lives of urban young women.

The Redirectors: Rebels with a Cause

Adolescent rebellion is the poster image of the teenage years. Whether interpreted as resistance to pressure to conform or to comply, it is a demonstration of the assertion of independence and individuality challenging the powers that be. The *Redirectors* are characterized by a recently developed ability to refocus the course of their lives and deliberately rechannel their forms of resistance. Out of all the girls I met at Altavista, the Redirectors were the most passionate and committed activists. However, their resistance had not always been channeled in empowering ways. At Altavista, the Redirectors learned to be reflexive about their forms of resistance— from the individual to the collective—and to move from reckless opposition to intentional agency.

Diana and Gabriela are good examples of Redirectors, and, to some extent, Iliana also fits this group. Generally speaking, the girls represented by this group had been restless and had expressed their discontent with society from an early age. It is also possible, as in the cases of Diana, Gabriela, and Iliana, that activism and social and political consciousness were initially fostered by at least one family member. Because the Redirectors could easily sense impositions, injustice, and coercion, they were not easily tamed. Often misunderstood, these girls might have behaved and/or have been perceived as rebellious, obstinate, aggressive, and in some cases conceited.

Typically perceiving themselves as different or as the outcasts, the Redirectors might have become somewhat isolated or might have joined other groups of kids or even adults who exhibited the same kind of behavior and/or perspectives. As activists, initially they might have been followers rather than organizers. And although their awareness of power and oppression compelled them to participate in important grassroots forms of social action, at the personal level they were not always successful at differentiating empowering and liberating forms of resistance from self-damaging activities.

While bright, these girls experienced disapproval from teachers and even peers prior to attending Altavista due to their defiant behavior. Unmotivated by subtractive and domesticating schooling experiences, they had almost given up on their pursuit for formal education. Arriving at Altavista was a lucky and timely opportunity for reflection and liberation. The freedom and nurturing that these girls received at Altavista, a growing critical consciousness, and new destabilizing experiences in their lives helped them reflect on their past, present, and future, and to develop more strategic and thoughtful forms of resistance. This reflexivity is the crucial element that characterizes the Redirectors' self-authoring process. As they began to reflect on the self, they were able to redirect the course of their lives and their agency in more deliberate ways.

Portrait of a Redirector: Gabriela

Gabriela was seventeen years old when I met her, and she described herself as sincere, inquisitive, and strong. As I got to know her, I realized she could not have chosen better descriptors. Gabriela had a sweet smile and carried herself with confidence. Far from the typical "feminine" look, she wore torn sneakers, old clothes with a distinct "hippie" style, her hair in dreadlocks, and no makeup except for the occasional lipstick. I would see her hang out by herself, just with the girls, or with her boyfriend or big groups of friends. She was an artist who enjoyed playing music; writing songs, raps, and poetry; painting; and making bracelets. Bob Marley and the Beatles were among her favorite musicians.

Gabriela intrigued me since the first time I observed her in class. What got my attention were not only her unique dress style but also her contemplative demeanor—relaxed and intense at the same time, almost mysterious. She listened intently in class as if hanging onto every word that came out of the teacher's mouth. Gabriela was also one of the most participative and inquisitive young women. She asked questions and offered insightful comments during class discussions and seemed to be a leader among her peers.

It did not take long to confirm that Gabriela was a very intelligent and independent young woman, and one of the most active students in the school. She spoke a vernacular barrio Spanish, interspersed with advanced academic vocabulary as she eloquently articulated her point of view. She was not afraid to say what she thought, but she spoke calmly and whoever was around always listened. It was clear that other students, male and female alike, gravitated toward her. During recess I would often see Gabriela hanging out with the "hippies," teachers, or other mixed groups, smoking a cigarette, playing her guitar, or singing songs.

One of the first things I learned about her was that employers usually rejected her job applications due to her appearance. Not willing to change her style, Gabriela would try to make a few pesos selling her crafts on the streets and boulevards, while her boyfriend did his torch juggling routines. Other times she sold candy or homemade burritos.

Indeed, experiencing rejection and discrimination due to her appearance was part of everyday life—she was dark skinned, her working-class background was evident in her dress, and she simply looked "different," as she intentionally rejected hyperfeminized styles and the latest fashion. One afternoon after school, I took Gabriela and her cousin Iliana to the administrative offices of the Autonomous University of Ciudad Juárez (UACJ) to claim a scholarship for their college application. As soon as they walked into the administrative building, the security guard looked at Gabriela suspiciously and asked her to provide a photo ID. I did not see him do this to the other girls of middle-class appearance who walked in before us.

Gabriela grew up in a single-parent, working-class home. She had one brother and two older sisters who left home long ago to form their own families, so at the time of the study she lived only with her mother and her sixteen-year-old sister, Alejandra. Her mother was a supervisor at a local supermarket, where she worked very long hours and earned the equivalent of about $150 a month. Some weeks, entire days went by without Gabriela being able to see her mother due to conflicting schedules. She often expressed feelings of loneliness growing up, which, coupled with her curious and inquisitive personality, led her to a path of hasty explorations that got her into much trouble.

Growing up, then, had been a turbulent journey. As a child, she had witnessed violence in the home until her mother divorced her abusive father. Later, Gabriela's mother found a new partner whom neither Gabriela nor her sister Alejandra ever liked. He had lived in their home for some years, causing much conflict until he was murdered a few months before I met her—another casualty of the cartel turf wars. Therefore, the scarcest resource for Gabriela was not money or material possessions but peace. The feelings of anxiety and fear caused by the violence and loneliness she witnessed at home were only exacerbated by the context of the city: "From the beginning with the feminicides I shaped my perspective of Juárez, and since those times I used to be afraid. Then later came all these murders, and I do feel somewhat stressed out to think that we have never overcome this violence," Gabriela confessed.

Despite, or perhaps precisely because of, these everyday challenges, Gabriela had cultivated a love for reading and writing, and her inquisitive nature had made her a good student since she was a little girl. But school had not always been a joyful place either. As mentioned in chapter 3, Gabriela had attended a middle school that had been extremely repressive of her racial identity and demanded a physical appearance that followed white normative attributes, such as forcing her to tame and straighten her Afro-textured hair with a flat iron on a daily basis. That Gabriela obeyed her middle school's racist hairstyling demands did not necessarily mean that she did it without objection. She resisted in various ways the arbitrary impositions from the school.

> They would make us stand up to greet any adult that entered
> the classroom. I thought it was so ridiculous, so I began messing
> with them by standing whenever one of my classmates who was
> eighteen years old walked in. The teachers would get annoyed and
> I would respond, "He's an adult too, isn't he? You said you wanted
> me to do that with every adult." Of course, I was being sarcastic,

but it seemed to me that they just wanted to keep us students down and blindly obedient.

Gabriela's tendency to interrogate the ways in which authorities demanded subjugation was fostered from an early age. Although very young, Gabriela already had a long history of activism. Since she was about eleven years old, she would join her brother, an urban artist and musician, at various shows and help him paint murals in bars and other parts of town. That is how she got to know many of the barrio artists and musicians whose work was of social critique. Moreover, her oldest sister, a law school graduate and community organizer, got her involved in the NGO CASA Promoción Juvenil as well as in feminist workshops and other activist events in the community.

The feminicides had been Gabriela's first issue of concern. Growing up in the discourse of danger for women did cause fear, but it also prompted her to action.

> Ever since I was a little girl I would hear about the murders and the things they did to women. In fact, that was the first issue that I undertook. Ever since I had use of reason, I would be working on campaigns with my sister Paty. We did marches and organized activities for the International Day for the Elimination of Violence Against Women on March 28 and other dates commemorating all the Mexican women who were raped or murdered. So from the beginning I was involved in those things and I shaped my perspective of Juárez.

With this background, it was not surprising that one of the most important characteristics that attracted Gabriela to Altavista was the school's reputation and contributions to grassroots movements among local activists. When Gabriela heard about Altavista's critical orientation, she knew it would be the best fit for her.

> I was involved in a group called Rezizte [a group of urban artists whose work highlights border culture and social critique] and I knew a girl who would talk a lot about Altavista. She told me that Subcomandante Marcos had visited the school. I also talked to another girl who knew Juan [the curriculum specialist and

language arts teacher], and she told me everything about it. So I enrolled and decided to stay here because I liked it a lot.

Indeed, Gabriela's perspective of Juárez was shaped by growing up in the discourse of the feminicides, her life in the barrio, and her involvement in various local social movements before and during her time at Altavista. To her, her activism and her education were not necessarily two separate things. In fact, she often invited the activists she knew in the city to events that she helped organize at school, such as Altavista Fest.

Contributing to the grassroots culture of the school was not difficult for Gabriela. She was acquainted with many of the barrio activists in the city, including women like La Oveja Negra, an underground hip-hop MC and rap writer whose lyrics denounced the injustices in Juárez, and Arminé Arjona, a poet, writer, and urban artist whose graffiti of social critique appeared on various walls around the city. Gabriela had also been a friend of Géminis Ochoa, the leader of the street vendors union "Che Guevara." She recalled the summer of 2009, when the longtime dreadlocked activist had been gunned down in broad daylight in downtown Juárez while organizing a demonstration against the army's abuse of vendors.

> Did you meet Géminis? Last year he told Eduardo [her boyfriend] and me, "Do you have any artwork or crafts that you want to sell? Come here tomorrow and I'll have a stand for you." He spoke with us in the morning and by the afternoon they had already killed him. They killed him because he was the leader of the street vendors, and since he was making too many waves the soldiers killed him right there in downtown in the midst of all the people. It was all over the news. I went to support his wife because they had always helped the people . . . and they killed him for being a revolutionary. And now there is no leader, and many of the vendor stands are going down because there are only a few people who really want to do something good for the people. Géminis was one of them. If you told him, "We have a colonia where the children have nothing to eat," he would raise the money and buy milk and bread for everyone.

This was not the only time Gabriela had witnessed the repression of the state against those who spoke up. She had also been part of the group who got Lolo—one of her Altavista teachers—out of jail when he was arrested during a demonstration a couple of years earlier. Gabriela and her friends had also been persecuted by the police and the military multiple times, in part because of her appearance and her involvement in social movements. Gabriela's involvement with CASA Promoción Juvenil contributed to her development of a strong activist network, but much of her grassroots activity also stemmed from her experiences of being alone and hanging out in the barrio. She explained that although many of the things she had seen and experienced had been very intense and disturbing, they had helped her develop her critical consciousness.

One morning in April, I noticed that Gabriela had skipped her first two classes. Later that afternoon, I saw her standing all by herself under a tree's shade. When I approached her, she explained to me that she had been late because a terrible incident had occurred that morning. She was going to meet with some of her friends from the barrio before coming to school, but she had arrived to the meeting place late and found some of her friends crying. Apparently the police had been chasing one of them, and a few minutes later they found him dead on the ground. Although she did not see what happened, she was sure it had been the police.

They are always after us. When we went to the last march [a city-wide demonstration against the violence and impunity in Juárez], a couple of police officers told us, "We know who you are, you better watch out because we're going to hunt you until we get each one of you." And yeah, you'll see them roaming in the barrio threatening us.

Gabriela seemed extremely sad and angry, but she appeared surprisingly calm. "It's always like this," she said with a mix of resignation and deep anger. "Everyone was crying, and yes I cried a lot too, but I have to be strong."

How can a young woman remain so strong and poised after all these dramatic experiences? As I got to know Gabriela better, she revealed that she had not always been this calm, and that while the streets had taught her important lessons, she had also been harmed.

Sometimes I think that other kids at my age would have never experienced what I experienced. It would be a new world for them. I might be very young, but I've been through a lot. I learned about everything out on the streets. There I was in all those movements

since I was a young girl. It helped me open up my vision to the leftist world. But it also led me to fall into other things, like drugs and
all that.

She explained that a teacher-activist who was visiting one of the movements from Zacatecas once commended her for getting involved in all
those social movements, but he warned her of hanging out with the wrong
crowd and of the dangers of doing drugs like some of the barrio activists.
At the time, however, she was young and naïve and did not listen to his
advice. She let herself get carried away and believed that drugs would help
her think at deeper levels and increase her creativity. Therefore, during
her early adolescent years, Gabriela's forms of resistance, rather than being
productive and liberating, in many cases were aggressive and caused great
grief to her family. Gabriela's testimonio of her aggressive behavior (see
chapter 3) revealed the anger and sense of superiority or perhaps a necessity to feel powerful that moved her to mistreat others.

I used to be real crazy; I got into drugs and everything, but I began
to change because I got into a lot of trouble. Since in my mind I
was superior, I thought I could do anything, and I didn't give a shit
about what anyone thought. I would get all drunk and all that. . . .
I got into punk culture and that really messed me up. I used to hang
out with guys all the time, with punks, who trained me real good to
be aggressive. This one guy, he would hit me and I would punch
him in the face with all my strength, like *a vato* [guy]. Out of
nowhere, they would make my anger come out. I behaved like a
chola [female gang member], and I was an anarchist, so *la chota*
[the police] meant nothing to me.

These forms of oppositional behavior should not only be considered as
poor choices or reckless rebellion (see Willis 1977). Rather, Gabriela's resistance stems from an accumulated anger resulting from witnessing impunity, hypocrisy, and repression on the part of the authorities against the
poor, women, the youth, and activists for years. "You don't know how many
times I've seen *chotas* [police officers] come to the bars to sell cocaine,
pot, *chiva* [heroin], all kinds of stuff," she explained, "but most people
don't know about that, and if I told them they wouldn't believe me." This,

coupled with the control of young women's bodies and movement at home, in schools, and in the streets, resulted in a nonstop chain of repression and regulation that provoked a continuous state of resistance. These conditions blurred the real reasons for Gabriela's discontent and acts of rebellion and made it difficult for her to reflect on whether her forms of resistance were beneficial.

However, in the last few years at Altavista, Gabriela embarked on a journey of self-reflection in which she began to see some of her acts of resistance as counterproductive. She attempted to align her behavior with who she really wanted to be. Gabriela explained how a process of reflection initiated this transformation that was still taking place.

> Then I started to think that that attitude didn't match who I really was, so I began to change. I still like the same music but I left that life behind. I changed because I saw how it was affecting my family, especially my sister. You know my younger sister? I was always fighting with her, and she couldn't defend herself because she was younger than me. I would pull her hair and hit her, and with a lot of anger, but I didn't know where that anger came from. And I was making my mother ill. Like I didn't know what it was that I wanted or anything. But one day something got into me. I don't know what it was, but I realized that I couldn't keep living like that. . . . I saw myself in the mirror, how skinny I was getting and I thought, if I continue on this path, I'm gonna die.

While Gabriela did not attribute her transformation directly to Altavista, during an interview, Gabriela revealed that the school offered her a safe space where she could reshape her identity and take a new direction without being judged. She contrasted this environment to her experiences in middle school that aimed to tame and discipline not only her behavior but also her way of dress and even her hair under white normativity.

> It did affect me in some way what they did to me in middle school because I used to love my hair, and they wouldn't let me be who I was. But I have changed. . . . When I saw the freedom here [at Altavista], I knew that nobody would tell me anything, so I started by dreadlocking my burnt hair. . . . I have liberated myself, as some

would call it. I have felt freer because I can wear my hair any way I want and dress any way I want, and I can now think what I want to think.

This freedom offered Gabriela a relief from a life of constant and continuous resistance, and provided a peaceful space to reflect on her identity and the direction she wanted to give to her life.

I used to listen to punk music, and I had the same ideas that I have always had, but punk culture was aggressive, it was an aggressive stage. . . . So then I thought, no, that's not worth it. I've always been calm and I like to think things through, even when I'm with really loud and reckless friends. It was like I didn't belong to that because they are aggressive and like to fight. And I like to fight too, but with real reasons and arguments.

In other words, the changes that she experienced did not imply that Gabriela became silent or stopped resisting the oppression in her life but rather suggested that she became more thoughtful about expressing her resistance in ways that were congruent with the identity she wanted for herself.

Gabriela's transformation was also apparent in the way she related to others. Her relationship with her sister improved significantly, and although she had some relapses with marijuana, she had made major progress in staying away from drugs. In school, she went from being an angry and self-isolated person who refused to talk to anyone to a friendly young woman with a keen eye toward identifying those who needed a friend. She began to reach out to peers, especially those who appeared isolated or were new to Altavista. As will be evident in the stories of other young women, she was often the one who offered friendship in vulnerable times. Three of the other girls I interviewed pointed to Gabriela as the first person who ever reached out to them and helped them get acclimated to the school.

In this and other ways, Gabriela played a major role as a socialization agent and actively contributed to the cultural and philosophical dimensions of the school. She was often the initiator or leader of various cultural activities, both formal and informal, and she even recruited her friends who were often like-minded to enroll at the school.

There were no bands when I enrolled at Altavista. Almost everyone was kind of normal. . . . I mean, they just came to school and
that was it. So we started spreading the word about the school and
other kids from other high schools would say, "I'm going to get out
of that prison and come here."

Therefore, by the time I met her, Gabriela was probably the most popular girl. Her popularity, however, was not manifested in the same ways
as Hollywood portrays popular high school girls. She did not seem to be
interested in getting the boys' attention, being the prettiest one, or wearing
the latest fashions. In fact, Gabriela appeared to give little importance to
how people perceived her. She was known for her unusual style that challenged the prototypical girly look, her openness and sincerity, as well as
her initiative in promoting cultural and social justice activities.

Gabriela also distinguished herself, especially among other young
women, for her poised demeanor, confidence, and wisdom, which was
another way in which she contributed to the cultural production at Altavista. In fact, Marsella, one of her peers, firmly asserted that if she had to
pick a role model, it would be Gabriela. Marsella admired Gabriela's confidence and self-love. "Some say that she's gross, that she doesn't shower
because she wears her hair in dreadlocks. But she doesn't care what people
say. She says what she thinks and she's not afraid to be herself," Marsella
explained with great respect.

A couple of other girls also shared the high regard they had for Gabriela
by sharing a story that occurred the previous semester. Gabriela had been
picked up by the military and had been kept hostage for about three days.
Apparently she had been taking a cigarette break outside one of the meeting places for an NGO that she was involved with. A group of soldiers
patrolling the neighborhood found her suspicious and put her in the jeep
with several other people. Her reaction was completely different to the
way she would have reacted in the past. Cristina expressed her version of
the story with much admiration.

There were elderly people and even a young pregnant girl in that
jeep. But those soldiers don't care about anything. They kept
Gabriela there all those days, and her family and all of us at
Altavista were desperately looking for her. They didn't give them

water, and they didn't let them call their families or anything. The pregnant girl started getting really sick, and it was Gabriela who tried to calm her down and who tried to reason with the soldiers, until finally they dropped them all off in downtown.

Another progressive transformation in Gabriela in the year I got to know her was her perspective on women. In the past and even during our first interview, she had indicated that she preferred to hang out with men. In her view, women tended to be superficial, worried about boys way too much, and were conflictive and easily manipulated: "Some girls look like telenovela characters, literally! They dress like them, they talk like them, and they think like them." Gabriela had resisted hegemonic expectations of women by separating herself from other girls and by engaging in typically masculine activities, such as skateboarding and playing the guitar. "I like to show them [the boys] that I can also do things just like them. One time a guy asked me how come I could play the guitar if I was a girl. 'Well and why not?' I said, 'if I have fingers and a brain!'"

As time progressed, there was a small but noticeable change in Gabriela's attitude toward girls. Although she still felt that she could not see eye to eye with most girls, and she continued to engage in the same activities as before, such as making music and hanging out with skaters, she had now more girl-friends. In particular, at Altavista, she tended to spend most of her free time with other girls when she was not with her boyfriend, playing the guitar, or writing by herself. She also held several of them in high esteem. This transformation and reflection allowed her to begin to look at women's behaviors as part of a social context from a much more critical perspective.

Some girls are very *truchas* [smart]. And I understand that sometimes we need those woman-to-woman conversations. . . . But I often wonder why girls don't participate as much as boys in class. I sit there and observe, and I wonder why, if they are also smart.

Therefore, in recent years, rather than rejecting women and dismissing them as foolish like she did in the past, she began to question the factors in society that led women to behave in certain ways, and to find ways to express solidarity with them. During her last semester as a senior at Altavista, Gabriela organized a women's group.

We wanted to do the women's group. It's because I would like to help the girls destress. Like us girls think about a lot of stuff, we worry a lot. So what I wanted to tell them was to have a variety of activities, like arts and crafts, or something like that to destress. The plan was to also establish a theme. First a game or activity, then a reflection, maybe a debate. Even if you don't know anything, to share your opinions, whatever you want to contribute, and then a time to relax, I don't know, to have some food. . . . We've already done it twice and we had a lot of girls. The first time we introduced ourselves, the things we liked, our age, zodiac sign, and shared one positive thing and one negative thing about us. And so we started getting to know each other.

Interestingly, although she eventually wanted to be able to discuss topics that would allow the women to engage in critical consciousness raising, at the moment what she found most imperative was to have a space for young women to be themselves and "destress," revealing her understanding of the pressures, fears, and control to which many girls were often subjected. Also, while Gabriela was the main organizer of this activity, she still spoke as "we," acknowledging how at the end of the day this was always a collective effort. Although Gabriela became busy with other things at the end of the school year and her women's group only met twice, it had been well attended, and it revealed a redirection of the ways she resisted hegemonic impositions on women. Rather than avoiding women, she began to reach out to them and redirected her efforts to build a space for authentic women's voices to emerge.

This is just one example of how at Altavista, with a much more peaceful and self-reflexive state of mind, Gabriela continued to be as critical and radical as before, and to focus on social justice issues in new ways. She wrote raps and poetry of social critique and continued to participate in and organize social movements. However, she now focused on developing tools for deliberate collective resistance rather than following any form of rebellion without a clear mission. Gabriela was one of the main organizers of the march on October 2, as well as the Altavista Fest, which was a prelude to the citywide march against the violence in Juárez. Her goal through all these efforts was to raise consciousness and build capacity for mutual support.

I tell teacher Lolo that I like to invoke people to clear things out because right now many people are very confused. Right now you can say just about anything and they immediately believe it. That's why we need to keep people informed, but not through the mainstream media because that's nothing but manipulation. But we have to inform each other, among ourselves. Right now we, the students, are going to organize a march, and that's where we can hope for the best. That's where we can talk to them and clear things out and let people know about what's happening and about what they can do to come out and help each other and themselves.

Although Gabriela never ceased to maintain her idealism, she was not naïve either. She had wanted to organize a social movement against the violence in the city but knew that very little could be expected from people paralyzed by fear.

Everyone is scared. "What if they kill us?" they say. You don't know who the enemy is; it could be your neighbor, or it could be the authorities. So I do think that the people can rise and lift up their voices, but they're scared. . . . At the march, I saw the expression of my people, because there were elderly women marching and jumping. And the people inspired me *machín* [a lot]. But then again, it might be just a movement and nothing else, a movement that comes and goes.

Despite the little impact these movements might have in creating actual change, Gabriela refused to give up. During one of our last conversations, Gabriela talked with enthusiasm about the many postgraduation projects she had in mind. Indeed, Gabriela's ideas were quite radical: "I want to have my own little house, and plant a garden, and live off of that, outside of capitalism." Gabriela's utopian dream was to develop a self-sustained community in the most organic sense of the word. But at the same time, Gabriela was practical and realistic. She explained to me that at first she had thought of going to college to major in music, but she was very aware of the fact that she would not be able to make a living as an artist. Philosophy was another major she had considered, but she thought her prospects with a degree in philosophy would be the same as with a degree in the fine arts. Thus, with a mix of practicality and idealism, she considered teaching as the ideal career for her. As an educator she would have greater possibilities to utilize her artistic talents, continue to do critical work and make a difference in her community, *and* put food on the table. She thus dreamed of having her own school one day, a school similar to Altavista where the talents from the barrio were seen as assets. This revealed that she saw schooling as a potential and effective vehicle from which to enact autogestión and social change.

On graduation day, after the formal speeches were over, Gabriela stood up without being called on. She walked decidedly to the stage and took over the podium. The students and teachers looked at her with enthusiasm and anticipation as she prepared to read from a wrinkled piece of paper torn out of a notebook. With great emotion, Gabriela expressed the love she had for her school and her gratitude to the teachers for allowing her and her peers to embrace their own individuality and to experience freedom. Moved by her words, several students wiped tears of joy.

Portrait of a Redirector: Diana

Diana was another clear example of a Redirector. I was immediately drawn to Diana due to her visibility in the school, inside and outside the classroom. A second-year Altavista student, Diana was participative in her classes, articulate, inquisitive, and extremely active in school-wide projects. Diana had big dark eyes, and long, dark, wavy hair. Light skinned, petite, and slender, Diana was a little shorter than I. But her smile and her personality seemed greater than life. She dressed in a variety of styles, from bohemian and punk to simple jeans, layered tank tops, and lots of bracelets. Diana described herself as straightforward and open.

> I feel like I don't have any taboos. I am very sincere and sometimes too much. Sometimes I hurt people with my sincerity. I am very much a perfectionist. I easily trust others, and almost anyone can be my friend. And that's why I've been hurt in the past. And my faults? I am proud, very proud. Just like my mother. I am not patient.

As I have noted before, Diana was very excited to participate in the study. To her, this was an opportunity to have a voice in the public discourse about young Juárez women. Therefore, she was always enthusiastic and took her participation in the study seriously.

The daughter of an educated woman, Diana enjoyed relatively more privilege than the rest of the young women. Her mother, a lesbian single parent, had taught Diana about the strength that was needed when a woman lived against the current. This was particularly true considering that Diana's grandmother was somewhat conservative. Diana deeply admired her mother, who, in addition to the boldness she demonstrated in her personal life, was also a psychologist and an activist dedicated to women's issues. The influence of her mother, coupled with her own strong personality, made Diana naturally outspoken and critical. This critical awareness and boldness, however, had not always been an asset in Diana's life. Diana had not enjoyed a good relationship with schools, neither teachers nor students.

> In middle school I was "*la apestosita*" [the stinky one, the undesirable person], like "Ugh here she comes, the feisty one, the one who argues about everything, the one who can never keep her mouth shut." Because that's how I am; I mean, if I don't like something, I speak up. And I don't care who it is. So they did not like me in middle school.

While smart and capable, Diana had been unmotivated and discouraged by her disciplining middle school. She learned to view school as nothing more than a meaningless routine:

> So before I was very monotonous, I would think, "Ugh school!" Like in eighth and ninth grade, I was so reluctant to get up to go to school, to put on my uniform, to go and put up with my teachers, pretend that I'm listening to them. And that was it, every day.

It was not surprising then that Diana maintained mediocre grades all through middle school. Her analysis of her low academic performance and discouragement, however, underscores that her problem was more than boredom.

> This is the problem that most of us have, that in middle school they tell us, "Look, here is the honor roll," and if I am the one who has the best grades, the rest are the stinky ones, the dummies, the ones who can't learn, the ones who never do anything. Then,

instead of striving to be interested in what they are teaching you . . . your motivator has to be to become like somebody else, or having to compete. . . . And so before, I used to care a lot about grades, and I thought I was putting in a lot of effort, but I still would get 70s and 60s.

Diana was not afraid to speak about her discontent with the traditional Mexican education system. In fact, she considered it a stumbling block for intelligent kids, who, like her brother, ended up dropping out. This would probably have been Diana's destiny as well if it had not been for her mother's persistence. Given the selective process of most high schools, Diana's grades would not have opened many doors. It was instead due to her success in athletics that Diana still had a chance after middle school to be admitted into a reputable high school in her neighborhood. However, her experience trying to enroll led to further disappointment with schooling.

I was in track and field and I was going to enroll directly at [one of] the Centro de Bachillerato Tecnológico Industrial y de Servicios [CBTIS], but because of my lack of interest I did not enroll. And this was because one day I went to visit the school and I was assaulted and they stole my cell phone. And there were four young people who saw everything, two girls and two guys, and they did not offer me any help. That was another disappointment, that not even among us women can we support each other. So I rushed out, crying and trembling. I mean, it was too many things. And there was only an older woman who came out and helped me. And I thought, "Instead of caring for each other as young people, it's the opposite." So that was what caused my lack of interest. And so I didn't study the study guide and I didn't pass the admissions test. I spent the entire summer depressed and doing nothing. And my mother told me, "You're going to attend Valdés High School [pseudonym]." It's very close to my house and it's a Catholic school. And I said, "I don't believe in God, much less in the Catholic Church. It's one of the worst religions, one of the most disastrous. How am I going to attend a school like that if I don't believe in that? They're going to kick me out in two days!" So my mother told me, "Look, close to my job there is a school called Preparatoria Altavista."

So Diana and her mother headed to a women's organization where her mother worked to ask for directions and the director told Diana, "If you want to attend CBTIS, I can still enroll you there right now. Or do you want to go to Altavista instead?" Diana was not interested in CBTIS anymore and insisted on going to Altavista. It did not take long for Diana to confirm that she had made the right choice.

> We got here on a Friday and classes were starting on the following Monday. So there were a lot of young people around, some with long hair, etcetera. And when I saw them, I thought, "Look this is cool!" . . . So from the first time I came and saw the green areas, which I love, I felt this peace. And I'm very prone to that, to feel the energy of a place as soon as I get there. I can feel the different emotions. And as soon as I got here I told my mother, "Look, this is very nice," and my mother enrolled me that same day. . . . And after I finished my first semester here, I had very good grades, and my grandmother told me, "With those grades, I'm going to enroll you at Preparatoria El Parque [a highly reputed high school]. And I said, "I'm not leaving this school; I'm going to spend eternity here!" The love of my life is this school.

Loving a school had definitely not been part of Diana's experience in the past. What is it that caused such a change? And, more important, in what other ways did her life change and why? In previous chapters, I have discussed how the core principles of Altavista made an impact on Diana and her attitudes toward her own education. For example, she explained how her learning was no longer motivated by grades.

> My perception of grades has changed. I don't care anymore about grades. What matters to me is that I learn, and now I get 100s! . . . I don't care about grades. I mean, OK, they give me my grade, and I come and show it to my mother and that's it. But I don't need to know my grade, but rather that I know that I actually learned something in class. . . . What makes one a good student is to actually be interested in what is being covered in class. But school also has to incite that interest, that hunger to want to know more—it doesn't just impose what you have to learn: "Learn this, learn that, memorize this paper." Why? "Because that's what will be

on the test, so you have to learn it." No, instead I want to be left
with a desire to know more. . . . So, to some extent, a good student
is one who is curious, who wants to learn more. Not someone who
gets along and obeys all the teachers, but someone who seeks
clarity and answers to her questions.

At Altavista, Diana was not only allowed to pursue her own interests
but also treated with the respect and dignity she did not experience in
other schools. The freedom and lack of policing that Diana experienced
humanized her and allowed her to engage in her own learning without
extrinsic motivators. It is no wonder why her grades immediately improved.
It appeared as if the pessimism and disappointment that she had learned to
live with began to dissipate as she met other youth who shared her views.

What I love about Altavista is other students. Yes, there are many
that I see that are like me, enthusiastic. For example, David, a guy
who is very curious and always wants to learn more and more. And
the teachers because they are all so wise and open.

Having restored her trust in humanity and, in some way, in school, Diana
began to open up to reflection. It was the consequences of freedom as
experienced by her, but also by others, as well as opportunities to engage
with teachers and students who demonstrated authentic caring that supported her transformation and the rechanneling of her energies from self-
centered resistance to collective caring and action. By experiencing caring,
she also felt compelled to care.

I have changed a lot! In every way! Because I've become more
tolerant. I used to be worse! Yes, you know how I am right now,
that I'm like "OK, you don't want to follow me? Fine, I'll go alone!"
Well, I used to be worse. I wouldn't even ask if anyone wanted to
come with me. I would just go for what I wanted without looking
back. So I've started to leave my pride behind. ¡Híjole! Altavista has
really helped me with that because I'm very prideful. Because there
have been times that I've been hurtful. For example, with the
things I say, because I'm very sincere and straightforward. But
sometimes I'm extreme. So being here has helped me unsettle my
pride and reflect and say, yes, you messed up here and in this

way. . . . This school and my peers made me change. My first
semester was like before, that people were like "Why don't you
shut up, Diana?" So I didn't think I would make it here. But then
I met Marta and we became friends and that was it; she helped me
develop. And the freedom itself that the school gave me.

As Diana explained, this reflexive process began to help her see the consequences of her words and actions on other people, which before would be
blurred by her pride. At Altavista, she could no longer be that self-centered.
The emphasis on community and understanding that Altavista promoted,
in conjunction with Altavista's insistence on eschewing judgment through
the freedom that it encouraged, helped Diana begin to trust people and
relate to others.

As discussed in chapter 3, a natural consequence was Diana's improved
relationships with her teachers. But this reflexivity and movement from
the self to others also led, as in Gabriela's case, to a significant transformation in her ideas about other women, and it all started with a restored
ability to form friendship relationships with other young women. This
is noted by the fact that she attributes much of her evolution to the influence of her best friend, Marta. Ironically, while Diana admired her mother
and shared most of her feminist beliefs, she had not been very fond of
female friends before attending Altavista. Her ideas of women, however,
needed to change if she wanted to follow her mother's footsteps of feminist activism.

I also changed in my perception of women. Because in middle
school, all of them were so superficial. They were in their own
world, and I often said that I would not hang out with women.
I had two friends, and that's just because they were lesbians, so
they were different. . . . But now I see that not all women are like
that. Before I thought that all women only cared about the clothes
you wore. Or for example, it would get on my nerves that on
Mondays they would be like "This weekend I went to the mall and
I bought clothes at Mango and Express [brand name clothing
stores]," as if it was a competition. They were not my friends.
Instead, it was more about who bought more, or who had the
cutest boyfriend, or who dressed the best, or who had more
money, and things like that. Those are empty conversations and

to me that is superficiality. But here, it's nothing like that. It's very unusual to find a person like that. And I have noticed that.

It is possible that because Diana had access to at least lower-middle-class spaces, she was more prone to find herself in contexts where the pursuit to be considered a member of a higher class was prominent among her peers. But at Altavista, the collective identity was definitely working class, and neither teachers nor most students were interested in pretending to be something they were not. In this way, the intersection of gender and class that affected female discourse in other spaces took a different turn at Altavista, where women also were encouraged to participate in critical discourse and action, and this allowed Diana to be exposed to and explore other ways of being as a young woman.

> Here I have many girlfriends, and in our conversations, we debate, we engage in constructive talk. I mean, we talk about controversial topics. Or for example, I want to go to Cuba for college, and we talk about that and why I want to go. And I mean, they question me, you know? And in fact that has helped me because it has made me do more research so that I could explain to them with strong arguments why. My girlfriends have made me grow a lot.

This new perspective on women also helped Diana be more reflexive and understanding of other women's behaviors without immediately judging them negatively. Diana strongly believed that women and men had the same abilities and potential, and she refused to assume a position of weakness. While she understood that women were often positioned as inferior, she recalled her own attitudes toward women whom she perceived as weak and how these began to change.

> I have a friend who is the oldest among her siblings. So nobody does anything at home but her. I mean, she cleans the house and everything. And in middle school she used to hang out with a lot of guys so that she could go out whenever she wanted. So the teachers would tell her that she would end up getting pregnant before she even finished middle school. Yet she's here today, and she's very intelligent. And in a way, people who didn't know her had that conception of her. At first we didn't like each other. I

didn't like her because I thought that she was too easy, because she would go out with a lot of guys. That's how I judged her at first. But once you get to know her, you realize many things. I mean, her father abuses her and her mother pretends that she doesn't see anything, that she doesn't hear. So in a way she's learned to frame herself as someone who has to be hurt, vulnerable, and who has to tolerate it. . . . It is like if she had become dependent on that. And then she takes care of all the young children in her family. And sometimes she comes to school late because she has to take her little brother to school and then she leaves early because she has to pick him up, like if he was her son. It's like if she had like seven little children. So that is very hard on her. Even at her *quinceañera*, her father was putting on her shoe [a tradition in which the father changes the shoes on his daughter from flats to high heels to symbolize her initiation into adulthood], and he tells her, "You should have told me it was going to be so much hassle and I wouldn't have come." But of course they will never kick her out of her home because she's the maid and the nanny.

Thus, at Altavista, by being able to form new kinds of relationships with women, Diana was able to reflect on her own judgments and began to be more understanding of those who appeared so different from her. Although Diana later shared her testimonio (see chapter 4) of the devastating assault at a veterinary clinic in which she was raped by an armed man, and which most likely connected her even more to other women's struggles, she had already begun her participation in feminist activism through her involvement in women's conferences. At those venues, she had opportunities to read her poetry, which revealed her solidarity, compassion, and understanding of women's issues.

Her transformation into a more patient and tolerant young woman did not subdue her critical consciousness, nor did it dissuade her enthusiasm to take action. On the contrary, it cultivated her ability to be a leader, which is the way she saw herself. Altavista gave her the opportunity to engage in community leadership workshops and in whatever projects she envisioned, while at the same time learning from the setbacks and her work with people who were different from her. This was perhaps the most important lesson from her leadership of the ecological committee discussed in chapter 4. While the committee eventually disappeared, it taught Diana about the importance of tolerance and caring if any effective collective work was to get done.

> I am patient in many things, but one of my faults is that, for example with the ecological committee, I get impatient very easily because sometimes I feel that they don't show interest. I want everything to get done smoothly, but people don't follow my pace. But there are people who are slower and we get impatient with each other.

While Diana spoke about her impatience, in my observations of her behavior during their meetings, I was struck by how democratic she was. She definitely led, but her leadership was characterized by dialogue, even if it took a long time to come to consensus.

Another Redirector: Iliana

Although I did not get to know Iliana in as much depth as Gabriela and Diana, she also expressed that her time at Altavista had resulted in transformation. Iliana was Gabriela's cousin and had a strong indigenous identity. During middle school and in her first year of high school at a different institution, she had developed cynicism about schooling due to the repressive nature of her schools. Her choice of schools was extremely limited due to her financial situation; thus her response to her feelings of oppression was an internalized anger and passive aggression. Tired of these contexts, she came to Altavista, largely motivated by the recommendations of her sisters, who were also Altavista alumni. As in the case of Gabriela and Diana, the freedom she enjoyed at Altavista was something she valued very highly, particularly as this had allowed her to embrace her indigenous identity and tap into alternative knowledges without repression or shame, as well as to pursue her own interests. There were no signs of passive aggression or anger in her. Instead, both teachers and peers viewed her as a pacifist and a trustworthy friend. As calm and quiet as she appeared, Iliana was one of the most involved students in activist initiatives, such as theater for social change, marches, and the ecological committee. In this way, Iliana found ways to express and redirect her resistance from internalized anger and cynicism to collective action.

In sum, Gabriela, Diana, and, to some extent, Iliana exemplify the pathway that Redirectors take in authoring their identities. While these young women might have come to Altavista with a background of critical ideas and activist experiences, they lived at the intersection of multiple oppressions of race, class, and gender, which caused anger to accumulate and made resistance a continuous way of life. This state of constant defensiveness made life confusing and resulted in negative consequences, like isolation in the case of Diana, or affiliation with oppositional groups without questioning their purposes and engagement with self-damage resistance, as in the case of Gabriela. The freedom and authentic caring that Altavista offered allowed Redirectors like Gabriela, Diana, and Iliana to experience a period of relative peace, which fostered reflection and a purposeful self-authoring. In this way, they were also able to refocus their passion for social justice on actual liberating forms of resistance. Moreover, the Redirectors were able to explore the possibilities of collective agency.

The Reinventors: From Caterpillars to Butterflies

When the *Reinventors* entered Altavista they were shy, quiet, and/or repressed to a certain degree, but at Altavista they began to blossom into new personalities. Karla and, to some extent, Mónica fit in this group. For various reasons, these young women had learned to be silent and fearful of people, or had learned to silence their ideas and dreams. In contrast to the Redirectors, the Reinventors did not have a history of oppositional behavior or rebellion. They had learned to follow the rules without much resistance, displaying many of the behaviors attributed to "good girls."

It could be argued that Altavista played a crucial role in the self-authorship of some of these women. The freedom and opportunities for critical discourse offered by the school, in addition to the support from caring teachers and peers, helped these young women begin to explore new ways of being. They progressively abandoned their old suppressed selves and acquired a new voice and the courage to participate or engage in activities and behaviors that they had never envisioned for themselves. They started voicing their opinions both in school and at home and began to shape their own aspirations for the future, relatively more independently of what others might have expected from them in the past.

While these girls participated with great enthusiasm and passion in the activist and social justice projects promoted by the Redirectors, they were seldom the initiators. Instead, they were invested in the project of reinventing the self and helping others do the same. If they initiated any projects, these had as their main goal to help others come out of their shells as well. Eventually, some of these girls may become just as activist oriented as the Redirectors, so it could be argued that some Redirectors were at some point Reinventors as well.

Portrait of a Reinventor: Karla

Before entering the field, I never thought I would feel so self-conscious. I constantly questioned my right to enter the students' lives and to even ask any questions. My fear of being too intrusive might have paralyzed me forever had it not been for Karla, the young woman whose story introduced this book. Warm and bubbly, she approached me one morning during recess as if she had known me for years, "Hi! How are you? I haven't seen you in the past few days! Do you want to come with me to the classroom? We're just doing our homework." And just like that, a few minutes later she was showing me photographs she kept in her bag and telling me all about her family, the boy she had a crush on, her friends, and even her recently murdered uncle.

Karla was seventeen years old when I first met her, and lived with both of her parents. The youngest among her siblings, she was the only child left at home. Karla's father worked as a kitchen supervisor at a maquiladora, and her mother occasionally sold clothes at a flea market. Karla's parents meant the world to her; one of the most important motivators in her life was to make her parents proud. "They have sacrificed so much for me that I don't ever want to let them down," she often said. Karla had a very good relationship with her parents and trusted them completely: "Some girls can't talk with their fathers about anything. My father even knows when I'm on my period." She admired her mother's strength and determination and loved how open minded her father was.

Karla dressed in jeans, colorful T-shirts, and sneakers. But on special occasions she did not hesitate to wear sleek and sexy dresses and very high heels. Very open and proud about her sexuality, she described herself as a "blondie, chubby, with green eyes, and a little crazy" kind of girl. Karla was quite an extrovert and was an especially popular friend among gay and lesbian students and many of the younger students. She liked to study and learn, and her teachers and peers knew her as a very dedicated student. She was also very involved in the arts, such as theater, singing, and painting.

Nonetheless, had it been only three years earlier, she would have probably appeared completely different, and I doubt that she would have approached me. Much to my surprise, she revealed how quiet and shy she used to be when she was in middle school.

> I didn't talk to anyone; I only had one friend. I was very reserved, like I couldn't trust anyone. I used to be very afraid of speaking in public. Whenever I had to do a presentation, I would rather fail than get in front of the class. Thankfully, I was a good student, so none of the teachers ever gave me a failing grade. Some of them would force me to speak in front of the class, but I couldn't speak; I would get stuck.

Although Karla recalled being able to get along with adults much better than with kids her age when growing up, her insecurity caused her to silence herself whenever she was treated unfairly at school or at home. Karla attributed much of her shyness to the fact that she was often bullied for her weight, which made her feel self-conscious. In addition, Karla had developed physically earlier than her peers, and her womanly body was a target of harassment when walking in the streets and another reason to feel self-conscious around her peers. She tried to pass as invisible and became an introvert.

Advised by some of her cousins, Karla decided to enroll at Altavista. As former students, her cousins had described the quality of the school and the teachers very positively, and the autonomy offered to students was without a doubt very attractive to her. But to Karla, the unpretentious culture of the school and the convenience of being close to home had been the determining factors.

> This school doesn't use repression to motivate you. Instead, they let you mature and begin to do things on your own. Also, there aren't those differences in social class, like you know, at El Parque High School, the "juniors" drive their cars and all that, and I don't relate to that. . . . But here, I can relate to everyone very well. So I thank God that I ended up here, otherwise I would've been stuck in the same repression as before. . . . I wanted to be here, to get to know this school. Plus it's so close to my house. Imagine if I had to go all the way to those faraway high schools, with all those men

harassing me? No, no, no! Plus, I wouldn't have met all the friends
that I have now. I wouldn't have met Armida, or my teachers whom
I adore. I wouldn't have met you!

Clearly Karla loved her school and felt grateful to be there. The way she
spoke, she did not even remotely resemble the girl that she used to be in middle school. The freedom and caring offered by her teachers, coupled with
the various resources the community contributed to the school (such as the
theater workshops offered by Telón de Arena and mentioned in chapter
3), provided a safe space for Karla to explore new ways of being and embark
on a process of self-discovery through which many new talents came to the
surface. She attributed this transformation almost completely to Altavista.
A group of actors had come to offer theater workshops during Karla's first
year at the school and this is how she was able to take the first risk.

> My school has a very important meaning in my life because it has
> allowed me to grow on my own. I wanted to be an artist, but that
> dream had always been repressed. . . . And I said, I want to get out
> of this cage that has trapped me. . . . I can't be closed to people. I
> have to open myself up, discover, I want to be an actress. And so
> I thought, here is the beginning. So I got into theater. My first
> performance was here at the high school, and I felt so comfortable
> with myself. I found out that that was really what I liked. It also
> helped me open up to people. . . . Without my school and that
> opportunity, I wouldn't have realized that I had that potential.
> I said to myself, I have to be strong. And I found something that
> I didn't know about myself. I would be acting, and I would think,
> is that really me? Is that the repressed girl from middle school?

Karla's experience with theater helped her change her self-perceptions.
She began to take better care of herself by eating more healthfully and
exercising. Although she lost some weight, she did not achieve the slender
figure that many girls aspire to, but she did not seem to be interested
in that. I could tell that she had embraced her body the way it was. She
enjoyed showing me photographs of herself, thanking me gracefully when
I noted how beautiful she was, and she loved to dress up in her own unique
and sophisticated style for special occasions. I could definitely not see one
drop of insecurity when it came to her appearance.

Karla's transformation, however, was not limited to gaining confidence and exploring her talents; it was also about acquiring a voice and the ability to think critically. She revealed that the teachings and the opportunity for critical dialogue at Altavista helped her learn to stand up for herself, to question and find answers on her own, but most important to gain confidence in her own knowledge production.

> The things that I learn here I can go and apply them out there in my surroundings. People may come and question me, tell me that I'm wrong, and whatnot. But I tell them that there are ways to demonstrate what's true. Here I have learned to trust that what I know is right because I have a solid basis for my arguments.

This ability to take a stand for herself also transferred to the way she behaved at home.

> I used to be that girl who would lower her head whenever adults said anything to her. For example, if my parents scolded me unjustly, like if my little nephews did something wrong and then blamed it on me, my parents would scold me and I would just lower my head and remain silent. But now I defend myself, I let them know when something is unfair. I defend my rights at home. . . . I think I learned that here, from the classes and the conversations we have with the teachers.

Karla's agency was also evident in the orchestration of the various messages she received from multiple social and cultural realms. For example, she was a devout Catholic who went to church and followed many of the religious traditions and values that her parents had inculcated in her since she was a little girl, but she crafted her own beliefs based on her own perspective and experiences.

> I am religious, and I like church. I've been taught that you can always rise above the problems when holding onto to God's hand. Every time I wake up in the morning, I thank God for a new day. Or when I eat, I thank God for my food. Before, I didn't use to believe in anything, but I experienced times of bad luck when bad things started happening . . . and like one time I prayed to God for

my mother's healing and she recovered quickly from her illness. So I thought, "Yeah, God exists," and I started changing on my own, my way of thinking.

However, some of the beliefs she adopted were not completely congruent with her religion. She indicated that although she was Catholic and believed in God, she did not believe in saints like most other Catholics do. But the clearest evidence that she was willing and able to make her own conscious choices even when they went against Catholicism was her perspective on homosexuality. Her two best friends were gay and she embraced them completely.

> I accept people the way they are, as long as they don't mistreat me. I accept them because they are like anyone else, the only difference is that they're attracted to people of their same sex, and so what? What's wrong with that? I don't see anything wrong. I'm very liberal. . . . I hang out with men and women, with gays and lesbians, with everyone. I respect everyone's right to be the way they want to be. I feel lucky because homosexual kids follow me a lot. They tell me all kinds of stuff; they trust me very much. They tell me when they feel scared to come out of the closet. And I tell them, it's your decision, be free to be yourself, it's your life; be yourself and keep pressing forward.

Indeed, kids from all grades enjoyed her friendship. Her self-confidence, energy, openness, joyful attitude, and determination were contagious. Perhaps it was the memory of having been an outcast in the past that made her so sensitive to students who felt oppressed by normative social standards. She was also notable among the senior students for reaching out to the younger kids. It appeared as if she wanted everyone to have the same liberating experience that had transformed her life. Hence, she created a theater club and a voice club through which she strived to help students emerge from their shells and discover their talents. She also offered help and support to students who lived in difficult family circumstances and constantly encouraged academically underperforming peers.

To be sure, much of the support Karla offered to her friends was the result of the involvement of her caring parents. They were always welcoming to her friends, who in turn found in them additional adult guidance and affection. Karla truly appreciated the way her parents took part in her life, and pleasing them was one of Karla's priorities. But how much influence did Karla's parents have in her decisions and identity formation? At times Karla had to negotiate the expectations that her parents had for her and her own conflicting goals and ideals. This negotiation process became apparent in her career choices. Since the first day I met her, Karla expressed her passionate interest in attending law school to become a criminal attorney. She often talked about her dream with excitement and mentioned that she had decided on this career path a long time ago. When I pointed out that this was a difficult profession for women in México because they were often discriminated against and objectified, she replied with determination: "I don't know how I will do this, but I will. I don't care how hard it might be. It has always been my dream, and I'm going to do it." A few months later she even started dating a law student, whom she liked precisely because they had the same interests. Both were very academically oriented, and they had discussions about law together. Although they had much in common, they differed politically, as he had some conservative ideas, but she enjoyed debating controversial topics with him. "I tell him what I think, and I've even made him change his perspective on some things because my arguments are strong."

But by the beginning of the spring semester, Karla seemed to have changed her mind. Her mother had told her that the current conditions of the city were too unfavorable to practice criminal law and she feared for her life. "My mother knows how I am. She knows that I won't be silent about the injustices I see, and she's very afraid." Karla then decided to look into other career pathways. She considered education, reasoning that it fit her love for children and her desire to make an impact on the new generations. She was also interested in majoring in psychology and becoming a school counselor. She loved and admired Altavista's counselor and thought that she would like to follow her footsteps. When I asked her if she was afraid too, or if she was changing her mind just because of her parents, she sounded as though she was trying to convince herself.

> It's 50 percent my parents and 50 percent my own choice. I am
> afraid. I mean, yes, it is a dream, but I'm scared. . . . And it's also
> for my parents. What if I ended up working for the police and
> had to defend cases there? It would be very stressful. And I like
> psychology a lot because everything I've learned here in class has

made me become very interested in it; all the mental processes and all of that seems very fun to me.

Karla applied to the psychology program at the Autonomous University of Ciudad Juárez (UACJ). I was able to get a waiver for her college application and a scholarship for her first year. She only had to pass her admissions exam. Karla was a very high achiever, so I was confident that she would not have any problems. But the day after the exam, she came to me in absolute agony because she felt she had not done well. She explained to me that her mother had told her right before the test that if she did not pass it, she would be completely disappointed and would not allow her to continue studying, so she would have to start working full time immediately. Although her mother's words seemed rather harsh, they were not completely surprising. Karla would be the first one in her family to ever attend college, and the entire family had invested in and sacrificed a lot to support her education.

The path to reinvention is not as linear as was evident in the way Karla reacted to her mother's expectations. Needless to say, the pressure to do well was overwhelming and her nerves caught up with her in the middle of the test. All the questions got jumbled up in her head, and she ended up in the restroom throwing up without finishing the exam. After graduation, Karla found out that she had not passed the test. She was inconsolable, feeling that all her work had been for nothing. "I feel worthless," she told me in an e-mail. It was as if the academic identity that she had built for years had just suddenly crumbled down, and her greatest worry was that she would be a disappointment to her parents. I had never heard her speak like this before, so I tried to encourage her and help her see that this was not the end of her life, that she could try again in the spring.

Fortunately, her mother did not react as Karla had expected. Her parents were supportive and allowed her to take art and theater classes while she waited to apply again at the university the following semester. But in October, she e-mailed me telling me that her dream to be a lawyer had not died and that she was considering applying to law school instead of going into the field of psychology. I asked her about her previous concerns, and she explained that she did not want to give up her dream out of fear.

Karla began to go with her mother to sell clothes at the flea market in order to save for her application, and she studied very hard during the fall for her admissions exam. This time she passed it, but she had more hurdles to overcome. She was accepted at a new campus, which was over an hour away from her home. She went several times to the main offices to request a transfer to the closer campus, but to no avail. This, however, did not stop her from pursuing her dream. Karla completed her first semester of law school with the same passion she expressed the first day she talked about it.

Another Reinventor: Mónica

Light skinned, slender, and with long, straight, light brown hair, Mónica dressed in simple jeans and T-shirts. She enjoyed reading, drawing, and listening to music. Mónica's demeanor was of kindness and quiet tranquility. Nonetheless, her life had been far from tranquil. Mónica had been raised in an orphanage and only recently, when she turned eighteen, had she been released. She lived with a sister and her sister's husband and daughter but felt very lonely. While she seemed excited about participating in the study and took it quite seriously, she struggled to get any words out during interviews. This nervousness, she explained, was perhaps the result of having grown up in an orphanage, where the rules were extremely strict and the girls' talk was highly constrained and repressed.

Given that Mónica was so different from Karla, one might wonder how they both fit in the same category. However, Mónica had in fact experienced a transformation that, while still in progress, had quite liberating effects. Although Mónica was quiet, it did not compare to the way she was when she began to attend Altavista.

> When I started here, I didn't hang out with anyone, I didn't talk to anyone. I was always hiding in this little room. I would help Armida to clean up her office and organize her papers. I started hanging out with a couple of friends, but then they left, so I ended up alone again.

Mónica explained that her previous experiences with making friends in middle school had been very hard. As in the case of Karla, the girls who surrounded her seemed to be very interested in clothing and appearing of a higher social class. Mónica felt different and awkward for living in an orphanage and being poor. This experience made her fear people, even when she entered Altavista as a new student. Therefore, Mónica spent her entire first year at Altavista isolated and hiding from her peers. Armida seemed to have given her a safe space to come to school without feeling too vulnerable. It was not until the second year that things began to change and she started coming out of her shell.

> In my second year, I started talking to more people. Well, they talked to me first. And I started to hang out with Rosy, Gabriela, and Lizette, and with all those guys. And I don't know how it happened but now I have more friends. . . . I think that it is this school that has changed me because if I had attended another high school, I would be like before.

Mónica explained that it was the freedom at Altavista that had helped her change because she realized she wouldn't be criticized or ostracized for being different or poor. The caring that her peers and teachers expressed also gave her the confidence to do things she did not do before. Moreover, the critical discourse and cultural activities of the school allowed Mónica to refocus her introspection and reflection to how her external environment and its history contributed to her own identity. She expressed that learning the story of the massacre of Tlatelolco, or even the reason why certain traditions existed, helped her "to know more about me too because it's like if a person had something, and didn't know about it, like something is missing."

Mónica felt so comfortable at Altavista now that sometimes she wished she could live there. Indeed, Mónica had many friends and I never saw her alone. She was quiet but always smiling. But what was more, she did not intend to simply remain in this comfort zone.

> Sometimes I like to be quiet because that is my personality and I also enjoy tranquility. But sometimes I feel very happy for having people around me who help me and care about me. And I want to express that. Or sometimes I want to talk to other people that I feel curious about—to get to know them better—but I can't because I'm so shy, and that is an aspect of me that I want to change. The fear I have of talking in front of other people, like I have scenic panic. I don't like that. That happens to me a lot when I am presenting in class and I want to change that.

With the supports that Altavista provided, Mónica was deliberate about her own transformation and wanted to continue to challenge herself to one day be able to express herself better. For that reason, she never said no to assignments that required her to speak in public. The patience that her peers and teachers had toward her during presentations might have helped her continue to challenge herself. In fact, participating in the study was another way in which she was confronting her fears. When I asked her whether the audio recorder was making her too nervous and whether she preferred that I turn it off, she said, "No, that's fine. It's that . . . well . . . what I think is that it's OK because that is like a challenge and I have to confront it until I feel no more embarrassment."

In sum, Karla and, to some degree, Mónica illustrate how the Reinventors may be able to transform their silenced selves into agents of their own destiny. Karla's experiences of freedom, caring, and critical dialogue helped her regain her voice, affirm her own knowledge, and explore hidden talents and ways of being. The result was a new self-love and self-acceptance that radically transformed her personality. Mónica also was going through a process of reinventing herself, authoring her own emergence from repression and isolation and into a more open and expressive young woman. While not completely invulnerable to the pressures or opinions of others, they strived to identify their own desires and dreams and pursue them. With this newly acquired confidence, the Reinventors like Karla also contributed to the cultural production of diversity and freedom at Altavista. She played an important role in the creation of safe spaces for self-authorship for those who had also been injured in the past or were afraid of not fitting into the mold that society imposed.

The Redefiners: Fighting Off the Demons

In contrast to the Redirectors and the Reinventors, who have been able to define and embrace their identities and the direction they want to give to their lives, the Redefiners were going through the process of unlearning oppressive definitions of themselves that they had acquired throughout the years. Marsella, Cristina, and, to some extent, Nora fit this group. While still vulnerable to hegemonic notions of femininity and beauty that significantly affected their feelings of self-worth, they utilized a variety of strategies to resist the damaging consequences of negative messages of inferiority instilled by family members, boyfriends, or peers as well as by the media and other public discourses that imposed limitations on them. The structural constraints in their lives might have also defined the world and the future for them. Not naïve about their position as working-class women, they often hesitated between hope and hopelessness about their life prospects. While the Reinventors went through a process of redefining themselves as well, the Redefiners are those who did not yet seem to have arrived at a liberating destination during their high school years, yet were in the process of defining what liberation and empowerment meant for them. In other words, although these girls had developed a critical consciousness that allowed them to question the oppressive messages and expectations from family and society, they still struggled to liberate themselves from them.

For Redefiners like Marsella and Cristina, for example, a major area of difficulty was the self-image. Dominant notions of beauty and/or a pursuit of social mobility left these girls feeling inferior and socially uprooted as they attempted to fit into the world of the middle class to get an education. And in the case of Marsella, extremely difficult experiences of rejection, abuse, and abandonment exacerbated feelings of inadequacy.

As the Redefiners became socialized in the culture of Altavista, they were exposed to a new way of thinking and seeing the world. Being like everyone else was no longer necessary, and achieving an upper-class "Barbie look" was no longer a requirement to be accepted. Instead, as these girls engaged in critical discourse, they became more conscious of the power dynamics that contributed to their everyday realities and discourses and began to perceive the oppression of classism and imposed definitions of womanhood and beauty. Moreover, the emphasis on autogestión at Altavista offered them a glimpse of possibility that encouraged them to actively pursue their dreams. But while the critical orientation of their school helped them unlearn the lies they had believed for years, the voices in their heads that implanted feelings of worthlessness or self-loathing were sometimes louder than their critical consciousness. It was then that they engaged in a process of self-contestation in which they tried to negotiate and create new definitions of self-worth, beauty, and possibility that they could believe for themselves.

The Redefiners' journey was one of ups and downs, in which context played a crucial role. As they were accepted and validated by others, or as they encountered indications of possibility to pursue their aspirations, their confidence and feelings of self-worth improved. But at the same time, as in the case of Marsella, every insult or insinuation that pointed to their shortcomings resulted in an injury that required substantial reflection and active steps toward self-reassurance. In the case of Nora, every time she faced the economic and gendered limitations imposed on her life, she felt defeated and at the verge of giving up her dreams. Nevertheless, despite the inevitable influence that their context and those around them had on their feelings, they were not passive victims of their environment. Instead, they constantly engaged in a process of self-contestation. Conscientious of the effect that external factors had on them, they drew on their critical consciousness to identify oppressive messages. Thus, despite feeling injured, they resisted these messages through different strategies, such as speaking back or separating themselves from the context or people who hurt them and engaging in activities that uplifted and encouraged them.

Portrait of a Redefiner: Marsella

I was never personally introduced to Marsella, nor did I ever approach her. But from the first week of my fieldwork, she would stop what she was doing to cheerfully greet me with a kiss whenever I walked by her. Our interchanges were brief—simple "hi, how are you?" conversations—but it appeared she was eager to be part of whatever I was doing. Little did I know that our relationship would last beyond my year of fieldwork.

Marsella was an eighteen-year-old third-year student at Altavista. She was of medium build and taller than most of the other girls, and dressed in a rocker style—usually wearing a black jacket, skinny jeans, and a thick, metal embellished belt. Her straight and dark shoulder-length hair was cut in a modern style with bangs framing her big brown eyes. She was outgoing, lively, and articulate, and I usually saw her hanging out with many friends—mostly males.

Marsella's family life had been extremely difficult. Her parents divorced when she was very young, and her father, who had been a journalist, was murdered when she was a little girl. Although custody was granted to Marsella's mother, she resented the fact that her mother had never paid much attention to her.

> After my parents divorced, there were many problems. My mother remarried and my father died when I was five years old. . . . He threw me a birthday party and a month later he died. I've always felt the need for my mother's attention, but I've never had it. . . . My mother never took care of me because she was always working. It was always my maternal grandmother who looked after me. When

[my mother] remarried, she had four more daughters. Then, when I was fourteen, she moved away with her husband and my four sisters, but she didn't take me. I didn't want to go with her either though, because [my stepfather's] presence was too uncomfortable for me . . . and now I don't even consider her my mother. I see her more as a sister and I call her by her first name.

It was her maternal grandmother whom Marsella considered her "mamá." The two of them lived in a small old house that was literally falling apart. Upon entering her home, one could immediately notice the moldy smell caused by the leaky ceiling. During the winter, the cold winds coming through the cracks and holes in the walls made it difficult to stay warm, intensifying Grandma's aches. Grandma was in her midseventies and her legs were always in pain. Although she could not walk well, she still cooked in her wood-burning stove and both women did their best to keep the house spotless.

Their financial resources were extremely scarce. Grandma received a pension that hardly amounted to the equivalent of sixty dollars a month, and Marsella's uncles sometimes gave her an extra few pesos, the equivalent of eight to fifteen dollars. Considering the high cost of living in Juárez, they sometimes had to choose between paying the water bill and buying food. They lived day to day. When Marsella showed me her shopping list, it consisted of "one potato, a package of spaghetti, an onion, a tomato, and a cup of beans," and all of that was supposed to last them a week.

Marsella felt that her mother did not care much about their situation. "She doesn't even visit her own mother," Marsella complained. Her mother and sisters lived nearby, but though Marsella sometimes saw her sisters, who would come to visit Grandma, she hardly ever saw her mother. Much of the pain Marsella felt had to do with her mother and had begun in her childhood, but it had continued through her adolescent years.

When I was a little girl, I was always wishing that my mother would show me love. But I'm eighteen now, and I've lived without her for four years. I don't wish for her love anymore because my grandmother has known how to care for me and has given me the love that I always needed. I will always miss my mother, obviously. . . . I will always wonder why my mother didn't care about me, but I guess that's the way it had to be.

From the first interview, Marsella was an open book. She immediately told me about her life history and confessed some of her deepest struggles.

> I am very joyful and I love talking with people. I can talk nonstop about any given topic. But I'm very insecure and many times when someone says something about me, even if they're joking, I misinterpret it and take it the wrong way. I always feel criticized. If I walk by and someone laughs, I immediately think they were laughing at me. . . . My self-esteem is very low. If someone tells me that I look ugly, I believe it and that's it. But if someone says, "You look pretty," I feel that they're making fun of me, like why do they say that if it's not true.

These feelings of insecurity had clearly developed over time. While in middle school, Marsella attended a school outside her neighborhood. In order to fit into the middle-class culture of her peers, she tried to achieve a *fresa* (preppy) look, which included wearing brand-name clothes that she obviously could not afford. She worried about her physical appearance and was bothered by the way her boyfriend at the time dressed. "He would get annoyed and ask me, 'Why do you care so much about what people say? Why are you so superficial?'" she explained. Her boyfriend's comments made her reflect on her behavior. "I don't have money, why would I want to appear to be something I'm not?" she reasoned. So Marsella changed her style and adopted a rocker style like her boyfriend. This did not appear to be much of a problem, but as her body changed, she began to internalize messages of inadequacy in reference to prototypical images of female beauty.

In middle school she strived to achieve the idealized image of beauty and even lapsed into eating disorders. The pressure from other women, including her girlfriends, her mother, and even her grandmother, to look a particular way began to make her self-conscious. "Sometimes my friends will say, 'The chubbiest person will do this or that,' and so of course I end up losing because I hang out with very petite girls, and so that type of comment makes me feel down," she explained. While she recognized the unrealistic expectations of looking like her smaller friends, she still felt hurt. Moreover, her boyfriend's eventual betrayal, mistreatment, and even an instance of physical abuse exacerbated her feelings of lowliness and rejection.

Loving her body was Marsella's greatest struggle. Whenever I asked the girls if there was anything they would like to change about themselves, they all mentioned things about their personality, with the exception of Marsella.

> I wished I could change my body. I don't like it. I don't like to be chubby. I don't know, I don't know, I hate many things about myself. I hate my face, my hair, my body. Sometimes I feel like I don't love myself. . . . Or maybe it is that I'm not very feminine. It's not natural for me to wear makeup or things like that. It's always my girlfriends who push me to do that. Sometimes I wonder why I don't have a boyfriend if I'm a cool person, but then I tell myself, oh, it's because I'm not pretty. . . . I also wish I could change my self-esteem.

Just as Marsella had learned to accept her mother's abandonment as an inevitable fact of life, she learned to accept as true the normative messages about femininity and beauty both implicit and explicit in society. One sunny afternoon, Marsella confessed to Karla and me that her mother had always compared her to her sisters.

> Every time that I'm around my real mother and my sisters, my mother will tell me, "Oh, look how pretty these girls are, they have nice boobs and butt, and they're skinny. This dress would look very pretty on them," but not on me because I'm flat chested and I'm not skinny like them.

Her mother's words had more impact than she probably intended. "How can I think of myself as pretty if even my mother doesn't think I am?" she told Karla and me. Sometimes she would urgently pull me aside to vent about emotional breakdowns that she experienced. "I don't know. . . . I feel like I want to hurt myself." And every time she expressed these feelings of frustration and self-hatred, they were related to her self-image. "I feel so ugly, no matter what everyone says. If you tell me that I'm pretty, I don't believe you because I think you're just saying that because you love me, but not because it's true." It was surprising that with such intense feelings she managed to do well in school. But what I soon realized was that it was indeed school that in part helped her keep her sanity.

As contradictory as it may sound, while Marsella struggled with self-damaging thoughts, she simultaneously refused to completely conform to idealized images of femininity.

> My girlfriends will tell me, "Why don't you wear this or that?" But I'm not very feminine. I don't like to wear skirts or shorts. I like men, I'm not lesbian, I'm heterosexual, but I don't like it. My grandma jokes and says that I'm very masculine because she sees that other girls my age wear miniskirts and little tops showing their belly buttons, and earrings, and stylish haircuts, and all that. But I tell her that I don't like that. . . . You see, I don't like to show my belly button because you can see the rolls in my stomach, and I don't like skirts because they're uncomfortable. I'm a woman who likes to climb trees and all of that, and it's just not practical.

In a way, Marsella resisted the normative expectations for being a woman, even when she had to pay the emotional consequences for not abiding by them. What is it that helped Marsella counter the imposed definitions of femininity and beauty rather than strive to achieve them like in the past? What kept her from giving up or rebelling against the world in self-damaging ways? And how did her school help her in the areas that meant the most to her?

Answers to these questions are difficult to determine, but it could be argued that, on the one hand, she had a strong sense of responsibility for her grandmother, which motivated her to survive in spite of emotional turmoil. On the other hand, she was motivated by the hope that education offered her. Altavista in particular helped her develop the ability to debunk social myths, which in turn might have contributed to her resistance to hegemonic definitions of beauty and her damaged feelings of self-worth.

Indeed, Grandma had been able to love and support Marsella throughout the years, and Marsella loved her deeply. Christina, one of Marsella's closest friends, confessed to me that even though she once had problems with Marsella, she remained there for her because she knew her circumstances were exceptional: "She cannot live her life like other teenagers. She can't go to parties and hang out with friends all the time. She has to take care of her sick grandmother because she has no one else, and I know how hard this must be for a girl her age."

Marsella's grandmother was perhaps her greatest fan and the most important motivator to keep her going despite the many difficulties in her life. She had always encouraged her to continue her education and to go to college.

> *Mi Mami* [referring to Grandmother] has always made great efforts so that I can go to school. I wasn't going to enroll in middle school because we didn't have money for it, but she went and got me a scholarship and found money so that I could do it. Also to come here, we went to many governmental offices, with the PRI, with the PAN, with the PRD, with everyone. All she wanted was to get me financial help so that I could go to school. She has always told me that no matter what happens I should not stop studying, that it's the most important thing. Sometimes we don't even have food to eat, we don't even have money for a kilo of tortillas, but she saves so that I can have money to pay for public transportation to go to school.

Nevertheless, Marsella admitted that her investment in her education was not only motivated by her grandmother's sacrifices.

> I was going to tell you that if you don't go to school you will be a nobody. But that's not true. I don't just do it for my grandmother either. For me it's important to go to school because I like to learn. I want to have an education because I think it's an important way to defend oneself.

This is one reason why despite her financial needs and emotional injuries, Marsella was a very good student. She attended every class, completed all her assignments, and was attentive and participative in every lesson. As one of the most underprivileged students, the only reason why she was able to come to school was that she had gotten a scholarship; Rigoberto, the history teacher, paid for her tuition. He explained how this happened.

> Marsella started with a half scholarship and was a good student since her first semester here. But by her second semester, she had already dropped out because she didn't have money to pay for the

rest of her tuition. I noticed, however, that she kept coming to
school. She wouldn't attend any classes, but she would be hanging
out in the courtyard almost every day . . . so I decided to give her a
scholarship.

When looking at her high school options, Altavista had not been Marsella's first choice. The negative reputation that the school had among her
middle-school peers created many misconceptions for her.

I had heard that the students were lazy and skipped all their classes,
that they were drunkards and drug addicts. There were also older
kids when I came to enroll and I felt too young and vulnerable to
be around them. I was very scared during the first days. But once I
started to discover new things, I loved it. My whole perspective
about the school changed, and now I think this school is perfect.

Therefore, it was not just her grandmother's and her own valuing of
and high hopes in education that motivated her. In reality, it would be hard
to believe that the future benefits of formal schooling would be relevant
enough when going through deep depression. Instead, it was the meaning
that Altavista gave to her life in the here and now that supported Marsella
during her darkest times. Marsella found in Altavista a space of caring and
freedom where she could be validated and loved no matter what she
looked like. She often went to her teachers for advice, and even called
Rigoberto "mi Papá" (my Dad) or "mi Padrino" (my Godfather).

I don't know what this school means to other people, but it means
a lot to me. Like I tell you, I've always had my self-esteem ups and
downs, and here, it seems that my lows last less. Maybe it is
because I talk with the teachers about how I feel, or they ask me
what's wrong when they notice that I'm sad. And they tell me
things that help me feel much better. I feel more comfortable with
myself here.

Marsella was aware of the origin of her low self-esteem, and she was also
cognizant that her self-worth did not depend on fulfilling arbitrary notions
of beauty. Having opportunities to explore new talents gave Marsella a
space to resist her feelings of inadequacy and begin to internalize new

feelings of self-worth. Like Karla, she participated in the theater workshop offered by a local NGO. Her talent was more evident to her when she was selected for a play to be performed at UACJ, the most prestigious university in the city.

She had also learned from other young women at Altavista that it was possible to love oneself no matter what other people thought. As I previously mentioned, when I asked her if there was a woman that she admired and saw as a good role model, she immediately answered, "Gabriela." In addition to admiring her confidence despite people's opinion or the stigma that her appearance carried, Marsella admired Gabriela's ability to respect herself.

> Many people say that she doesn't shower, that she's not clean, but to me that person deserves much respect because in spite of all that criticism, she always stands up for herself, she defends her position, her way of being. She's very confident and I can tell that she has a high self-esteem; she values herself. She's not aggressive or mean, but she always voices her opinion. She's not afraid to be embarrassed or to be countered. She's authentic and says what she wants. If she feels like asking a boy out, she goes and does it. She doesn't think, "Oh no, am I going to look bad? What are people going to think of me? What if he doesn't like me?" No, she goes and asks him, and if the guy says no, she doesn't feel less. She's like "OK, let's just be friends then." And she's not afraid to wear pants, clothes that aren't brand name, or clothes that look old. She doesn't care and wears whatever she wants.

Finally, the critical discourse at Altavista also helped her to challenge oppressive messages and attitudes from the larger society. She enjoyed being able to question what in other schools was taught as truth, to analyze social inequalities, to critique the government, and to go beyond superficial historical accounts. Issues of gender were perhaps the most important to her, as they helped her redefine the roles and expectations for women.

> If I hadn't enrolled at this school, I wouldn't have learned many things. For example, . . . in middle school if something was spilled, they would have us girls clean up while the boys could just go out and play. When I came to this school, I understood that mopping

the floors is not a female's job. Both men and women can do it.
And I learned that if I wasn't the one who made the mess, I didn't
have to clean it up just because I was a woman. . . . At other schools
they teach you to work, but they don't teach students to value and
respect women; here they do. They teach us that women are just
as capable as men. If the men can do something, you can too.
You're not disabled for being a woman. So in a way they teach us
to value ourselves, not to feel superior, but not inferior either, to
feel equal.

It was perhaps this critical orientation that helped her work tirelessly to
redefine her self-image. She could not change her feelings immediately, but
she could challenge her actions. During her high school years, Marsella's
forms of resistance consisted of dressing the way she liked, even when
people's criticism hurt her. She also enrolled in theater classes and acted
in front of people, all the while knowing that she would be subjected to
people's scrutiny. She finally took the greatest risk of rejection when she
went up to the guy she liked and asked him out. She came to me expressing
how nervous she felt, but this was an important step of self-authorship.
Fortunately, he said yes, and five years later, they were still in an exclusive
and serious romantic relationship.

In addition, Marsella took preventive measures by seeking spaces to
protect her mind from reproducing hurtful thoughts. That was the reason
why she preferred to hang out with boys and separate herself from the
groups of girls who made her feel inferior by focusing too much on or crit-
icizing her physical appearance. Rather than attempting to fight negative
thoughts on her own, she sought help from teachers.

Clearly, while injured and struggling, Marsella, like other Redefiners,
was in no way a passive victim of her environment. Although the type of
autogestión in which Marsella began to engage at Altavista resulted more
in a reflexive, intimate, and slow and nonlinear transformation that did not
appear too revolutionary during her high school years, it could be argued
that Marsella was among those on whom Altavista had a profound and
long-term impact. The self-reflexivity stemming from critical consciousness that Altavista promoted has continued to shape her self-authorship
during her college years, where she has increasingly engaged in and organized activist projects, moving from self-consciousness to a collective
consciousness.

After graduation, Marsella wanted to attend the state university to major in communication studies. There were absolutely no scholarships available for first-year students, but with the help of a friend of mine and due to her good grades and the superior test scores she achieved on the college's admissions exam, the president of the university was willing to give her a half scholarship. After my year of fieldwork, Marsella and I stayed in contact via Facebook and phone, and she would explain how things were going at the university.

Academically, her first semester was an absolute success. She was the top student in most of her classes and was clearly the most well-read and thoughtful student in her cohort. However, she was also the most critical and outspoken, and this began to bother professors and students alike. Marsella began to feel the insults and criticism again for not being able to live up to middle-class expectations. She hardly had any money for public transportation, yet her peers would demand that she participate in all kinds of fundraisers and join them for lunch at expensive restaurants. "I don't know why you even try to come to college if you know you're poor," a professor told her when she tried to explain she did not have the resources to comply with his policy of wearing formal outfits for class presentations. Moreover, during an audition for a university TV show, she realized that women were only selected on the basis of their looks. And those who were selected were only assigned to discuss superficial topics like fashion and music, while men spoke about politics, current events, and cultural topics.

In one of her classes she once had to speak up against her professor and classmates' criticisms of the working class and the people from her barrio, whom they judged to be mediocre and conformist.

> So I got up and told them, "You all don't know what you're talking about. You can criticize them because when you complain that you don't have money, it means you can't buy your brand-name clothes for the week or gas for your new car to go out partying. When the poor say they don't have money, it means they have no food on the table and no electricity."

Marsella eventually grew tired of having to constantly battle the superficiality of her classmates and the banking education she received from her teachers. Realizing that at that program and university she would only be judged by her appearance, and that as a woman she would never be considered for communicating important topics, she decided to separate herself from that social world.

> I'm the feisty and rebellious one here; I'm an outcast. But I wasn't trained in high school to be a robot. I was prepared to think for myself. I don't want to talk about makeup, fashion, and gossip. I want to talk about topics that matter. This school is not for me.

After finishing the first semester, she dropped out of her program and spent the following semester taking care of her elderly grandmother, reading, and writing. She often shared with me about the books she was reading, mostly history books and novels by Isabel Allende. She also sold used clothes, empty milk containers, and aluminum cans in order to earn some income and made jewelry and gifts out of paper clips and any other materials she could use and recycle herself while she waited to enroll in the education program at UACJ. Though I worried that too many obstacles would erode her dream of going to college, she was determined.

> I was the only one in my barrio who was going to college, and everyone viewed me with admiration. It encouraged me a lot, and I know I have to do this. . . . I'm going to finish college, and when I graduate I will show my mother that I was able to do it, and that I didn't get pregnant like she predicted.

Because Altavista was like a home to her, Marsella visits the school periodically, and her favorite teachers continue to support her with advice and to foster her critical consciousness. "They always know what's wrong with me, and they always help me feel better," she explained to me. Now in her third year of college, she is a much more confident young woman whose identity resembles more that of the Redirectors.

Other Redefiners: Cristina and Nora

Cristina

Cristina described herself as overly cheerful and a good friend. Other girls often trusted her with their secrets and asked her for advice, and she had many male friends as well. Cristina also had very strong convictions about how a woman must protect and defend herself against vulnerability and the social constraints that attempt to limit her. Cristina was feminine and flirtatious, with expressive sparkly eyes, and always laughing and smiling—definitely a social butterfly. However, she was also very sensitive and proud, and was easily hurt. She had not had very good luck in romantic relationships, and she had also experienced conflict in her friendships.

Although Cristina spoke candidly about her opinions and experiences in school, and even about some of her insecurities, there were some other things that troubled her in her intimate life. During interviews, we often had to stop for a few minutes as she sobbed or recovered from the memories that would bring her to tears. Yet she only shared partial information about these issues. Her struggles appeared to be a combination of gender and economic struggles with some other personal issues that had brought much distress to her mother and that she was still struggling to overcome completely.

On the one hand, Cristina's father was very domineering and chauvinistic. He treated her mother with disrespect and disdain and expected women to constantly serve him. As an attempt to empower herself, Cristina's mother had attended beauty school and had opened her own beauty salon. She did this also to be able to pay for Cristina's education since her father refused to support her. "Why do you want to go to school if you're a woman?" he would ask her. So her mother paid for all of Cristina's expenses. With a working mother in such a patriarchal home, Cristina had to rush home daily after school to prepare dinner for her father, clean the house, and take care of her two younger brothers.

Cristina did this without objection, as she knew that this was necessary if she wanted to complete her high school education. But she was also compelled by the need to recover her mother's trust. When Cristina started high school, her parents enrolled her at a different institution, a highly reputed state high school. She did not do well there. The same pressures along gender and class that other girls like Marsella and Karla experienced began to take a toll on Cristina.

> I became a little . . . like before I could care less about my physical appearance, but I began to worry a lot about that. So sometimes I feel down because I can spend hours in front of the mirror—yes, too many hours. So that is something that started about two or three years ago when I started high school at [another school]. . . . I was very plain and simple, but there were a lot of people very

different from me at that school. . . . So I started to isolate
myself. . . . For example, the girls there would only talk about looks,
looks, and looks: "I look like this and I want to look like that." But
my looks were simple and I wasn't as interested in that. So when
they saw that I didn't have the same interests, they began to stay
away from me. So then it was just me and another girl who was
simple like me that remained friends. Since then my self-esteem
went down a lot. Since then that idea stuck with me. I have tried to
change that and I'm working on it, but it still affects me.

Her emerging insecurities due to her peers' pressures to look in a particular way were not the only struggles she had to confront at the time.

There was a time in which my mother was helping me with a
problem I had, but my frustration was that I could not get out of
that problem. I got out and then I went back to it. That's what
frustrated me—that she supported me, and there I was again. . . .
Because my mother and I have always been best friends, above
all else. And she would tell me, "It's just that I don't trust you
anymore." And that was very painful. But things are getting better
with her now.

Cristina never shared details about what exactly her recurring problem
was. However, she expressed how deeply this had affected her, as it had
serious consequences for her mother and it had impacted the most important relationship in her life.

One time, my father beat up my mother. So that is also my
frustration because it was because of what I did. So I felt awful
that he took it out on her. He had never done something like
that and my mother didn't do anything. If it wasn't for my grandmother, who arrived right on time, I don't know what would have
happened.

In this way, Cristina felt guilty and frustrated with her own behavior, but
she also developed a growing anger against her father and struggled to shape
her identity as a strong woman given what she viewed as her mother's tolerance to abuse.

The day after my father beat up my mother, he had the nerve to act as if nothing had happened. So I saw his hypocrisy and I have this rage against him. And I would have liked for my mother to defend herself, to at least try. . . . He often yells hurtful and offensive words, but that's usually directed at me, and I never remain quiet, I always speak back, but my mother is always trying to pacify us, and she says, "It's OK, just leave him alone. We'll figure it out tomorrow," etcetera. So it makes me angry that she can't speak back.

Given Cristina's struggles, her grades declined significantly, so she was rejected by her former high school and was not able to enroll in her second semester of tenth grade. Therefore, she enrolled in beauty school, but she must not have done well, as she indicated that she ended up losing six months in which she didn't study. This, along with her continued struggles with her "problem," led her mother to enroll her at Altavista, more than anything as a way to discipline her. Given Altavista's stigma and Cristina's increased attention to appearances, her mother saw it as a suitable punishment. But the school ended up surprising them.

It turned out that I loved it here. Because the original plan was that I was going to return to [my former school], but no way. I stayed here even though I struggled a lot with the paperwork so that I could stay. But wow, it's been great here! Because people here are humble and simple . . . and they give us a lot of freedom and that feels very good—that there's freedom in every way. And so here there are people with whom I've been able to identify, like Gabriela, who was my first friend here, . . . and I really feel the difference. . . . I was afraid when I just started here that everybody would have their friends and I would be alone. But people immediately reached out to me. Because that's what we do when we see somebody new. . . . And nobody judges others based on how they look. If I don't like him or the way he dresses, well, that's my problem. Because we have all kinds of people here, from the sloppiest to the most put together. And all people say is "That's the way she dresses, and that's her, and that's it."

The absence of judgment on the basis of appearances meant a lot to Cristina, as this helped her begin to reshape her own perception of herself. In addition, the critical focus at Altavista was allowing her to relay her attention to things that were more meaningful and less superficial.

> I began to change because when I started here I had already become more *"fresita."* I made sure my clothes matched and that I wore the right shoes, etcetera. But after being around people here I began to change. . . . And another thing is that here they give us the weapons to keep going without fear of what is going on outside. Because here we pay attention to the social issues that are going on and they help us get interested in other things beyond looks. So I tell my mother that despite what most people think, I'm sure that at this school, there is more cultural knowledge, more art, more interest on the part of students than in other schools.

Cristina, then, was still going through her own transformation, which was a difficult process because it involved not only eschewing the internalized pressures on her physical appearance but also overcoming her personal problem, recovering her mother's trust, and dealing with her father's machismo. In between sobs, she confessed:

> I get like this because my mother has put so much trust in me, and I have disappointed her in many ways, and I lost her trust. But I'm good with her right now, and I am beginning to recover it. When I started to struggle with this problem, I asked her not to tell anyone, for it to remain between the two of us, and that's how it was. So she has helped me so much. . . . But I don't know; with my father, I have this anger against him and I can't talk to him or agree with him. . . . He treats my fifteen-year-old brother as if he was the dumbest thing in the world. He can make you feel like that. So I'm like, enough! When I was little, it was a big trauma for me, but now I try not to listen to him anymore. . . . So I want to keep changing. Like I tell you, I was never interested in looks; I always looked at people's character first. So that is something that I really want to change, and I have tried for like a year, and it has been hard, but I'm trying, I'm trying.

Cristina had been doing very well academically and was able to earn a half scholarship, which was very important to her, as this could be a relief to her mother financially but also because it contributed to her efforts to regain her mother's trust. Nonetheless, during the last couple of months of my fieldwork, Cristina seemed to be struggling with her classes. However, I was unable to interview her again and she did not participate in the photography activity. Due to a rumor that caused much distress to Cristina, she had stopped hanging out with Marsella, who had been one of her closest friends but whom she thought was the one to blame. Since Marsella had become very close to me, it is possible that Cristina did not trust me enough to remain in the study and she seemed to avoid me. This was never clear to me, but I did not want to be intrusive and thought it was best to give her space. What I did observe was that she had become more truant and spent much of her time outside in the school courtyard hanging out with friends and skipping her classes. This could have very negative consequences, as it could result in declined grades and thus in losing her half scholarship. Fortunately, her teachers took notice and began to address the issue. What should be noted is that for a Redefiner, these lapses are not unusual. In the end, she was able to pull herself through and was able to graduate successfully from high school.

Nora

Although Nora did not appear to struggle with issues of self-esteem or physical appearance, her struggles in redefining herself had more to do with her aspirations for the future as a young, working-class woman. As previously mentioned, Nora once asked me to bring her information about how to enroll at the University of Texas at El Paso (UTEP). One afternoon I was waiting in the hallway for a teacher when Nora came out of her classroom and immediately approached me to say hi. We had a brief conversation about the picture on my bag of Gloria Anzaldúa. Then she asked me where I was a student and where I had attended college. When she learned that I had a bachelor's degree in education from UTEP, she got excited and said she was interested in going there too and majoring in education as well. I promised her that I would bring her updated information.

A couple of weeks later, when I had gathered all the necessary information, including requirements for obtaining a student visa and placement exams for international students, I arranged a meeting with Nora. She showed up with her boyfriend, César. I was not surprised about that. Nora spent most of her time with him; very rarely did I see her hanging out alone or with girlfriends.

Nora sat quietly, listening to all the information as I spread the materials on the table. She looked overwhelmed, but soon I realized that the feelings had to do with other things beyond the amount of information I was sharing. Her eyes were watery and she stood silent for a minute. She thanked me and then looked at her boyfriend with sadness. He then tried to encourage her to speak to me. Stumbling with her words, and shedding tears, she explained that it would be impossible for her to attend UTEP, that she had too many siblings and she would feel guilty for even attempting it. The expense would be too high on her family, pretty much impossible to cover, and she explained that although it was her dream to go to school in the United States, she would never be able to do it.

I tried to explain to her the different alternatives she had, such as getting scholarships and the fact that at UTEP Mexican students were able to apply for in-state tuition. I also explained that she could get her bachelor's degree in México and then go to UTEP for a master's degree once she was able to earn some money on her own. This did not seem to give her any hope.

César then tried to explain what he thought the problem was. He believed that Nora did not want to pursue dreams of her own. "I have told her that I have applied at the Autonomous University of México [UNAM] in México City. And if I get admitted into their sociology program, I'm definitely going. But she is very upset by this." He indicated that Nora wanted to simply follow him wherever he went, but since this would be hard, she would get resentful with him for wanting to pursue his dream. He said that he would try to encourage her to also pursue her own dreams, but that she didn't seem to have any, that she would be happy just getting married, having babies, and staying at home. "I don't want her to stay attached like that to me. I want her to have other dreams and follow them."

Although this seemed to be César's perspective, I was not too sure that this was completely true. I had observed Nora participate with great passion and enthusiasm in her classes when César was not around. She appeared independent, critical, and articulate as she expressed her point of view. But when she was with him, she was slightly different, quieter and almost as if hiding behind his shadow. Nora, however, did not counter César's interpretations. In fact, she added that indeed that's how it was, and that in addition she was very jealous and almost possessive of him. When I asked if it was true that she did not have any dreams, she only looked down and sobbed. "I am expected to follow my mother's footsteps. I cannot be selfish and think of college when my mother sacrifices everything for the family." The meeting ended on this sad note. I told her that I could continue to help her if she needed more information about UTEP or anything else. Toward the end of the semester, I asked Nora what her plans were after graduation. She said that she had already been admitted at the National Pedagogical University in Juárez and that she would attend there. Altavista teachers had tried to convince her to apply to the education program at UACJ instead, but she said that it was more expensive and she was happy with her decision.

A year after my fieldwork, I was pleased to get a friendship request from Nora on Facebook. I immediately accepted and we began to communicate frequently and became close friends. She shared with me that her relationship with César had changed a lot, since they were not able to see each other more than once or twice a week. She was working in order to pay for her college education and although he was still in town, they lived far away and it was too difficult to bridge the distance with their busy schedules. She also confessed to me in a message:

I was able to enroll at the National Pedagogical University to major in Educational Intervention and the truth is that I have loved my program. . . . Do you remember that my original idea and dream was to be able to study in the U.S. and that due to lack of money I couldn't do it? Maybe I never told you, and it may sound childish, but I always saw you like a model of what I wanted to be when I grew up because you studied what and where I wanted to study. And for a moment I felt so motivated and began to believe that it was possible. Today I am doing what I can, what is in my hands. But I haven't forgotten that dream. . . . Sometimes you feel that you can do the things you want, but you need a push. . . . Sometimes we are what we can, but I want to be able to be what I want.

A couple of months after this message, Nora decided to break up for good with César. She was extremely sad, but this did not preclude her from pressing forward. I had the opportunity to meet with her several times and stay in touch, and she was completely different from the girl she had been around César, resembling more the young woman I had observed in classes. She was driven and had many dreams, which she pursued with passion and hard work. Sometimes she was discouraged by the realities of her context. For example, one time she was assaulted by a couple of armed guys. She had just cashed her paycheck, worth two weeks of work and intended to pay for her tuition, and the robbers took all the money and her cell phone. Needless to say, she would often get frustrated and discouraged by the conditions of the city, her own physical exhaustion, and her financial situation, but she did not give up.

After getting to know her, I learned that she had begun a process of self-definition at Altavista, where her critical consciousness was awakened and where she was able to dream beyond the limitations imposed on women. However, her relationship with César constrained her, as she devoted most of her attention to him. This was her daily struggle: choosing between what seemed impossible by defining herself beyond the parameters of her realities and suppressing her dreams to appease others or for what offered her immediate reward and comfort.

In sum, although the Redefiners might not have been able to become who they wanted to be during high school, they had a defined vision and they were working toward that. They fell and got up again, affected by their context but responding with great agency. At first sight they might appear contradictory, chaotic, or hopeless. But a closer look reveals that by developing a critical consciousness, observing real models of self-authorship, and experiencing the freedom, caring, and opportunities for challenging the self at Altavista, they were able to engage in an autogestión that starts with the self and deliberately strives to author their identities and redefine their self-perceptions as they swim against the current.

Conclusion

The portraits in this chapter offer insights into some of the innermost processes of autogestión and forms of self-authorship that young women experienced at Altavista. The school was not the only influence in the girls' lives, which was relative to that of their families and peers, life histories, and their own agency in orchestrating all the messages from these various realms. What is also clear is that these young women were not passive victims of Juárez violence and that Altavista played an important role in their path to liberation.

According to Pastor, McCormick, and Fine (1996), the challenges of racism, sexism, and classism, rather than debilitating young urban women, have caused them to develop a keen awareness of power dimensions. In this way, the process of individuation characteristic of adolescence is embedded in critical ideas of justice consciousness for young urban women (hooks 1991). As opposed to young women who enjoy a relative degree of privilege and find comfort in being part of the dominant group, poor women of color have to develop strategies to defend themselves (Pastor, McCormick, and Fine 1996). This development of critical consciousness was evident in varying degrees in all the girls in this study. While living in the barrio was enough for the Redirectors and others to develop an oppositional consciousness, Altavista helped the young women understand how to better direct their resistance in the midst of oppression. Altavista thus fostered what Duncan-Andrade calls a critical hope (2009), which "demands a committed and active struggle" against despair and against the social inequalities that shape these youth's reality (185). It is precisely this active struggle that is crucial in autogestión and that takes place in both the intimate and the external realms of the young women's lives. For several of the girls in this study, including the Redirectors and the Redefiners, acquiring a class consciousness, and a warrior identity as a barrio intellectual and a *"mujer de Juárez,"* was key to developing not only a healthy self-esteem but also strategies for survival.

Initially sparked by feelings of dissatisfaction and a need for self-definition, the process of self-authorship may then involve actively striving to shape one's perspectives, goals, and a sense of oneself that, when clearly defined, can lead to congruent construction of meaning and actions (Baxter Magolda 2001). The Redirectors, the Reinventors, and the Redefiners have engaged in this process. But as their stories illustrate, the processes can be messy and nonlinear. For example, the Redefiners can begin to construct knowledge and act in ways congruent to their perspectives, even when their sense of self continues to be injured. On the other hand, this is not entirely true all the time. Marsella and Cristina, for example, on many occasions also acted against what they knew was right for them in their struggle to redefine their own self-worth.

According to Marcia B. Baxter Magolda (2001), experiences in which individuals face a disruption in their comfort zone, are forced to take risks and make decisions, experience dissatisfaction with a present situation, or are compelled to change may provoke the process of self-authorship. However, Baxter Magolda, whose research is situated in developmental theory, renders invalid the possibility of self-authorship in adolescence, attributing youths' regulation of behaviors to fitting into a peer group rather than to intrinsic self-definitions and goals.

Clearly, all the women in this study contradict these assumptions about adolescents in developmental literature to some extent. Their daily realities are such that taking risks, making difficult decisions, and being compelled to change or take action are almost unavoidable despite their young age. Moreover, as can be seen from most of the portraits provided, although all of them experienced a desire to fit in, Altavista also served as a space where they could undo this influence as to not let it override internal goals. On the other hand, when their goals did not match the women's behavior, the issue was far more complex than a desire to fit in.

The life histories of the young women presented here show that adolescent working-class girls who have had to overcome many obstacles throughout their lives may follow a different life trajectory and may engage in self-authoring processes much earlier than the women often studied, who tend to be older or in more privileged positions. This not only points to some gaps and biases in developmental literature on young women's self-authorship but also may suggest that young women's knowledge that emerges at the margins of society can be easily undermined and that meaningful opportunities to foster liberation and autogestión, like those provided by Altavista, can often be overlooked by the tendency to focus on economic gains or measurable results in discussions about the value of education for women in the so-called developing world.

As discussed in previous chapters, the type of empowerment that the Redirectors, the Redefiners, and the Reinventors revealed is not based on mythical ideas of meritocracy, consumption, or individualist pursuits. Even when stemming from a self-reflexivity that focuses on their internal sense of identity, the external results tended to go back to communal goals. Gabriela, Diana, Karla, and Marsella are all good examples of how their autogestión moved from the intimate self to connections with others and collective action in their external world.

Finally, Pastor, McCormick, and Fine's (1996) and Robinson and Ward's (1991) concerns that marginalized girls may manifest their critical consciousness through individual and seemingly chaotic or self-damaging forms of opposition could be addressed by recognizing the powerful ways in which Altavista promoted autogestión. The pedagogical and sociocultural context of Altavista offers insights into potential ways in which schools could provide tangible and meaningful benefits to improve youth's living conditions beyond the symbolic capital of a diploma or practical skills for employment—namely by fostering self-reflexive, strategic, and both intimate and collective forms of agency. Having unleashed students' autogestión, the possibilities are infinite and their chances of overcoming the unavoidable challenges that will come their way will most likely increase.

Life after Altavista

The most savory grape, the one that produces the wines with best texture and aroma, the sweetest and most generous, doesn't grow in rich soil but in stony land; the plant, with a mother's obstinacy, overcomes obstacles to thrust its roots deep into the ground and take advantage of every drop of water.

—Isabel Allende, *Portrait in Sepia: A Novel*

HIS BOOK HAS BEEN about hope in the midst of impossibility, and meaningful knowledge that liberates. It tells the story of both a group of young women holding on to their dreams and their right to a life of dignity despite extremely challenging circumstances, and a school that aims to support their journey.

The young protagonists of this book took on the challenge to reinvent themselves, all while living in the most precarious circumstances and in an unprecedentedly hostile era. The autogestión that they developed in the process was not the type of empowerment promoted in mainstream media and in shopping malls characterized by purchasing power. Nor was it about simply having enough grit. Instead, critical consciousness and a communal vision were identity elements that most of the girls in this study had in common, even when they did not completely feel independent or confident and when their lives were constrained in many ways. This *conscientization* is precisely what fueled their agency. It is a consciousness that cannot be easily co-opted by capitalist schemes of consumerism or the fallacy of meritocracy, nor eroded by the barrage of death and violence. Many of these girls embodied identities of activists, critics, organic intellectuals, and agents of change. They were also bearers of wisdom and dreamers searching for peace and a spiritual connection with their world—constantly changing, constantly remaking themselves. As anthropologist Jessica Taft (2011) asserts, for young women like these, "the vision of empowered girlhood is not based on individual success in a flawed system of inequalities and injustices, but in the belief that they have something to contribute to making the world a better, more just and more sustainable place" (79).

Although these women often felt lonely, they were not alone in their struggle. Altavista, with its relentless quest for utopia, became a sacred space (Soto et al. 2009) of human connection that served as both a safe refuge and a cultivator of their autogestión and critical reflexivity in connection with others. It existed against all odds and offered these women what they were not able to find in most places, and without requiring a complicated bureaucratic system, millions of dollars, or the counting and recounting of standardized test scores. Instead, it took revolutionary love, a bold vision, and committed teachers who viewed themselves as organic intellectuals and activists.

What Altavista makes clear is that knowledge does not always come from school, but it can be fostered by it. Much of it comes from everyone and everything we get to know and to experience, especially life struggles. Altavista and the young women also demonstrate that a school can take the courageous and revolutionary role of exposing and validating this knowledge—a role that goes against the colonial notion of schooling as a venue to domesticate and polish the "illiterate" and "simple minded." As Armida stated when I said good-bye, "Knowledge does not come from the universities. It comes from the social contexts where human beings are." This understanding, so crucial to Altavista, was what set it apart from other schools, and it is a lesson that the young women learned and demonstrated well.

The almost impossible task of offering a relevant and liberating education was bestowed on Altavista. Its teachers took on this challenge by eschewing hegemonic ideas of "success" and offering the hope of what could be possible through students' action, the validation of their identities, and the legitimization of subjugated knowledges. Thus, Altavista's goal was not so much to help students fit into the world as it is today but to provide a space where students could make and remake themselves, and in the process remake the world. Empowerment and autogestión for the young women in this book was then not only about becoming autonomous but also about learning that the world is theirs, about reading it and transforming it.

Pressing On

Today, Altavista continues to sustain itself and stay the course against the current, and the girls have taken on new challenges as young adults. As has been clear, Altavista does not offer any ideas for schools struggling in the current paradigm of competition, but it revives the possibility of utopian dreams. Altavista is not, however, a victory narrative. The teachers at Altavista understood that, in contrast to middle- and upper-class students, Altavista's students were not protected by a series of safety nets that will catch them or grant them second chances when they fail or when they make mistakes. The obstacles that Altavista's students confront on a daily basis require considerably more effort, sacrifice, strategy, and perseverance to overcome. Of the students who graduate, only about half of them apply to colleges and universities, and an even smaller number enroll. The reality is that many of the students do not finish high school or enroll in higher education institutions because they have to work. Some of the students take a year off with the goal of working and saving money for college. Part-time jobs after school are difficult to find in the area, and transportation and safety become important issues for students looking for jobs in faraway neighborhoods. Principal Armida has witnessed far too many times that once students stop going to school, they will probably not go back. For that reason, she took at least two entire class sessions in the spring semester to explain to students how to navigate the college world, encouraging them not to give up, to continue their education, giving them strategies to save money and to apply for scholarships. She would tell them:

> The disinherited like us will never have money. Instead, start saving before you graduate from high school so that you will at least have money for the initial enrollment fee, and then you need to study hard so that you can get a scholarship that will help you remain in school. But don't expect to have all the conditions necessary, a computer, etcetera, no. All of that will hardly ever come to us. So if you are waiting to study, you will never do it. You have to just go for it and pursue your goal.

Armida also guided them on which universities were more academically and scholarly solid, which ones were just for-profit institutions and academically weak, and which ones were more likely to offer merit-based financial support. She even talked to students about the importance of being deliberate about the decisions they made in life. "If you or your girlfriend gets pregnant, you want this to be a conscious choice. I'm not telling you that you shouldn't get pregnant. But I want you to know that life gets more complicated when you have a child," Armida told the students, "and even if you do have a child, don't let this stop you from pursuing college. I'm telling you from personal experience. I got pregnant when I was nineteen, and I still went to college and got my degree, but it was very difficult."

Many students make great efforts to overcome the barriers imposed upon them. Those who graduate from Altavista and manage to attend college take with them and continue to develop the identities and agency they cultivated in high school as well as their ability to read both the word and the world (Freire 1970). "University professors often know when a student comes from Altavista," Armida explained, "because they tend to be the most critical and vocal." Some students would be welcomed by university professors who appreciated this level of thought and social critique, but in many instances students would be faced with new challenges of repression and domestication at the university level.

The struggle also continued for Altavista. Just as I began to write this book, the school was at the verge of closing and being taken over by the state due to lack of funding. Once again, as many times before, its teachers and students had to rise and find creative ways to keep its doors open. Its story does not end here, but I hope that documenting this brief period in its history will contribute to its legacy for the generations to come.

Life after High School

The young women who shared their stories are no longer adolescents. They are now grown women—some are even mothers—who have embarked on new projects. Altavista most definitely marked an important time in their lives, but they continue to cultivate their wisdom as they overcome new challenges and reach and build new dreams. After my time in the field, I had the opportunity to stay in touch with most of them. With a few, including Marsella and Nora, I became very close. Almost every time I visit Juárez, I meet up with them, and we stay in touch through Facebook and phone when necessary. With others, including Alejandra, Gabriela, Diana, Karla, and Iliana, I have kept in touch to various degrees mostly through online social networks. On the other hand, I did not hear from others like Cristina and Mónica for a long time, and I completely lost track of Lizette. Below I briefly share some of the developments in their lives that I have had the honor to learn about or witness.

Alejandra

After my year of fieldwork, I learned that Alejandra had gotten pregnant and quit school. After she had her baby, the problems with Rafael escalated and he threatened to take away her baby. Afraid of what he could do, she moved with her son to a city in the United States, where she had a relative. She stayed there for a couple of years and was able to escape from her turbulent relationship, go back to school, and raise her son with much more peace. After having spent some time in the United States, Alejandra was deported back to México. Although I did not keep up with the various events of her life, it appears as though she was able to completely terminate her turbulent relationship with Rafael, the father of her son. Alejandra returned to Altavista and completed high school. She also started a new relationship and had two more children. She currently lives in Juárez and is in her fourth year of college at UACJ. Alejandra has maintained impressive grades and thus has been awarded a *beca de excelencia* (academic excellence scholarship). This scholarship is awarded each year only to a small percentage of students—those with the highest grades—and it covers their entire tuition. Alejandra has been able to remain a top student all while juggling her three small children and financial challenges.

Gabriela

After high school graduation, Gabriela participated in an internship project with an NGO that focused on building up the community by tapping into the resources and talents already present in its youth. She took a few trips to conferences in México and the United States focusing on collective action. She then enrolled in the teacher education program at UACJ, but after participating in an exchange program with the University of Guadalajara (UDG), she decided to change schools and majors. She was admitted and enrolled in the anthropology program at UDG. In 2013 she began a romantic relationship with her new partner, Oscar, with whom she recently had a baby boy.

Gabriela has shed her dreadlocks but continues to be interested in music, urban art, and activism. As a new mother, she has become passionate about motherhood, researching and promoting human and women's rights as well as women's ways of knowing in relation to birthing and caring for babies, particularly when it comes to underprivileged mothers. With every new stage, Gabriela continues to cultivate her wisdom and to serve as an advisor to her friends. Her relationship with her sister Alejandra appears stronger than ever despite the geographic distance between them, perhaps due to their new identities as mothers. Today, Gabriela continues to cultivate her own spiritual journey and pursue artistic projects, most recently involving painting and photography.

Diana

After the devastating experience Diana had in 2011, she continued to get involved in marches and other forms of activism in her community and continued to work on her own healing. After she graduated from high school, Diana began her studies in physical therapy in México City, but after struggling financially, she finally enrolled at a university in Puebla, México, where she has been pursuing her degree. Not only has she continued her studies, fueling her passion to help people through a combination of physical therapy and alternative ways of healing, but she has also continued to be actively involved in feminist activism.

While away from Juárez and after much reflection, Diana finally came to terms with her sexual orientation and came out to her family as a lesbian. As such, at the time this book was written, she was involved in a long-term relationship with her new partner, Samantha. Feeling that she finally identified the type of feminism that best fits her views, Diana has actively participated in *lesbofeminist* activism through a collective in Puebla that has provided her a nurturing and supportive community in the particularly conservative context of Puebla. In addition, this group has offered her a venue to express her forms of resistance in productive ways. Diana continues to organize workshops and marches against feminicide and sexual violence, among many other activities.

Karla

Karla's transition to college to attend law school was extremely difficult due to the dangers of the city, transportation and financial obstacles, not to mention the challenges that came with the university context itself. She also had to sacrifice time with her boyfriend due to the time-consuming commute to school and in order to study during the week. While she finished her first year successfully, she became emotionally exhausted and found that law school was not for her after all. She transferred to the psychology program, where she has been much happier.

Karla continues to pursue her degree in psychology at UACJ. Though she has continued to face multiple challenges, such as her mother's illness and her own health issues with anemia, she continues to press toward her goals. For example, she took a job at the maquiladora during a couple of summers to save for a car that would make her commutes to school safer and more feasible. Karla continued to be involved in theater and also started a new relationship with a young man. Together they had a baby girl whose pictures populate her Facebook timeline.

Iliana

Iliana became pregnant in the early spring of her last year of high school. She kept it a secret and was often absent due to morning sickness. Therefore, I did not see her very often that semester. Although Iliana tended to be one of the most reserved participants, she seemed withdrawn in the last weeks of my fieldwork. She continued to extend her sweet smile to me whenever I saw her, but having learned from another student that she was pregnant, and not wanting to put pressure on her or appear intrusive, I did not ask too many questions. A few months after graduation and after she gave birth to a beautiful baby boy, I reconnected with her through Facebook though mostly in a superficial way. Iliana married her longtime boyfriend and father of her son and has been a dedicated mother ever since. Although I do not know whether she attempted to attend college, as she had expressed to me during interviews, she did pursue her dream of engaging in community projects, particularly related to music and with children.

Marsella

From the first interview, I was intrigued by how open Marsella was with me about her insecurities and other intimate areas of her life. In part, I interpreted her confessional testimonios as a desire to have her story told to the world for other young women who found themselves in a similar situation, but also as a cry for sisterly intimacy and connection. I was perhaps right about this; as our friendship continued and grew after my fieldwork, she began to call me *"hermanita"* (sister). Indeed, that is what she became to me, a little sister. While she continued to struggle with self-esteem issues a few years after high school—granted, to a much lesser degree—her focus significantly changed. Disappointed by the communication studies program at the state university where she first enrolled, Marsella quit the program and spent almost a year preparing financially and academically to enroll in the education program at UACJ. As usual, Marsella had the highest scores in UACJ's admissions exam for their education program and every year she was a top student. While she has needed moral support, particularly when facing personal and economic difficulties, such as her grandmother's illnesses, family problems, and other consequences of living in very precarious conditions, Marsella has not been one to give up. A voracious reader, Marsella continues to redefine herself as an intelligent, critical, and sensitive woman of substance and action. She has enjoyed a high reputation among her professors, who admire her passion, critical voice, and insightful contributions to her classes. Her academic efforts and dedication have paid off as she, like Alejandra, has been awarded a *beca de excelencia* every year due to her high grades. She has also received other awards from the university due to her high academic achievement, including one that provided her a new laptop. Without these scholarships, she would not be able to continue her education.

But getting good grades has not been her only priority. Her commitment to social justice efforts and activism has grown stronger than ever. Therefore, Marsella continues to be involved in activist projects. She is a committed vegetarian due to her politics regarding humane practices toward animals. She also has participated in multiple marches and student movements against violence and other social problems at the local and national levels, including the national movement "Yo Soy #132."

Marsella no longer isolates herself from other women and has been able to find friends who share her views. Although she continued to struggle with her self-esteem, at times felt depressed by her dislike of her own image in the mirror, and had some brief relapses with eating disorders after graduating from Altavista, her boyfriend, Manuel, and her grandmother's love continued to give her strength in her battle to redefine her self-image.

In 2015 Marsella's grandmother passed away, which was a devastating loss. Nonetheless, in the past few years, Marsella has gotten closer to her mother, which has allowed her to learn from her and dispel myths about the past. For example, Marsella now understands that the reason why her mother left her father was that he was physically abusive and she did not want Marsella to witness or experience this kind of abuse. This has helped her see her mother in a different light, as she admires her mother's brave and difficult choices and can now better understand why she had to sacrifice her time with her in order to work. This new understanding has probably contributed to better feelings of self-esteem.

Throughout her college journey, Marsella continued to visit Altavista regularly, at least weekly, and has continued her relationships, especially with Armida and Rigoberto. Not surprisingly, her undergraduate thesis research focuses on college students' attitudes toward education, and whether these attitudes are focused on social transformation or conformity.

After six years in a serious relationship, she and her high school sweetheart began to question their relationship as apparently they wanted different things: Manuel was interested in marriage and children while Marsella still had many other goals that she wanted to accomplish. Marsella's determination to pursue her goals has convinced Manuel to compromise and wait until she is ready for a family.

At the time this book was written, Marsella had just graduated from college. This incredibly meaningful accomplishment was only shadowed by the unfortunate fact that her grandmother was no longer physically present to witness it. Still, Marsella glowed with pride during her graduation ceremony that I was honored to attend.

Marsella has grown into a very confident young woman who is clear about what she wants in life. She is currently enrolled in a postbaccalaureate program for a certificate in the study of feminicide in México that will be fully sponsored by her undergraduate thesis advisor. This reveals not only Marsella's commitment to learning and addressing issues of gender and violence but also Marsella's resourcefulness, determination, passion, and persistent approach to developing meaningful relationships with teachers. Marsella's next goals are to complete research for publication and enroll in a graduate program.

Nora

Although I did not get to know Nora very well during my year of fieldwork at Altavista, she and I became very close afterward. Nora and Marsella were good friends, so the three of us enjoyed getting together when I visited the city. As previously discussed, Nora asked me for information about the possibilities of attending the University of Texas at El Paso. Disappointed about the impossibility of this dream, she never attempted to apply. I worried that she would be paralyzed by this setback. Her boyfriend had characterized her as someone who did not have dreams of her own and was willing and almost adamant to follow him wherever he went. His plans were to study sociology in México City, so I was surprised when she told me she was going to study education at the National Pedagogical University in Juárez. And I was even more surprised when not too long after graduation, Nora and her boyfriend broke up. Apparently, like in Marsella's case, they wanted different things. This constituted an important act of self-authorship that allowed her to more fully engage in autogestión.

Nora was very successful in her education program. Not only did she earn very high grades but also, and opposite to the way her former boyfriend depicted her, Nora had many dreams. She completed a thesis whose research focused on students' social identities and that allowed her to continue to collaborate with Altavista. Soon after receiving her college degree, Nora applied for a competitive state grant that focused on the revitalization of cultural practices in low-income communities. This involved working with communities and children to bring back traditional Mexican games that use handmade toys and physical activity. Nora was awarded the grant, which allowed her to direct the project and learn from the communities where she implemented it. At the time this book was written, Nora had enrolled in and completed her first year of a master's program in urban development at UACJ and was conducting research in the state of Jalisco.

While Nora has had great academic success, and her collective actions are to be admired, there are other aspects of her life in which she has also demonstrated her wisdom and autogestión. In 2011 Nora started a new relationship with an old boyfriend. Soon, she got pregnant and got married. Although the couple was in love, the many responsibilities of marriage and parenting, particularly in their difficult economic situation, led to many problems and disappointments. Eventually, the situation became so dire that Nora felt compelled to leave her husband. These challenges, while discouraging and difficult to overcome, have not been able to destroy her spirit and determination. Nora's beautiful daughter is a source of inspiration, and someone for whom she wishes to model what it means to be a woman of strength.

Cristina and Mónica

I did not hear from Cristina or Mónica for a very long time. All I knew was that Cristina had been seen by other girls working at a department store, and Mónica had also started working at a maquiladora, but I was not able to keep in touch after high school graduation. Recently, however, I was thrilled to find a friendship request from Cristina on my Facebook account. Although we have not had the opportunity to converse much, I learned that she is the happy mother of a beautiful baby girl. I also heard from Mónica a few years after graduation through Facebook. She sent me a message to tell me that she had started college at UACJ. However, I did not hear from her again.

Final Words: Toward the Path of *Conocimiento*

If the role of a researcher is to come up with formulas and solutions for schools, I have miserably failed. If the role of a researcher is to objectively capture the truth and to remain detached from the story, I have failed again. The young women in this study have captured my heart. We have become accomplices of many stories, whose sharing contributed to the process of self-authorship, and by witnessing it, I was personally impacted as well. They have become my sisters, my friends, and my role models. I have learned lessons of hope, wisdom, and courage—lessons of what it means to be a woman. Today I remain friends with several of them, and I feel privileged to continue to be a witness of their lives.

Altavista, the girls in this study, and my journey in Juárez taught me about the path of what Anzaldúa (2002) calls *conocimiento:*

> a discourse of signs, images, feelings, words that, once decoded, carry the power to startle you out of tunnel vision and habitual patterns of thought . . . one that guides your feet along the path, gives you el ánimo to dedicate yourself to transforming perceptions of reality, and thus the conditions of life. . . . By redeeming your most painful experiences you transform them into something valuable, algo para compartir or share with others so they too may be empowered. (540)

This path of conocimiento that the young women have walked through is not a clean story of privilege and comfort, nor simply a response to a single identity crisis, nor the pursuit of a dream with grit and hard work. It began as soon as they started their journey into womanhood, when the ground shifted around them, as they were forced to confront their fears and face a collapsing new world in which they became aware of their vulnerability. Altavista then provided a liminal space where their inner life met the outer world of reality, resulting in new possibilities. Serving as what Anzaldúa (1987) would call *Nepantla*, or a state of in-betweenness, Altavista exposed them to new perspectives and to the opportunity to legitimize and access the knowledge derived from their own feelings, their bodily experiences, and a life at the margins. It is in this zone of new prospects and reflexivity that the young women could explore, individually and collectively, their own constructions of self, knowledge, and reality. At first they might have felt paralyzed, confused, and angered by a new awareness; they might have felt displaced by the chaos of navigating contradictory realms. But the alternative reality that Altavista was able to offer them, even if temporarily, pulled them out of their usual coping strategies. Here they were able to put the pieces together, re-create their life story, test it, and reenvision a new road map for their lives. As such, the young women authored new identities full of compassionate strategy and responded to a call to action to find common ground and form holistic alliances. Their story then becomes *algo para compartir,* a testimonio of wisdom that generates further agency.

During my year of fieldwork and beyond there was too much brutality and death in Juárez—so much that it could suffocate those who survived the most violent era in the city, leaving nothing but cynicism and numbness. But here Altavista and the young women offer a story of possibility, of conocimiento, of autogestión and courageous, critical, and hopeful life. I have been given the chance of living and the responsibility to tell about it. This book may not produce a formula for school reform or for women's empowerment. It certainly will not save any lives and prevent further tragedy. But I hope that at least it can be a testimony to the world honoring those who, like Altavista's teachers and the young women who have shared their stories, have resisted succumbing quietly to injustice and death.

Acknowledgments

THIS BOOK IS THE RESULT of a long journey that could not have been completed without the support of many family members, friends, mentors, colleagues, and organizations along the way. From the initial visionary stages to the data collection and writing process, this has been a collective effort.

Primero que nada agradezco a la Preparatoria Altavista y a lxs maestrxs y las jóvenes que generosamente compartieron conmigo y con el mundo su tiempo, sus historias, su esperanza, su valentía y su sabiduría. La amistad que resultó de este proyecto me ha tocado profundamente y más allá de la creación de este libro. Simplemente no tengo las palabras adecuadas para expresar el gran agradecimiento y admiración que siento por ustedes. Areli, Dafne, Valeria, Elizabeth, Lluvia, Jaqueline, Pamela, Dayana, Mayra, Nidia, Daisy, Armida, René, César, Ricardo, Gustavo, Miguel, Lalas, José, Rodolfo, Verónica, Perla y muchxs otrxs más: gracias por su tiempo, confianza y apoyo. Gracias también al Colegio de la Frontera Norte y a todxs aquellxs investigadores, maestrxs, activistas, artistas, poetas y miembrxs de la comunidad de Ciudad Juárez que generosamente me ayudaron a ganar mayor entendimiento del contexto social y educativo de la ciudad.

Support from various organizations, centers, and donors proved critical to bringing this project to completion, and I am forever grateful for their generosity and their belief in my work. This includes financial support from the American Association of University Women's American Fellowship and various sponsors from the University of Texas at Austin, including the Graduate School, the College of Education, the Center for Women's and Gender Studies, and the Mexican Center.

I am deeply indebted to my familia, who have supported this journey in the most personal ways. To my children, Emiliano y Natalia, I wish I could find the words to thank you for all that you have given to me and to this project without even knowing it. You have been part of this process since your conception and my greatest inspiration, *la luz de mi vida y mi razón de ser. Emiliano, gracias por ser paciente con mamá cuando no podía jugar contigo porque tenía que escribir este libro. Natalia, gracias cosita bella por patear mi pancita mientras me sentaba por horas en frente de la computadora, recordándome que tenía que apurarme a terminar de escribir para que pudieras salir.* I hope one day both of you will read this book and also gain wisdom and inspiration for your own lives. To Juanito, my soulmate, I wish I were a poet like you to thank you for your love and support in the way that you deserve. You have witnessed this journey from beginning to end, enduring my epiphanies, risky adventures, frustrations, and the many hours of secluded writing and years of work that this has required. Your heart, intelligence, spirit, and passion for knowledge and social justice never cease to inspire me. *Te amo; gracias por caminar conmigo.*

Especial agradecimiento se lo debo a mi padre, quien creyó en mí más de lo que yo podría hacerlo y quién prendió el motor para que comenzara este proyecto. Estaré eternamente agradecida por tener un hombre tan sabio en mi vida, que apoya mi idealismo y pasión, y cuya dedicación a la educación, la juventud y la igualdad social ha inspirado mi trabajo. Padre, desde la elección de la escuela, la investigación de campo y el proceso de escritura, tus consejos han sido fundamentales. A mi madre, el fundamento de mi vida y mi trabajo y a la que nunca dejaré de extrañar, eres la esencia de este libro. Tú has estado presente en espíritu y guiado cada palabra que he escrito. Como desearía que estuvieras presente físicamente para que fueras testigo del legado que ha dejado tu historia, la cual engendró este proyecto. Todo este trabajo es para honrarte a ti. A mis hermanitos, César y Flor Alejandra, gracias por todo su amor, apoyo, ánimo y presencia incondicional. Somos ramas del mismo árbol, having started the journey together *en el viejo Juárez* that led me to this point. *Mucho de lo que hoy soy y he logrado hacer es por ustedes*—the three of us, always against the odds.

Con gratitud especial también ofrezco reconocimiento a mi gente en la frontera—aquéllos que permanecen y también a los que se han ido a otras tierras. Gracias a mis madres postizas Chela, Tía Nacia y Tía Pack, así como a mi hermana Pina y mis grandes amigas Laura G., Laura M. y Marsella por nutrirme física y espiritualmente durante el transcurso de este proyecto durante altas y bajas. No hubiera sobrevivido sin ustedes. A Diana y Héctor, gracias por ver los diamantes dentro de la roca y por su gran generosidad y apoyo.

This project would not have been completed without the support of many mentors who motivated and supported it in many ways, including Angela Valenzuela, Luis Urrieta, Haydeé Rodríguez, Lourdes Díaz Soto,

Keffrelyn Brown, Cecilia Ballí, Aurolyn Luykx, and Elaine Hampton, who believed in my writing before anyone else. I owe special thanks to my ultimate mentor, Dr. Douglas E. Foley, *the Godfather.* Your incredible wisdom and knowledge along the way has supported every step. I am incredibly blessed and honored to have you in my life—as an ethnographer, as a scholar, and as a friend. Thank you for believing in the significance of my work and in the power of my ideas when it seemed like very few did. You have helped me gain confidence in my writing and have shown me what it means to remain authentic and true to my ideals throughout the years.

Also thanks to my *hermanas académicas* who have shared sacred spaces with me, saving me from intellectual isolation, discouragement, and even illness. Mónica Neshyba, thank you for your caring support, always thinking about what may seem like the smallest details yet are the most meaningful ones. G. Sue Kasun, Carol Brochin, Toni Avila, and Elizabeth Villarreal, brave scholar mommies and my *hermanas, siempre al pie del cañón,* have lifted me up when I've needed it the most. And to my brilliant and most caring graduate student, Esmeralda Rodríguez, you have done more than you could imagine. *A todas, gracias.*

Last but not least, I thank my Creator, holding my hand and breathing healing love, life, and insight into my body and soul throughout the entire journey that has led to this book. May this book honor life, hope, freedom, and revolutionary love of the Divine.

Notes

Introduction

1. Underpinning and driving economic globalization, "neoliberalism" is a term used for economic liberalism that promotes the reduction of rules and restrictions, privatization, free trade, open markets, deregulation, and reductions in government spending in order to enhance the role of the private sector in the economy. In Latin America, neoliberalism has extended via international financial institutions and transnational corporate hegemony. In order for many Latin American nations to deal with their economic crisis, they were pushed to cede democratic control of their economies to the international actors to whom they are economically indebted. In these neoliberal structural reforms, real democracy is obstructed and deformed by international economic interference in policy-making. In Latin America, neoliberal adjustments are directly associated with increased inequality, poverty, and lack of access to state-sponsored social supports, and have resulted in the degradation of worker, indigenous, and peasant lives, their rights, and their ability to protest (Kelly 2008).

2. I often make reference to the feminicides as a phenomenon that has marked the history and identity of Juárez as well as the lives of its young women. In doing so, I utilize the term "feminicide" rather than "femicide," following Rosa-Linda Fregoso and Cynthia Bejarano's (2010) conceptualization of the term, which points to the socially constructed notions of femininity and masculinity and the role of power: "In arguing for the use of the term *feminicide* over *femicide*, we draw from a feminist analytical perspective that interrupts essentialist notions of female identity that equate gender and biological sex and looks instead to the gendered nature of practices and behaviors, along with the performance of gender norms. . . . Instead of a scenario in which gender and sex necessarily concur, the concept of feminicide allows us to map the power dynamics and relations of gender, sexuality, race, and class underlying violence, and in so doing, shift the analytic focus to how gender norms, inequities, and power relationships increase women's vulnerability to violence" (3–4).

3. In the summer of 2010, precisely when Juárez was going through its deadliest year ever, the popular cosmetics company MAC paired up with Rodarte fashion designers to introduce their new fall collection, surprisingly inspired by Juárez. The preview was quite shocking and controversial, as it revealed the ghostly images of this "edgy" line: dead-looking models wearing white lipstick, and reddish brown hues all around their eyes. "Ghost Town," "Factory," "Badland," and "Juárez" were among the names of their shades, ranging from a $12 nail polish to a $19.50 eye shadow (Beck 2010). MAC, known for embracing racial and gender diversity and as a pioneer in the support of HIV/AIDS education and recycling programs, failed its reputation as a socially conscientious company and the ad was deemed offensive by the fashion community (Harquail 2010). While MAC changed the names in the collection, as well as offering an apology and a one-time monetary contribution to a Juárez charity, this does not change the fact that MAC had allowed the objectification of Juárez feminicides to happen without any sort of alarm, revealing the degree to which Juárez women have been "othered" and dehumanized. As one commenter stated in a response to a blog: "MAC has made a name for itself by catering to 'All ages, all colors, all races.' Apparently this 'inclusiveness' doesn't extend to the brown women lost in Juarez. Compassion is a wonderful quality . . . we are ugly without it. And no amount of makeup will cover up that kind of ugliness" (Harquail 2010).

1. Border Paradoxes, Dystopia, and Revolutionary Education

1. The total Juárez population in 2010 was 1,332,131 residents, according to the Instituto Nacional de Estadística y Geografía (INEGI 2011).

2. As of 2013, the minimum wage in El Paso, Texas, was US$7.25 *per hour*—about 95.70 pesos—(U.S. Department of Labor n.d.), while in Juárez the minimum wage was 64.76 pesos *per day*—about 8 pesos per hour (Secretaría de Hacienda y Crédito Público [SHCP] 1982–2015).

3. The Bracero Program (1942–64) included a series of laws and diplomatic binational agreements for the importation of temporary laborers from México to the United States. Braceros were brought to work in agriculture and in the construction of the railroad lines that would support the importation of U.S. goods into México and the exportation of Mexican raw materials and labor to the United States.

4. Maquiladora plants in México are factories, often owned by transnational corporations, that use temporarily imported materials and assemble goods for export. This stage in the process of global capitalist expansion involves relocating the labor-intensive phases of production to economically developing countries and benefiting from an abundant supply of cheap labor, in addition to policies that allow companies to import materials and technology duty free as long as the

assembled products are exported. They established factories in Juárez and other border cities because initially plants used for this purpose were only allowed within twenty kilometers of the U.S. border (Villarreal and Sakamoto 2008).

5. Meant to attract foreign investments, Export Processing Zones (EPZs) are parcels of territory with special laws regarding production that incentivize transnational corporations with extremely low production costs. EPZs are able to offer these low costs by allowing investors to import without tax, requiring minimal corporate income tax, and by offering cheap labor wages, freedom from labor unions, loosened regulations on the environment and labor, and state-subsidized infrastructure (Teeple 2000).

6. Andrés Villarreal and Wei-hsin Yu (2007) confirm that in México, foreign-owned and export-oriented firms employ significantly more women than nationally owned firms at the occupational level, partly due to greater employment for unskilled workers.

7. It has been documented that migration to Juárez has brought an influx of people particularly from indigenous and rural backgrounds whose native communities of small agricultural landowners and workers have been dramatically dispossessed by the very forces of economic globalization (Bacon 2008; Ponce 2012).

8. Sarah Babb (2005) asserts that the structural adjustment policies implemented in Latin America have brought about the erosion of institutions that promote social welfare due, in part, to the tendency of highly indebted countries to extract domestic resources and reduce spending on social services. Because peripheral nations are at a disadvantage when negotiating with foreign investors and multilateral organizations, they are incapable of building the institutions of social citizenship and instead lower wages and safety standards in order to attract foreign investors.

9. Portes and Hoffman (2003), in their Marxist analysis of the effects of neoliberal structural adjustment in Latin America, argue that an important consequence of neoliberal reforms has been the evolution of social classes during the last two decades in the region, giving way to greater economic disparities. They also underscore the evidence that the class of micro-entrepreneurs, or the informal proletariat (who range from small business owners to gum sellers in the streets), has seen a rapid increase.

10. According to sociologist Teresa Almada (in Moreno Acosta 2008), who has done extensive research with gang members and the challenges of drug addictions in the city, drug traffic from Juárez to the United States changed in three important ways in the 1990s. First, Mexican cartels began to grow larger and more powerful than those in Colombia. Supported by the Mexican state, Mexicans began to control the drug trade. Second, the Mexican cartels adopted a new strategy in which drugs would be infiltrated in multiple, but small or low-scale, deliveries. This necessitated the involvement of a greater number of Juárez residents to serve as the

"burros" to carry out these low-level drug dealing operations, as well as assassins to take care of pending issues. Third, payments began to come in the form of drugs.

11. Estimates about the number of *picaderos* in the city range from 1,800 to 10,000, many of which are protected by law enforcement officers (Dávila 2008; Frontera Norte Sur 2008; Moreno Acosta 2008).

12. México's education system is currently divided in four macro levels: (1) *educación inicial,* for small children up to five years old (the equivalent to pre-kindergarten); (2) *educación básica,* including pre-*escolar, primaria,* and the three years of *secundaria* (the equivalent to grades 1–8); (3) *preparatoria or bachillerato,* which includes grades 10–12; and (4) higher education. The SEP also offers two additional educational branches: indigenous education and technological education.

13. T. Almada, "Fw: Juárez se nos muere de tristeza," electronic mailing list message, February 11, 2010.

14. A month after the massacre, the nightmare returned to Villas de Salvárcar when a commando of seven trucks, with a group of armed and masked men claiming to be part of the ministerial police, arrived and picked up four young men who had survived the shootings and had been previously interrogated by the authorities. Desperate, the families went to the attorney general, who was unable to confirm whether that had been an official commando. President Felipe Calderón responded to their complaints that the students who had been targeted were most likely gang members. The infuriated families demanded to speak with the president, who had no other choice but to visit the city on February 11. A meeting with the city's Social Cabinet was organized at an elegant convention center. As hundreds of elegant people and politicians gathered to meet with the president, and after a series of formal introductions, Luz María Dávila, a maquiladora worker who had been devastated by the loss of her two sons in the massacre, stood to confront him. She took the microphone and said: "I will not remain silent because this is the truth. Excuse me Mr. President, I cannot tell you 'welcome' because for me you are not welcome. No one is, because for more than two years murders have been committed here. Many things are happening and nobody does anything. I want justice, not just for my two children, but also for all the other children. I cannot shake hands with you and say 'welcome,' because to me you're not welcome. I want this to be done right, so that Juárez becomes what it was before. Juárez is in mourning. It's not fair that my boys were at a party.... Now I want you to take back what you said, that they were gang members. That's a lie. One of my sons studied at the UACH [Autonomous University of Chihuahua] and the other one was in high school. They didn't have ... time, no. ... It cannot be, Mr. President, you cannot say they were gang members. They had no time to walk in the street. They studied and worked. I bet that if someone had killed one of your children, you would look under the rocks for the murderer. As I have no

resources, I can't look for the killers. You always say the same things Mr. President, Ferriz [City Mayor], Baeza [Former Governor of Chihuahua], they all say the same and nothing gets fixed here. Everything is worse, that's the truth" (Silvielena 2010). Outside the convention center, dozens of activists who blocked Tomás Fernandez Avenue to protest against the incompetence of the Mexican government were violently removed by the local and federal police. They were pulled by the hair, pushed, and kicked, paradoxically right outside a meeting that was supposed to seek ways to eliminate the violence in the city. Among the protesters were some of the victims' families as well as members of various NGOs.

15. A number of activists and families of feminicide and drug war victims have been aggressively repressed by the state and other unidentified enemies. On October 29, 2010, José Darío Alvarez Orrantes, a nineteen-year-old, first-year sociology student at the Autonomous University of Ciudad Juárez (UACJ), was shot in the back by the federal police during a peaceful march against the militarization of the city. In the days to follow several other students were victims of the police's harassment and violent repression (Hernández Navarro 2010).

Josefina Reyes Salazar, another activist, had been actively denouncing the abuses of the military before she was seized by armed men and shot in the head when trying to defend herself (Amnesty International 2010). Her relatives continued the protest for nearly a month but also became targets. Her two siblings and sister-in-law were killed in February 2011—adding up to six victims of homicide in the family since 2008. Other members of the family continued to receive threats, pushing as many as twenty of them to seek political asylum across the border. As if this were not enough, the family was accused of slandering Juárez's law enforcement's reputation and of organized crime.

Susana Chávez, 36, the poet and devoted feminicide activist who coined the slogan "Ni una más" (Not one more death) for a campaign against the killing of Juárez women, was found murdered and mutilated in January 2011 (King 2011). The authorities arrested three suspects, two of whom were under eighteen years old, and who had allegedly been drinking with her before they killed her for refusing to have sex with them. Those who knew Susana highly doubt the authorities' story, but as with the other victims of feminicide, the truth may never be known.

Less than a month before Susana's death, Marisela Escobedo, the mother of a feminicide victim, was also gunned down right in front of the governor's office building in the city of Chihuahua, where she had been camping to demand the arrest of the killer of her sixteen-year-old daughter, Rubi Frayre. The main suspect was her live-in boyfriend, Sergio Barraza, who was captured and eventually set free despite having confessed to the crime. Marisela had received threats from Barraza, but she challenged the governor by stating in an interview outside the governor's palace, "What's the government waiting for, that he come and finish me? Then let him kill me, but here in front to see if it makes them ashamed"

(Ellingwood 2010). Her family also continued to suffer repercussions. Marisela's husband's business was set on fire and her brother-in-law was killed. Family members sought asylum in the United States, but immigration authorities responded by locking up Marisela's son and her brother in an immigration detention center in New Mexico (Frontera Norte Sur 2011).

Also forced into exile were Cipriana Jurado of the Worker Solidarity and Research Center and Paula Flores, mother of Sagrario Gonzalez—a 1998 feminicide victim—who actively advocated for feminicide victims' relatives and organized the disenfranchised community of Lomas de Poleo to keep youth away from crime. Other exiles include Malu Garcia, a founder of the organization May Our Daughters Return Home, whose house was burned down in 2011, and Eva Arce, a women's activist who has received numerous threats and attacks (Frontera Norte Sur 2011).

16. The devastating numbers of deaths caused by the drug wars in Juárez from 2008 to 2011, and particularly in 2010, when the tally of murders reached over three thousand for that year alone—the highest in the world (Campbell 2011)—led to media reports naming the city the "murder capital of the world." This title was used widely in headlines during these years and beyond (see, for example, Allen 2009; Vulliamy 2009; Holden 2010; Petersen 2010; Amey 2015).

17. Often described as both a postmodern and new Che Guevara, Subcomandante Insurgente Marcos was the spokesman and de facto leader of the EZLN, a Mexican revolutionary movement fighting for the human rights of the indigenous peoples of México. Subcomandante Marcos was a constructed persona that the Zapatistas used as a leader figure and to strategically establish visibility (Castells 2010).

18. This includes the ideological transformations that came with Vietnam War protests, the Cuban revolution, the Chinese revolution, the counterculture hippie movement, feminist movements, the civil rights movement in the United States, and the assassination of Che Guevara.

19. Ordaz's repression against student movements was particularly fierce given the upcoming Olympic Games. To Ordaz, giving an impression of peace, stability, and prosperity was crucial because México would be the first Third World country to host this event, and the Olympic Games represented an important source of income and potential multinational investment opportunities for the country.

20. Beginning in the summer of 1968, México City saw a series of student protests and rallies demanding the end of repression and the liberation of political prisoners, among other things. These student protests reflected the opposition demonstrated by various movements across the country. Their specific demands, part of a larger demand for a more open and democratic government, included the release of political prisoners, the dissolution of the government police force, the firing of the police chief and his assistant, compensation for acts of police brutality that initiated protests, the repeal of Articles 145 and 145A of the Mexican

Constitution (which defined "social dissolution" as a crime and sanctioned imprisonment of anyone attending meetings of three or more people, deemed to threaten public order), and the punishment of the guilty within the police and government. President Díaz Ordaz, however, strongly rejected students' demands. On October 2, thousands of students gathered in México City's Plaza of Tres Culturas in the Tlatelolco housing complex to organize their next steps, but little did they know that the soldiers would come to capture their leaders and turn the gathering into a massacre that lasted almost two hours and resulted in the injury, killing, and disappearance of many students (Richman and Diaz-Cortes 2008). Repression continued, as the government refused to investigate the massacre and concealed all the information (which was not released until recently), including the numbers and names of those who disappeared.

21. According to SEP's (2014) website (translation mine): "The ENLACE test is applied at the high school level to get to know the extent to which youth are able to put in practice, and in real situations, the basic disciplinary competences in the areas of reading comprehension and mathematics acquired throughout their schooling trajectory.

"ENLACE offers specific information to parents, students, teachers, administrators, educational authorities and society in general to improve the quality of education, promoting transparency and accountability.

"Adequate use of the ENLACE results can turn this evaluation into a powerful instrument of educational improvement by offering elements that contribute to establishing focused tutoring programs and implementing professional development programs for teachers, among other actions."

22. Prior to the meeting at Altavista, Marcos spoke for about thirty minutes during a demonstration that blocked the downtown international bridge. The audience included the media and a crowd of approximately eight hundred people, including academics and activists from both sides of the border who supported indigenous rights and demonstrated solidarity with striking Oaxaca peasant teachers and union members (Bellinghausen, 2006).

23. Granjas Lomas del Poleo is the subject of a legal dispute with wealthy Juárez magnates Pedro and Jorge Zaragoza, who wished to expropriate over 852 acres of land in the northwest of Juárez, where the inhabitants of the colonia established their farms over thirty years ago (Cano 2009). These moguls attempted to get the inhabitants to abandon their lands before the courts made their decision through violent forms of oppression and harassment (Enlace Zapatista 2008).

2. Through Girls' Eyes

1. Universidad Nacional Autónoma de México (UNAM) is located in México City. UNAM is perhaps the most prestigious public institution of higher

education in the country and the first university in the Americas. It is also known for its historical participation in social movements.

2. The Tarahumaras or Rarámuris are the indigenous people who inhabit the state of Chihuahua. After the arrival of Spanish colonizers, they retreated to the Sierra Madre Occidental—also known as Sierra Tarahumara—in the southeast of the state, but today they can also be seen, often begging or selling crafts in the streets, all around the cities of Chihuahua.

3. Enacting a Pedagogy of *Autogestión*

1. Although the principal used the term "gay" in describing the student, it is not clear whether the student self-identified as gay, transgender, or in another way, so the term "queer" has been used to better represent this ambiguity.

2. While the technological resources at Altavista were scarce, students used their cell phones in creative ways to record videos and take pictures, which they would later download into their PowerPoint presentations.

4. Building a *Mujerista* Space at Altavista

1. El Grito or Cry of Independence is a rite followed every year to commemorate the struggle of México's independence from Spain. On September 16, 1810, Miguel Hidalgo y Costilla, the priest of the parish of Dolores in the state of Querétaro and one of the leaders of the insurgent movement, arose, calling the peasants to rebel against the Spanish authorities. The peasants from the surrounding area responded to the ringing of the church bell by gathering in the courtyard of the church, where Father Hidalgo inspired them with a fiery cry: "Long live religion! Long live Our Lady of Guadalupe! Long live the Americas and death to the corrupt government!" Though it has evolved in some ways, being now characterized by the cry *"Viva México,"* the Cry of Independence is repeated every year by the president of México from the balcony of the National Palace in México City, and it is echoed by the governor of each state throughout the country.

2. *Permacultura* or permaculture was developed in the 1970s and is based on the application of universal ethics and design principles to create a self-sustainable future. It moves in a series of spiraling stages that begins at a personal and local level and then proceeds to the collective and global. Health and spiritual well-being, culture and education, finances and economics, land and self-government, and management of land and nature constitute some of permaculture's specific dimensions (TIERRAMOR n.d.).

Bibliography

Abrams, L. S. 2003. "Contextual Variations in Young Women's Gender Identity Negotiations." *Psychology of Women Quarterly* 27, no. 1: 64–74.

Adely, F. 2012. *Gendered Paradoxes: Educating Jordanian Women in Nation, Faith, and Progress.* Chicago: University of Chicago Press.

Akom, A. A., J. Cammarota, and S. Ginwright. 2008. "Youthtopias: Towards a New Paradigm of Critical Youth Studies." *Youth Media Reporter* 2, no. 4: 1–30.

Allen, N. 2009. "Mexican City Is 'Murder Capital of the World.'" *Telegraph*, October 22.

Allende, I. 2001. *Portrait in Sepia: A Novel.* New York: HarperCollins.

Amey, K. 2015. "The Most Difficult PR Job in the World? Mexican City Once Considered the 'Global Murder Capital' Is Now Attempting to Lure Tourists Back." *Daily Mail*, July 2.

Amnesty International. 2003. "Mexico: Intolerable Killings; Ten Years of Abductions and Murders in Ciudad Juárez and Chihuahua." August 10. AI index: AMR 41/027/2003. https://www.amnesty.org/en/documents/amr41/027/2003/en/.

———. 2010. "Mexico Urged to Protect Activists after Campaigner Shot Dead." January 6. https://www.amnesty.org/en/latest/news/2010/01/mexico-urged-protect-activists-after-campaigner-shot-dead-20100106/.

Antrop-González, R. 2006. "Toward the School as Sanctuary Concept in Multicultural Urban Education: Implications for Small High School Reform." *Curriculum Inquiry* 36, no. 3: 273–301.

Anzaldúa, G. 1987. *Borderlands/La Frontera: The New Mestiza.* San Francisco, Calif.: Aunt Lute Books.

———. 1990. *Making Face, Making Soul/Haciendo Caras: Creative and Critical Perspectives of Feminists of Color.* San Francisco, Calif.: Aunt Lute Books.

———. 2002. "Now Let Us Shift . . . the Path of Conocimiento . . . Inner Work, Public Acts." In *This Bridge We Call Home,* edited by G. E. Anzaldúa and A. Keating, 540–78. New York: Routledge.

Apple, M. W. (1977) 2004. *Ideology and Curriculum.* New York: Routledge.

Aronowitz, S. 1992. *False Promises: The Shaping of American Working Class Consciousness.* Durham, N.C.: Duke University Press.

Babb, S. 2005. "The Social Consequences of Structural Adjustment: Recent Evidence and Current Debates." *Annual Review of Sociology* 31: 199–222.

Bacon, D. 2008. "Displaced People: NAFTA's Most Important Product." *NACLA Report on the Americas* 41, no. 5: 23–27.

Bae, M. S. 2011. "Interrogating Girl Power: Girlhood, Popular Media, and Postfeminism." *Visual Arts Research* 37, no. 2: 28–40.

Ballí, C. 2009. "Murdered Women on the Border: Gender, Territory and Power in Ciudad Juárez." PhD diss., Rice University.

Bartolomé, L. I. 2008. "Authentic Cariño and Respect in Minority Education: The Political and Ideological Dimensions of Love." *International Journal of Critical Pedagogy* 1, no. 1: 1–17.

Baxter Magolda, M. B. 2001. *Making Their Own Way: Narratives for Transforming Higher Education to Promote Self-Development.* Sterling, Va.: Stylus.

Beck, L. 2010. "MAC Kisses Off Juárez-Inspired Product Names: Company Changes Plans for MAC Rodarte Collection after Explosion of Customer Outcry." July 21. http://www.nbcdfw.com/the-scene/fashion/MAC-Kisses-Off-Juarez-Inspired-Product-Names-98799069.html.

Belenky, M. F., B. M. Clinchy, N. R. Goldberger, and J. M. Tarule. 1986. *Women's Ways of Knowing: The Development of Self, Voice and Mind.* New York: Basic Books.

Bellinghausen, H. 2006. "Llega *la otra campaña* a Ciudad Juárez; se reúne con simpatizantes de ambos países." *La Jornada,* November 3. http://www.jornada.unam.mx/2006/11/03/index.php?section=politica&article=018n1pol.

Bettie, J. 2003. *Women without Class: Girls, Race, and Identity.* Berkeley: University of California Press.

Beverley, J. 2000. "*Testimonio,* Subalternity, and Narrative Authority." In *The Sage Handbook of Qualitative Research,* 3rd ed., edited by N. K. Denzin and Y. S. Lincoln, 547–58. Thousand Oaks, Calif.: Sage.

Bowden, C. 1998. *Juárez: The Laboratory of Our Future.* New York: Aperture.

———. 1999. "I Wanna Dance with the Strawberry Girl." *Talk,* September, 114–18.

Bowles, S., and H. Gintis. 1976. *Schooling in Capitalist America: Educational Reform and the Contradictions of Economic Life.* New York: Basic Books.

Brayboy, B. M. 2000. "The Indian and the Researcher: Tales from the Field." *International Journal of Qualitative Studies in Education* 13, no. 4: 415–26. doi:10.1080/095183900413368.

Brown, L. M., and C. Gilligan. 1992. *Meeting at the Crossroads: Women's Psychology and Girls' Development.* Cambridge, Mass.: Harvard University Press.

Brugués Rodríguez, A. 2005. "Relaciones económicas y niveles de bienestar de Ciudad Juárez: Un enfoque de género." In *Diagnóstico geo-socioeconómico de*

Ciudad Juárez y su sociedad, edited by L. E. Cervera Gómez, 66–113. Juárez, México: El Colegio de la Frontera Norte/Instituto Nacional de las Mujeres.

Bruner, J. 1985. "Narrative and Paradigmatic Modes of Thought." In *Learning and Teaching the Ways of Knowing,* edited by E. Eisner, 97–115. Yearbook 84, pt. 2. Chicago: National Society for the Study of Education.

Burbules, N. C. 2000. "The Limits of Dialogue as a Critical Pedagogy." In *Revolutionary Pedagogies: Cultural Politics, Instituting Education, and the Discourse of Theory,* edited by Peter Pericles Trifonas, 251–73. New York: Routledge.

Butcher, K. 2015. "Constructing Girlhood, Narrating Violence: *Desert Blood, If I Die in Juárez,* and 'Women of Juárez.'" *Latino Studies* 13, no. 3: 402–20.

Cámara de Diputados. 2007. "Anexo IV: Proposiciones." *Gaceta Parlamentaria,* no. 2355-IV, October 4. http://gaceta.diputados.gob.mx/Gaceta/60/2007/oct/20071004-IV.html.

Campbell, H. 2009. *Drug War Zone: Frontline Dispatches from the Streets of El Paso and Juárez.* Austin: University of Texas Press.

———. 2011. "No End in Sight: Violence in Ciudad Juárez." *NACLA Report on the Americas* 44, no. 3: 19–22, 38.

Campos Montero, J. M., and S. Dollinger. 1998. "An Autophotographic Study of Poverty, Collective Orientation, and Identity among Street Children." *Journal of Social Psychology* 138, no. 3: 403–6.

Cano, A. 2009. "Lomas del Poleo: Lucha entre pobreza y avaricia." *La Jornada,* March 19. http://www.jornada.unam.mx/2009/03/19/sociedad/048n1soc.

Carnoy, M. 2000. "Globalization and Educational Reform." In *Globalization and Education: Integration and Contestation across Cultures,* edited by N. P. Stromquist and K. Monkman, 43–62. Lanham, Md.: Rowman & Littlefield.

Castells, M. 2010. *The Power of Identity.* Vol. 2 of *The Information Age: Economy, Society, and Culture.* 2nd ed. Malden, Mass.: Wiley-Blackwell.

Castillo, D. A., and M. S. Tabuenca Córdoba. 2002. *Border Women: Writing from La Frontera.* Minneapolis: University of Minnesota Press.

Cervantes-Soon, C. G. 2012. "Testimonios of Life and Learning in the Borderlands: Subaltern Juárez Girls Speak." *Equity & Excellence in Education* 45, no. 3: 373–91.

———. 2014. "The U.S.-Mexico Border-Crossing Chicana Researcher: Theory in the Flesh and the Politics of Identity in Critical Ethnography." *Journal of Latino/Latin American Studies* 6, no. 2: 97–112.

Chant, S. H. 2003. *Gender in Latin America.* New Brunswick, N.J.: Rutgers University Press.

Cital Beltrán, P. 2005. "Desarrollo urbano." In *Diagnóstico geo-socioeconómico de Ciudad Juárez y su sociedad,* edited by L. E. Cervera Gómez, 12–37. Juárez, México: El Colegio de la Frontera Norte/Instituto Nacional de las Mujeres.

Coatsworth, J. H. 2004. "Globalization, Growth, and Welfare in History." In *Globalization: Culture and Education in the New Millennium,* edited by M. M. Suárez-Orozco and D. B. Qin-Hilliard, 38–55. Berkeley: University of California Press.

Combs, J. M., and R. C. Ziller. 1977. "Photographic Self-Concept of Counselees." *Journal of Counseling Psychology* 24, no. 5: 452–55.

Connell, R. 2015. "Gender and Embodiment in World Society." *Revista Lusófona de Estudos Culturais* 3, no. 1: 289–95.

Conti, A. 2011. "'Si esto sigue así, la impunidad va a matarnos.'" *La Voz,* March 11. http://www.lavoz.com.ar/noticias/mundo/%EF%BF%BDsi-esto-sigue-asi%EF%BF%BDla-impunidad-va%EF%BF%BDa-matarnos.

Coronado, I. 2008. "Public Policy Changes on the U.S.-Mexico Border." In *Transformations of* La Familia *on the U.S.-Mexico Border,* edited by R. R. Márquez and H. D. Romo, 289–308. Notre Dame, Ind.: University of Notre Dame Press.

Craigie, H. 2005. "Mujeres en la línea: Engendering Migration, Agency, and Urban Space on Mexico's Northern Border." Working paper 36, Southwest Institute for Research on Women.

Cruz, C. 2001. "Toward an Epistemology of a Brown Body." *International Journal of Qualitative Studies in Education* 14, no. 5: 657–69.

Darder, A. 2003. "Teaching as an Act of Love: Reflections on Paulo Freire and His Contributions to Our Lives and Our Work." In *The Critical Pedagogy Reader,* edited by A. Darder, M. Baltodano, and R. D. Torres, 497–510. New York: RoutledgeFalmer.

Dávila, P. 2008. "El inframundo." *Proceso,* July 9. http://www.proceso.com.mx/rv/modHome/detalleExclusiva/60528.

Delgado Bernal, D. 1998. "Using a Chicana Feminist Epistemology in Educational Research." *Harvard Educational Review* 68, no. 4: 555–83.

Delgado Bernal, D., R. Burciaga, and J. Flores Carmona. 2012. "Chicana/Latina Testimonios: Mapping the Methodological, Pedagogical, and Political." *Equity & Excellence in Education* 45, no. 3: 363–72.

Duke, L. 2002. "Get Real! Cultural Relevance and Resistance to the Mediated Feminine Ideal." *Psychology & Marketing* 19, no. 2: 211–33.

Duncan-Andrade, J. 2009. "Note to Educators: Hope Required When Growing Roses in Concrete." *Harvard Educational Review* 79, no. 2: 181–94.

Durham, M. G. 1999. "Articulating Adolescent Girls' Resistance to Patriarchal Discourse in Popular Media." *Women's Studies in Communication* 22, no. 2: 210–29.

Elenes, C. A. 2000. "Chicana Feminist Narratives and the Politics of the Self." *Frontiers* 21, no. 3: 105–23.

Elenes, C. A., F. E. González, D. Delgado Bernal, and S. Villenas. 2001. "Introduction: Chicana/Mexicana Feminist Pedagogies: *Consejos, respeto, y educación* in Everyday Life." *International Journal of Qualitative Studies in Education* 14, no. 5: 595–602.

Ellingwood, K. 2010. "Mexico under Siege: Mother Shot Dead at Anti-crime Vigil in Chihuahua." *Los Angeles Times,* December 18.

Ellsworth, E. 1989. "Why Doesn't This Feel Empowering? Working through the Repressive Myths of Critical Pedagogy." *Harvard Educational Review* 59, no. 3: 297–325.

Enlace Zapatista. 2008. "Embestida violenta contra Lomas del Poleo." January 29. http://enlacezapatista.ezln.org.mx/2008/01/29/embestida-violenta-contra -lomas-del-poleo/.

Faux, J. 2012. "A Tough Choice for Mexico." *The American Prospect,* May 30. http:// prospect.org/article/tough-choice-mexico.

Fernández-Kelly, M. P. 1983. *For We Are Sold, I and My People: Women and Industry in Mexico's Frontier.* Albany: State University of New York Press.

Fine, M. 1994. "Working the Hyphens: Reinventing Self and Other in Qualitative Research." In *The Sage Handbook of Qualitative Research,* edited by N. K. Denzin and Y. S. Lincoln, 70–82. Thousand Oaks, Calif.: Sage.

Foley, D. E. (1990) 2010. *Learning Capitalist Culture: Deep in the Heart of Tejas.* Philadelphia: University of Pennsylvania Press.

———. 2002. "Critical Ethnography: The Reflexive Turn." *International Journal of Qualitative Studies in Education* 15, no. 4: 469–90.

Foley, D. E., and A. Valenzuela. 2005. "Critical Ethnography: The Politics of Collaboration." In *The Sage Handbook of Qualitative Research,* 3rd ed., edited by N. K. Denzin and Y. S. Lincoln, 217–34. Thousand Oaks, Calif.: Sage.

Fregoso, R.-L. 2000. "Voices without Echo: The Global Gendered Apartheid." *Emergences: Journal for the Study of Media & Composite Cultures* 10, no. 1: 137–55.

———. 2003. *MeXicana Encounters: The Making of Social Identities on the Borderlands.* Berkeley: University of California Press.

Fregoso, R.-L., and C. Bejarano. 2010. "Introduction: A Cartography of Feminicide in the Americas." In *Terrorizing Women: Feminicide in the Américas,* edited by R.-L. Fregoso and C. Bejarano, 59–69. Durham, N.C.: Duke University Press.

Freire, P. 1970. *Pedagogy of the Oppressed.* New York: Continuum.

———. 1997. *Teachers as Cultural Workers: Letters to Those Who Dare Teach.* Boulder, Colo.: Westview Press.

Frontera Norte Sur. 2008. "Sushi, Sensimilla and Slaughter." *H-Net: Humanities and Social Sciences Online,* January 24. http://h-net.msu.edu/cgi-bin/logbrowse .pl?trx=vx&list=h-borderlands&month=0801&week=d&msg=vUW6YZsvq O9lMtyH93kyKQ&user=&pw=.

———. 2011. "The Silencing of Women's Voices." *La Prensa San Diego,* March 11.

Gilligan, C. 2014. "Women's Psychological Development: Implications for Psychotherapy." In *Women, Girls & Psychotherapy: Reframing Resistance,* edited by C. Gilligan, A. G. Rogers, and D. Tolman, 5–32. New York: Routledge.

Gilmore, L., and E. Marshall. 2010. "Girls in Crisis: Rescue and Transnational Feminist Autobiographical Resistance." *Feminist Studies* 36, no. 3: 667–90.

Giroux, H. A. 1988. *Teachers as Intellectuals: Toward a Critical Pedagogy of Learning.* Granby, Mass.: Bergin & Garvey.

Gómez Licón, A., and D. Borunda. 2010. "Juárez Massacre: Football Players, Honor Student among 16 Victims," *El Paso Times*, February 2.

González de la Vara, M. 2002. *Breve historia de Ciudad Juárez y su región.* Tijuana, México: El Colegio de la Frontera Norte; Las Cruces: New Mexico State University; Ciudad Juárez: Universidad Autónoma de Ciudad Juárez; & México, D.F.: Ediciones y Gráficos Eón.

Goodenow, C., and O. M. Espin. 1993. "Identity Choices in Immigrant Adolescent Females." *Adolescence* 28, no. 109: 173–84.

Goodman, S. 2011. "Mexico Drug War a Lost Cause as Presently Fought." *Huffpost World*, March 10.

Grupo Ocho de Marzo de Ciudad Juárez. 1993–98. "Estudio Hemerográfico." Casa Amiga Centro de Crisis, A.C., and Diario de Juárez.

Harding, S. 1993. "Rethinking Standpoint Epistemology: What Is 'Strong Objectivity'?" In *Feminist Epistemologies,* edited by L. Alcoff and E. Potter, 49–82. New York: Routledge.

Harquail, C. V. 2010. "Only a Cosmetic Apology? MAC's Juárez Controversy & Fauxial Awareness." July 23. http://authenticorganizations.com/harquail/2010/07/23/only-a-cosmetic-apology-mac-s-juarez-controversy-fauxial-awareness/#sthash.D5U4JP27.dpbs.

Harris, A. 2004. *Future Girl.* New York: Routledge.

Hernández, A. 1997. *Pedagogy, Democracy, and Feminism: Rethinking the Public Sphere.* New York: State University of New York Press.

Hernández Navarro, L. 2010. "Ciudad Juárez: Mexico's Nameless Dead." *Guardian*, November 9.

Hidalgo Glez., Y. 2013. "La Rosa del Desierto." *Zapateando,* May 9. https://zapateando.wordpress.com/2013/05/09/la-rosa-del-desierto/.

Holden, S. 2010. "Drug War on Doorsteps All Over Ciudad Juárez." *New York Times,* April 19.

Holland, D., W. Lachicotte Jr., D. Skinner, and C. Cain. 1998. *Identity and Agency in Cultural Worlds.* Cambridge, Mass.: Harvard University Press.

hooks, b. 1991. *Yearning: Race, Gender, and Cultural Politics.* Boston, Mass.: South End Press.

———. 1994a. *Outlaw Culture: Resisting Representations.* New York: Routledge.

———. 1994b. *Teaching to Transgress: Education as the Practice of Freedom.* New York: Routledge.

Hyams, M. 2003. "Adolescent Latina Bodyspaces: Making Homegirls, Homebodies and Homeplaces." *Antipode* 35, no. 3: 536–58.

Instituto Municipal de Investigación y Planeación (IMIP). 2002. *Plan de desarrollo urbano de Ciudad Juárez*. Ciudad Juárez, México: IMIP.

Instituto Nacional de Estadística y Geografía (INEGI). 2011. "Información nacional, por entidad federativa y municipios: Juárez." http://www3.inegi.org.mx/sistemas/mexicocifras/.

Jesús, M. 2007. "Los compas del Foro." Weblog post, October 20. http://centrodemedioslibresch.blogspot.com/2007_10_14_archive.html.

Joekes, S., and A. Weston. 1994. *Women and the New Trade Agenda*. No. 305.43 J64. New York: United Nations Development Fund for Women.

Juárez, J. M., and S. Comboni Salinas. 2003. "La educación en el proceso de integración de América Latina." *Política y Cultura*, no. 20: 54–77.

Kearney, M. C. 2007. "Productive Spaces: Girls' Bedrooms as Sites of Cultural Production." *Journal of Children and Media* 1, no. 2: 126–41.

Kelly, P. 2008. *Lydia's Open Door: Inside Mexico's Most Modern Brothel*. Berkeley: University of California Press.

King, J. 2011. "Poet Susana Chavez's Death Sparks Outrage in Juárez." *Colorlines*, January 14.

Latina Feminist Group. 2001. *Telling to Live: Latina Feminist Testimonios*. Durham, N.C.: Duke University Press.

Lather, P. 2001. "Postbook: Working the Ruins of Feminist Ethnography." *Signs* 27, no. 1: 199–227.

Leadbeater, B. J., and N. Way, eds. 1996. *Urban Girls: Resisting Stereotypes, Creating Identities*. New York: New York University Press.

———, eds. 2007. *Urban Girls Revisited: Building Strengths*. New York: New York University Press.

Levinson, B. A. 1996. "Social Difference and Schooled Identity at a Mexican *Secundaria*." In *The Cultural Production of the Educated Person: Critical Ethnographies of Schooling and Local Practice*, edited by Levinson, B. A., D. E. Foley, and D. C. Holland, 211–38. Albany: State University of New York Press.

Limas, A., and P. Ravelo. 2002. "Feminicidio en Ciudad Juárez: Una civilización sacrificial." *El Cotidiano* 18, no. 11: 47–57.

Lugo, A. 2008. *Fragmented Lives, Assembled Parts: Culture, Capitalism, and Conquest at the U.S.-Mexico Border*. Austin: University of Texas Press.

Luttrell, W. 2003. *Pregnant Bodies, Fertile Minds: Gender, Race, and the Schooling of Pregnant Teens*. New York: Routledge.

Luykx, A. 1999. *The Citizen Factory: Schooling and Cultural Production in Bolivia*. Albany: State University of New York Press.

Lykes, M. B. 1985. "Gender and Individualistic vs. Collectivist Bases for Notions about the Self." *Journal of Personality* 53, no. 2: 356–83.

Madison, D. S. 2011. *Critical Ethnography: Method, Ethics, and Performance*. Thousand Oaks, Calif.: Sage.

Maher, F. 2001. "John Dewey, Progressive Education, and Feminist Pedagogies: Issues in Gender and Authority." In *Feminist Engagements: Reading, Resisting, and Revisioning Male Theorists in Education and Cultural Studies,* edited by K. Weiler, 13–32. New York: Routledge.

Marcia, J. E. 1966. "Development and Validation of Ego Identity Status." *Journal of Personality and Social Psychology* 3, no. 5: 551–58.

Márquez, F. 1953. "Art: Mexican Autobiography." *Time,* April 27.

Martínez, O. J. 2006. *Troublesome Border.* Tucson: University of Arizona Press.

Matute-Bianchi, M. E. 1986. "Ethnic Identities and Patterns of School Success and Failure among Mexican-Descent and Japanese-American Students in a California High School: An Ethnographic Analysis." *American Journal of Education* 95, no. 1: 233–55.

McLaren, P. 1986. *Schooling as a Ritual Performance.* Boston, Mass.: Routledge & Kegan Paul.

McRobbie, A. 2004. "Post-feminism and Popular Culture." *Feminist Media Studies* 4, no. 3: 255–64.

Menchú, R. 1984. *I, Rigoberta Menchú: An Indian Woman in Guatemala.* Edited by E. Burgos-Debray. Translated by A. Wright. London: Verso.

Mendel, G., and C. Vogt. 1975. *El manifiesto de la educación.* México, D.F.: Siglo XXI Editores.

Mignolo, W. 2000. *Local Histories/Global Designs: Coloniality, Subaltern Knowledges, and Border Thinking.* Princeton, N.J.: Princeton University Press.

Mohanty, C. T. 2003. *Feminism without Borders: Decolonizing Theory, Practicing Solidarity.* Durham, N.C.: Duke University Press.

Monárrez Fregoso, J. E. 2005. "Violencia e (in)seguridad ciudadana en Ciudad Juárez." In *Diagnóstico geo-socioeconómico de Ciudad Juárez y su sociedad,* edited by L. E. Cervera Gómez, 273–314. Ciudad Juárez, México: El Colegio de la Frontera Norte/Instituto Nacional de las Mujeres.

Montero, M. T. 2005. "Estado actual de la educación en Ciudad Juárez." In *Diagnóstico geo-socioeconómico de Ciudad Juárez y su sociedad,* edited by L. E. Cervera Gómez, 229–72. Ciudad Juárez, México: El Colegio de la Frontera Norte/Instituto Nacional de las Mujeres.

Moraga, C. 1983. "Refugees of a World on Fire: Foreword to the Second Edition." In *This Bridge Called My Back: Writings by Radical Women of Color,* 2nd ed., edited by C. Moraga and G. Anzaldúa, n.p. San Francisco, Calif.: Aunt Lute Books.

———. 1993. *The Last Generation: Prose and Poetry.* Berkeley: University of California Press.

Moraga, C., and G. Anzaldúa, eds. 1983. *This Bridge Called My Back: Writings by Radical Women of Color.* 2nd ed. San Francisco, Calif.: Aunt Lute Books.

Moreno Acosta, H. A. 2008. "Situación de la seguridad." In *La realidad social de Ciudad Juárez*, vol. 1, edited by C. Jusidman, 241–79. Ciudad Juárez, México: Universidad Autónoma de Ciudad Juárez.

Moya, P. M. 2002. *Learning from Experience: Minority Identities, Multicultural Struggles*. Berkeley: University of California Press.

Noblit, G. W. 1993. "Power and Caring." *American Educational Research* 30, no. 1: 23–38.

Noddings, N. 1988. "The Moral Life of Schools." *American Journal of Education* 96, no. 2: 215–30.

Noland, C. M. 2006. "Auto-Photography as Research Practice: Identity and Self-Esteem Research." *Journal of Research Practice* 2, no. 1: 1–19.

Nowotny, H. 1981. "Women in Public Life in Austria." In *Access to Power: Cross-National Studies of Women and Elites*, edited by C. Fuchs Epstein and R. Laub Coser, 145–58. London: George Allen & Unwin.

Oakes, J. 1985. *Keeping Track: How Schools Structure Inequality*. New Haven, Conn.: Yale University Press.

Office of Special Prosecutor Ignacio Carrillo Prieto. 2006. *Informe histórico a la sociedad mexicana*. Procuraduría General de la República. Washington, D.C.: National Security Archive. http://www.gwu.edu/~nsarchiv/NSAEBB/NSAEBB209/#informe.

Orner, M. 1992. "Interrupting the Calls for Student Voice in 'Liberatory' Education: A Feminist Poststructuralist Perspective." In *Feminisms and Critical Pedagogy*, edited by D. Luke and J. Gore, 74–89. New York: Routledge.

Palmer, C. 2008. "An Overview of Children and Youth in the Northern Mexican Border." In *Transformations of* La Familia *on the U.S.-Mexico Border*, edited by R. R. Márquez and H. D. Romo, 53–76. Notre Dame, Ind.: University of Notre Dame Press.

Pastor, J., J. McCormick, and M. Fine. 1996. "Makin' Homes: An Urban Girl Thing." In *Urban Girls: Resisting Stereotypes, Creating Identities*, edited by B. J. Leadbeater and N. Way, 75–96. New York: New York University Press.

Paterson, K. 2006. "The Zapatistas' Other Campaign Hits Ciudad Juárez." *La Prensa San Diego*, November 13.

Pérez Molina, I. M. 2008. "Relaciones de convivencia y familiares." In *La realidad social de Ciudad Juárez*, vol. 1, edited by C. Jusidman, 35–66. Ciudad Juárez, México: Universidad Autónoma de Ciudad Juárez.

Petersen, B. 2010. "Juarez, Mexico—Murder Capital of the World." *CBS Evening News*, August 12. http://www.cbsnews.com/news/juarez-mexico-murder-capital-of-the-world/.

Pipher, M. 1994. *Reviving Ophelia: Saving the Selves of Adolescent Girls*. New York: Ballantine.

Polkinghorne, D. E. 1995. "Narrative Configuration in Qualitative Analysis." *International Journal of Qualitative Studies in Education* 8, no. 1: 5–23.

Ponce, A. 2012. "Racialization, Resistance and the Migrant Rights Movement: A Historical Analysis." *Critical Sociology* 40, no. 1: 9–27.

Portes, A., and K. Hoffman. 2003. "Latin American Class Structures: Their Composition and Change during the Neoliberal Era." *Latin American Research Review* 38, no. 1: 41–82.

Pratt, M. L. 1986. "Fieldwork in Common Places." In *Writing Culture: The Poetics and Politics of Ethnography,* edited by J. Clifford and G. Marcus, 27–50. Berkeley: University of California Press.

Reeve, J., E. Bolt, and Y. Cai. 1999. "Autonomy-Supportive Teachers: How They Teach and Motivate Students." *Journal of Educational Psychology* 91, no. 3: 537–48.

Reinharz, S. 1992. *Feminist Methods in Social Research.* New York: Oxford University Press.

Richman, J., and A. Diaz-Cortes. 2008. "Mexico's 1968 Massacre: What Really Happened?" *NPR,* December 1.

Rickert, T. 2001. "'Hands Up, You're Free': Composition in a Post-Oedipal World." *jac* 21, no. 2: 287–320.

Rincones, R., E. Hampton, and C. Silva. 2008. "Teaching for the Factory: Neoliberalism in Mexican Education." In *The Global Assault on Teaching, Teachers, and Their Unions: Stories for Resistance,* edited by M. F. Compton and L. Weinter, 37–42. New York: Palgrave Macmillan.

Ringrose, J. 2007. "Successful Girls? Complicating Post-feminist, Neoliberal Discourses of Educational Achievement and Gender Equality." *Gender and Education* 19, no. 4: 471–89.

Rippberger, S. J., and K. A. Staudt. 2003. *Pledging Allegiance: Learning Nationalism at the El Paso–Juárez Border.* New York: Routledge.

Robinson, T., and J. V. Ward. 1991. "A Belief in Self Far Greater Than Anyone's Disbelief: Cultivating Resistance among African American Female Adolescents." In *Women, Girls, and Psychotherapy: Reframing Resistance,* edited by C. Gilligan, A. G. Rogers, and D. L. Tolman, 87–117. New York: Haworth Press.

Rosaldo, R. 1989. *Culture & Truth: The Remaking of Social Analysis.* Boston, Mass.: Beacon.

Rubio Salas, R. 2005. "Características socio-demográficas." In *Diagnóstico geo-socioeconómico de Ciudad Juárez y su sociedad,* edited by L. E. Cervera Gómez, 38–65. Juárez, México: El Colegio de la Frontera Norte/Instituto Nacional de las Mujeres.

Saldaña-Portillo, M. J. 2003. *The Revolutionary Imagination in the Americas and the Age of Development.* Durham, N.C.: Duke University Press.

Saldívar-Hull, S. 2000. *Feminism on the Border: Chicana Gender Politics and Literature.* Berkeley: University of California Press.

Sánchez, S. 2012. "Ser padre sin fronteras con amor y trabajo: El caso del padre mexicano/Fathering without Borders with Love and Work: The Case of the Mexican Father." PhD diss., University of North Carolina at Chapel Hill.

Schmidt Camacho, A. 2005. "Ciudadana X: Gender Violence and the Denationalization of Women's Rights in Ciudad Juárez, Mexico." *New Centennial Review* 5, no. 1: 255–92.

Schutz, P. A., and R. Pekrun. 2007. "Introduction to Emotion in Education." In *Emotion in Education*, edited by P. A. Schutz and R. Pekrun, 3–10. San Diego, Calif.: Elsevier.

Secretaría de Educación Pública (SEP). 2014. "ENLACE en Educación Media Superior." http://www.enlace.sep.gob.mx/ms/.

Secretaría de Hacienda y Crédito Público (SHCP). 1982–2015. "Cuadro histórico de los salarios mínimos." http://finanzas.tamaulipas.gob.mx/uploads/2015/09/CARTEL_SEPTIEMBRE_2015.pdf.

Silva, C. 2006. "La reforma para el Bachillerato: Una mirada desde Ciudad Juárez." In *Chihuahua hoy, 2006: Visiones de su historia, economía, política y cultura*, edited by V. Orozco, 351–90. Juárez, México: Universidad Autónoma de Ciudad Juárez.

Silvielena. 2010. "Luz María Dávila, Whose Two Sons Were Killed at a Party in Ciudad Juárez, Faced President Felipe Calderón in a Public Event." Weblog post, December 30. http://mexicohr.blogspot.com/2010/12/luz-maria-davila-whose-two-sons-were.html.

Simon, R. I., and D. Dippo. 1986. "On Critical Ethnographic Work." *Anthropology & Education Quarterly* 17, no. 4: 195–202.

Smith, L. T. 1999. *Decolonizing Methodologies: Research and Indigenous Peoples.* New York: Zed Books.

Soto, L. D. 1997. *Language, Culture, and Power: Bilingual Families in the Struggle for Quality Education.* Albany: State University of New York Press.

Soto, L. D., C. G. Cervantes-Soon, E. Villarreal, and E. E. Campos. 2009. "The Xicana Sacred Space: A Communal Circle of Compromiso for Educational Researchers." *Harvard Educational Review* 79, no. 4: 755–76.

Stacey, J. 1988. "Can There Be a Feminist Ethnography?" *Women Studies International Forum* 11, no. 1: 21–27.

Staudt, K. 2008. *Violence and Activism at the Border: Gender, Fear, and Everyday Life in Ciudad Juárez.* Austin: University of Texas Press.

Stern, L. 1991. "Disavowing the Self in Female Adolescence." *Women & Therapy* 11, nos. 3–4: 105–17.

Strack, R. W., C. Magill, and K. McDonagh. 2004. "Engaging Youth through Photovoice." *Health Promotion Practice* 5, no. 1: 49–58.

Stromquist, N. P. 1995. "The Theoretical and Practical Bases for Empowerment." In *Women, Education and Empowerment: Pathways towards Autonomy*, edited by C. Medel-Añonuevo, 13–22. Hamburg: UNESCO Institute for Education.

Stromquist N. P., and K. Monkman. 2000. "Defining Globalization and Assessing Its Implications on Knowledge and Education." In *Globalization and Education: Integration and Contestation across Cultures*, edited by N. P. Stromquist and K. Monkman, 3–26. Oxford: Rowman & Littlefield.

Subcomandante Insurgente Marcos. 2001. "In Our Dreams We Have Seen Another World." In *Our Word Is Our Weapon: Selected Writings*, edited by J. Ponce de León, 18. New York: Seven Stories.

Subedi, B., and J. E. Rhee. 2008. "Negotiating Collaboration across Differences." *Qualitative Inquiry* 14, no. 6: 1070–92.

Taft, J. K. 2004. "Girl Power Politics: Pop-culture Barriers and Organizational Resistance." In *All about the Girl: Culture, Power, and Identity*, edited by A. Harris, 69–78. New York: Routledge.

———. 2011. *Rebel Girls: Youth Activism and Social Change across the Americas.* New York: New York University Press.

Taylor, G. 2010. "The Abject Bodies of the Maquiladora Female Workers on a Globalized Border." *Race, Gender & Class* 7, nos. 3–4: 349–63.

Teeple, G. 2000. *Globalization and the Decline of Social Reform: Into the Twenty-First Century.* Toronto: University of Toronto Press.

Téllez, M. 2005. "Doing Research at the Borderlands: Notes from a Chicana Feminist Ethnographer." *Chicana/Latina Studies* 4, no. 2: 46–70.

TIERRAMOR. n.d. "¿Qué es Permacultura?" http://www.tierramor.org/perma cultura/permacultura.htm.

Trinidad Galván, R. 2001. "Portraits of Mujeres Desjuiciadas: Womanist Pedagogies of the Everyday, the Mundane and the Ordinary." *International Journal of Qualitative Studies in Education* 14, no. 5: 603–21.

———. 2011. "Chicana Transborder Vivencias and Autoherteorías: Reflections from the Field." *Qualitative Inquiry* 17, no. 6: 552–57.

———. 2014. "Chicana/Latin American Feminist Epistemologies of the Global South (Within and Outside the North): Decolonizing El Conocimiento and Creating Global Alliances." *Journal of Latino/Latin American Studies* 6, no. 2: 135–40.

Urrieta, L. 2007. "Figured Worlds and Education: An Introduction to the Special Issue." *Urban Review* 39, no. 2: 107–16.

U.S. Department of Labor. n.d. "Minimum Wage." Wage and Hour Division (WHD). http://www.dol.gov/whd/minimumwage.htm.

Valdés, G. 1998. "The World outside and inside Schools: Language and Immigrant Children." *Educational Researcher* 27, no. 6: 4–18.

Valenzuela, A. 1999. *Subtractive Schooling: U.S.-Mexican Youth and the Politics of Caring.* Albany: State University of New York Press.

———. 2008. "Ogbu's Voluntary and Involuntary Minority Hypothesis and the Politics of Caring." In *Minority Status, Oppositional Culture, and Schooling*, edited by J. U. Ogbu, 496–530. New York: Routledge.

Valverde Cabral, A. 2015. "Prepa Altavista: Educar para emancipar." http://allim ite.mx/prepa-altavista-educar-para-emancipar.

Vila, P. 2000. *Crossing Borders, Reinforcing Borders: Social Categories, Metaphors, and Narrative Identities on the U.S.–Mexico Frontier.* Austin: University of Texas Press.

———. 2003. "Conclusion: The Limits of American Border Theory." In *Ethnography at the Border,* edited by P. Vila, 306–41. Minneapolis: University of Minnesota Press.

Villamil, J. 2003. "En Ciudad Juárez, *tocada* contra impunidad y guerra." *La Jornada,* March 9. http://www.jornada.unam.mx/2003/03/09/006n1pol.php?origen=politica.html.

Villarreal, A., and A. Sakamoto. 2008. "Bringing the Firms into Globalization Research: The Effects of Foreign Investment and Exports on Wages in Mexican Manufacturing Firms." Unpublished manuscript in author's possession.

Villarreal, A., and W. Yu. 2007. "Economic Globalization and Women's Employment: The Case of Manufacturing in Mexico." *American Sociological Review* 72, no. 3: 365–89.

Villenas, S. 1996. "The Colonizer/Colonized Chicana Ethnographer: Identity, Marginalization, and Co-optation in the Field." *Harvard Educational Review* 66, no. 4: 711–32.

Villenas, S., F. E. Godinez, D. Delgado Bernal, and C. A. Elenes. 2006. "Chicanas/Latinas Building Bridges: An Introduction." In *Chicana/Latina Education in Everyday Life: Feminist Perspectives on Pedagogy and Epistemology,* edited by D. Delgado Bernal, C. A. Elenes, F. E. Godinez, and S. Villenas, 1–9. Albany: State University of New York Press.

Visweswaran, K. 1994. *Fictions of Feminist Ethnography.* Minneapolis: University of Minnesota Press.

Vogel, R. D. 2004. "Stolen Birthright: The U.S. Conquest and Exploitation of the Mexican People." *The Hispanic Experience: Perspective on the Frontier.* Houston Institute for Culture Special Feature. http://www.houstonculture.org/hispanic/conquest5.html.

Vulliamy, E. 2009. "Life and Death in Juárez, the World's Murder Capital." *Guardian,* October 3.

Wallerstein, N., and E. Bernstein. 1988. "Empowerment Education: Freire's Ideas Adapted to Health Education." *Health Education & Behavior* 15, no. 4: 379–94.

Wang, C. C. 2006. "Youth Participation in Photovoice as a Strategy for Community Change." *Journal of Community Practice* 14, nos. 1–2: 147–61.

Washington Valdez, D. 2005. *Cosecha de mujeres: Safari en el desierto mexicano.* Barcelona: Océano.

Weiler, K. 1991. "Freire and a Feminist Pedagogy of Difference." *Harvard Educational Review* 61, no. 4: 449–74.

Willis, P. 1977. *Learning to Labor: How Working Class Kids Get Working Class Jobs.* New York: Columbia University Press.

Woolfolk, A. E., B. Rosoff, and W. K. Hoy. 1990. "Teachers' Sense of Efficacy and Their Beliefs about Managing Students." *Teaching and Teacher Education* 6, no. 2: 137–48.

Wright, M. W. 2001. "A Manifesto against Femicide." *Antipode* 33, no. 3: 550–66.

———. 2004. "From Protests to Politics: Sex Work, Women's Worth, and Ciudad Juárez Modernity." *Annals of the Association of American Geographers* 94, no. 2: 369–86. doi:10.1111/j.1467-8306.2004.09402013.x

Zembylas, M. 2007. "Emotional Capital and Education: Theoretical Insights from Bourdieu." *British Journal of Educational Studies* 55, no. 4: 443–63.

Zembylas, M., and L. Fendler. 2007. "Reframing Emotion in Education through Lenses of Parrhesia and Care of the Self." *Studies in Philosophy and Education* 26, no. 4: 319–33.

Ziller, R. 1990. *Photographing the Self: Methods for Observing Personal Orientations.* Newbury Park, Calif.: Sage.

Ziller, R., and D. Lewis. 1981. "Orientations: Self, Social, and Environmental Percepts through Auto-Photography." *Personality and Social Psychology Bulletin* 7, no. 2: 338–43.

Ziller, R., H. Vern, and C. Camacho de Santoya. 1988. "The Psychological Niche of Children of Poverty or Affluence through Auto-Photography." *Children's Environment Quarterly* 5, no. 2: 34–39.

Index

NGOs, 65, 174, 175, 217, 223, 255, 273, 289n14

Noblit, George W., 154

Nora (student), 74, 168, 172, 258; academics and, 96, 264; assault on, 265–66; friends and, 83; home life of, 81, 181; life after high school, 277–78; personality of, 79; as Redefiner, 263–66; relationships with, 82, 272; on support, 69

Normal School of Salaices, 52, 54

North American Free Trade Agreement (NAFTA), 34, 58

objectification, 162, 171, 193, 202, 203, 242

obstacles, 92; financial, 274; overcoming, 89, 109, 268, 269, 271, 272

Ochoa, Geminís, 218

Office of Public Education, 59

oppression, 15, 91, 129, 152, 180, 182, 187, 194, 291n23; awareness of, 214; internalized, 87–88; resisting, 83, 177, 202, 222; social/political/economic, 169

organized crime, 43, 58, 289n15

"Oveja Negra, La" (Molina), 43, 218

Overcoming Addictions, 67

Pablo (student), arrest of, 66

Pachucos, 105, 106

Pancho Villa, 170

participation, 9, 37, 74, 105, 106, 175, 194, 197, 227, 234, 292n1; encouraging, 143, 144

Pastor, Jennifer, 11, 266, 268

patriarchy, 15, 18, 36, 37, 39, 87, 92, 140, 179, 187, 193, 203, 259; challenging, 180–85; expectations of, 7; impact of, 4; issues of, 183

Paula (counselor), 150, 155

peace, 131, 179, 192, 204, 216, 225; looking for, 180, 201

peasant movements, 54, 56

pedagogical tool, testimonios as, 180, 192–96

pedagogy, 19, 22, 73, 147, 150, 169–70, 178, 180, 194, 195, 199, 200; critical, 13, 14, 15–16, 27, 69, 128, 131, 133, 134, 148, 164, 165, 177, 210; engaged, 160; foundation of, 149; mujerista, 8–9, 11, 17, 20; theorization of, 18

Pedagogy of the Oppressed (Freire), 14, 211

philosophy, 14, 27, 184, 194, 226; teaching, 133–34

photovoice activity, 2, 22, 23, 27, 73, 74, 100, 212, 263

physical appearance, 83, 136, 216, 263; concerns about, 250, 257–58, 261, 262; judgments based on, 261–62

picaderos, 41, 67, 288n11

Pipher, Mary, 6

poetry, 200–204, 225

police, 40, 199–200, 219, 220, 288n11; harassment by, 289n15; impunity of, 72; students and, 66, 67

political orientation, 52, 75, 128, 206

politics, 10, 12, 17, 39, 178, 257, 276; feminist, 25

Portes, Alejandro, 40, 287n9

Portrait in Sepia (Allende), 269

postfeminism, 9

postindustrial society, 168

postmodern society, 168

poststructuralism, 15

poverty, 34, 37, 48, 52, 170

power: awareness of, 214; critique of, 11, 14; exclusionary, 163; gender and, 39; hegemonic representations of, 9; purchasing, 269; role of, 154;

responsibility, 37, 77, 93, 158, 207, 252, 280

Reyes Salazar, Josefina, 289n15

Rezizte, 217

Ricket, Thomas, 15

Rigoberto (teacher), 29, 56, 78, 146, 150, 154–55, 156, 170, 183, 184, 277; relationship with, 159, 160, 161–62, 190–91; story of, 160–61; teaching by, 157; tuition from, 253–54

Rio Grande, 46, 58, 61, 118, 170, 204

risks, 7, 71, 267; macronarratives of, 87

Robinson, Tracy, 11, 268

sabiduría, 128, 195; testimonios and, 198–202

sacred space, 4, 19, 27, 270

safe space, 99, 139, 176, 244–45, 246; Altavista as, 86, 87, 128, 180, 185

safety, 35, 84, 98, 102, 137, 271, 272; increase in, 66, 67

salir adelante, 91, 100, 108–10

scholarships, 95, 181, 215, 243, 253–54, 257, 273; applying for, 271; earning, 68, 263, 264, 276, 277

schooling, 58, 93, 131, 142, 182, 211, 254; caring about, 149; centrality of, 26–27, 28, 49; colonial notion of, 270; by cooperation, 48–49; counterhegemonic, 20, 56; economic analysis of, 51; framing, 148; hegemonic ideas of, 185; heritage of, 52; images of, 108–10; private, 48, 132; public, 48, 132; revolutionary, 20; right to, 41–42; on U.S.–Mexico border, 19–20

school queen, 138, 140

Secretariat of Public Education (SEP), 60, 62, 64, 159, 170, 288n12, 291n21

self: -care, 163, 164; concept of, 100, 120, 212; -confidence, 90, 241, 255;

-consciousness, 237, 238, 250, 256; construction of, 280; -definition, 10, 266, 267; humanization and, 13; -identity, 13, 72; liberation and, 13; -love, 223, 246; -perception, 81, 157–58, 239, 261–62; -reflection, 145, 225; -reflexivity, 19, 256; reimagining, 99–100, 236; -respect, 89–90; sense of, 121, 267; -transformation, 195, 199

self-authorship, 8, 9, 13, 20, 108, 177, 181, 192, 211, 213, 279; adolescence and, 267; agency and, 29, 212; autogestión and, 19, 266; elements of, 256; identity, 206; knowledge and, 268; process of, 5, 28, 200, 267; Redirectors and, 214; safe spaces for, 246

self-esteem, 12, 67, 89, 255, 260, 263, 277; healthy, 267; increasing, 254; low, 216, 250, 276

self-image, 247, 256, 276; struggles with, 250–51, 252

self-worth, 246, 247, 255, 267; damaged feelings of, 252; increasing, 254, 256

SEP. See Secretariat of Public Education

sexism, 170, 179, 193, 266; challenging, 97, 180–85; resisting, 87–93, 182–83

sexual assault, 116, 118, 159–60, 196–97, 265–66

sexuality, 85, 127, 237, 285n2; hegemonic representations of, 9; questions about, 152

sexual orientation, 152–53, 274

sex workers, 39, 170

Shakur, Tupac, 210

single motherhood, 36, 81, 228

social action, 119, 143, 147, 210, 214; engaging in, 129

Social Cabinet, 288n14

social: change, 178, 203, 227; conditions, 21, 54, 132; constraints, 125,

CLAUDIA G. CERVANTES-SOON is assistant professor of bilingual/
bicultural education in the Department of Curriculum and Instruction at
the University of Texas at Austin.

CPSIA information can be obtained
at www.ICGtesting.com
Printed in the USA
FFOW02n1120080718
47349004-50409FF

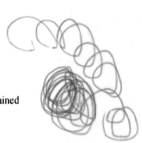